THE CHILD BEFORE THE COURT

RHETORIC, LAW, AND THE HUMANITIES

THE CHILD BEFORE THE COURT

Judgment, Citizenship, and the Constitution

TIMOTHY BAROUCH

THE UNIVERSITY OF ALABAMA PRESS
TUSCALOOSA

The University of Alabama Press
Tuscaloosa, Alabama 35487-0380
uapress.ua.edu

Typeface: Arno Pro, Trajan Pro and Scala Pro

Cover image: Illustration by David Nees, based on the
US Constitution; National Archives, Washington, DC
Cover design: David Nees

Cataloging-in-Publication data is available from the Library of Congress.
ISBN: 978-0-8173-2098-0
E-ISBN: 978-0-8173-9365-6

To Sam and Stella, you kept me going.

CONTENTS

ACKNOWLEDGMENTS

I WOULD LIKE TO THANK DAN WATERMAN, THE EDITOR-IN-CHIEF AT University of Alabama Press, and Clarke Rountree, the series editor. A first-time author couldn't have asked for better guidance and support throughout the process, at every step of the way. They have taught me invaluable lessons. The anonymous peer reviewers read the manuscript closely. They challenged my arguments, identified the project's value, and spotted my mistakes. Joanna Jacobs brought a keen eye and a thoughtful approach to her review of the manuscript. Irina du Quenoy combed over my prose, clarifying the expression of my ideas. Blanche Sarratt provided timely support so that the book would reach a wide, interested audience. Much of the production work was accomplished amidst the COVID-19 pandemic; may their effort serve as a reminder about the values of care and engaged teamwork at a time when many of us have lost so much. Needless to say, everyone involved in the process at the University of Alabama Press made sure that this book is as strong as it could be. Whatever shortcomings it has are mine.

I benefited greatly from strong mentorship throughout this undertaking. Robert Hariman has been my most trusted guide since the project's inception. He introduced me to successful professional habits of reading and writing. He gave me honest and direct feedback. And he offered me the kind of friendship that acknowledges the emotions associated with hard work, and that it is good to feel them and keep at it. It's no exaggeration to say that he showed me a path to living life as an academic at a time when I couldn't really see one. Steve Lubet took me under his wing as a "co-teacher" of a seminar on memoirs about the practice of law. His understanding of fairness, sharp mind, sense of humor, and frank attitude about writing taught me lessons that I still rely on when the words just don't come out. He showed me how to write a book proposal, which is no small feat. Just as important, he provided an impromptu education in music appreciation on our rides from Chicago back to the north suburbs.

I am especially grateful for the support at my academic home, the Department of Communication at Georgia State University. Mary Stuckey made me feel welcomed at GSU and encouraged my growth with her criticism. She kindly read early drafts of chapters and also helped me to develop professional discipline and to find my bearings in the classroom. Carol Winkler gave the project her exacting eye in its later stages, and her input and guidance helped me see it in a new light at a time when it needed her clear perspective. She continues to be a trusted mentor. David Cheshier has provided friendship, intellectual conversation, and encouragement to follow my interests. Greg Lisby has supported my passion for legal communication from the start of my time at GSU, first as our department chair and then as a coauthor. James Darsey's artful criticism, depth of disciplinary knowledge, and sense of humor helped me move forward. Jaye Atkinson, Nate Atkinson, Michael Bruner, Patricia Davis, Carrie Freeman, Marian Meyers, Maria Repnikova, Tillman Russell, Patrick Wade, Dror Walter, and Holley Wilkin each encouraged me by providing academic fellowship. I would especially like to thank Caleb Cates, John Hendry, and Chris Wernecke for their careful reading of the manuscript and their research support.

I also benefited from the intellectual approaches and critical questions of colleagues. Early on, Brian Edwards, Dilip Gaonkar, Angela Ray, and David Zarefsky each shaped my professional habits with their thoughtful reading of my work. They educated me, patiently pointing out my errors and helping connect my interests to broader academic conversations. I tried out early versions of some of my ideas at conferences in front of Jim Jasinski, Michael Kaplan, Katie Langford, John Lucaites, and Isaac West. Their feedback made my own thinking clearer. Calum Matheson has been a great friend since the outset of both our careers. His succinct way of getting to the nub of an issue and his consistent reminders about the relative importance of anything have made life more bearable. I hope that I have returned the favor. I should listen to him more.

My parents have been a constant source of support. They also taught me the value of persistence and hard work, which comes in handy for a project like this. I hope they understand how grateful I am. Kevin Tessier provided constant encouragement, helping me to stay focused on the future instead of the immediate obstacles. Mark Bixler's friendship helped me get over the hump. Finally: my family has sacrificed the most for the book. My kids—who are tired of my boring lectures—have made life fun and reminded me about the simple joys of serving each other. They gave up a lot of family time so I could write. I hope I can make it up to them. Lastly, Katie has been at my side throughout the writing of the book. Thank you for the long talks, the dancing, the pizza, the trips, the art projects, and everything else that goes into a full family life. I love you very much.

INTRODUCTION

The Child as a Representative Anecdote for the Citizen

In a time marked by a seemingly endless crisis of governance, young protagonists have been at the center of some of the greatest public controversies. On February 14, 2018, a former student allegedly entered Marjory Stoneman Douglas (MSD) High School in Parkland, Florida, killing seventeen students, teachers, and staff and injuring seventeen more.[1] Surviving students spoke out on social media and broadcast networks. A day after the shooting, they founded Never Again MSD, and an affiliated Facebook group (#NeverAgainMSD) attracted thousands of followers. By the time a week had passed, the group had announced the March for Our Lives on Washington, DC.[2] The movement supported a national school walkout, claimed legislative success, and mobilized for elections.[3] Its leaders have relentlessly answered critics and organized supporters.

That same spring featured another story with young victims—the separation of immigrant families attempting to cross the U.S.-Mexico border. As a part of the Trump administration's immigration policy, federal officials arrested adults at the border, sent them to federal jails for the crime of illegal entry, and took their children into the custody of the Department of Health and Human Services (HHS). Multimedia stories documented children crying in anguish and confinement.[4] After Trump announced the cessation of the policy, thousands of children remained separated from their parents, and media coverage continued to track whether families had been reunited. The slogan "Kids in Cages" indexed outrage over inhumane treatment.[5] The treatment of these children has been held up as evidence of a corrupted and morally lost polity.

In August 2019, sixteen-year-old climate activist Greta Thunberg set sail on a zero-carbon transatlantic trip from the United Kingdom to New York. Thunberg's millions of social media followers engaged with her weekly protests against the collective failure to curb runaway climate change. Inspired by the Never Again MSD students, Thunberg called for "climate strikes" at schools around the world, coining the term "Fridays for Future." After she arrived in New York, she addressed the United Nations, observing that she "shouldn't be up here. [She] should be back in school on the other side of the ocean. Yet you all come to us young people for hope. How dare you!"[6] Her notoriety sharply increased after the speech, with coverage emphasizing her "Pippi Longstocking braids" and her "extreme teenager-ness" as key to her influence.[7]

These controversies point to children's possession of some but not all of the traditional characteristics of citizenship.[8] The question of children's status marks a failure of democratic representation that is under increasing strain. The youth involved in these controversies were at the center of three of the largest problems of our times. Each problem raises fundamental questions about the relationship between citizens and their broader political communities. What do we owe each other by virtue of common membership in a shared community? Are exclusions from membership in the community justified, and if so, under what circumstances? How is the relationship structured between the state and those excluded, and who decides these questions?

The aforementioned public crises feature children and adolescents whose significance stems from their (in)ability to exercise judgment as citizens.[9] The child's position in the public sphere activates disputes about inclusion/exclusion in democratic representation, who decides whether the child qualifies for citizenship, and on what authority. This book argues that the child's status is *constitutional* in nature because it determines their rights to resist state authority, to speak, and to choose. As Elizabeth F. Cohen has observed, "Law . . . play[s] an important constitutive role in determining how children experience the early years of their citizenship. How a democratic polity engages or evades its minor citizens will shape how they see themselves, how others see them, and what options they have to change their position."[10] This book uses the term "constitutional" in two senses. The first is the one in which most readers would likely understand the term: the legal principles governing the United States, as written down in the Constitution. The second sense is the one in which Cohen uses the term "constitutive," meaning that it has the power to establish something. This sense is active in a sentence such as "Language is constitutive of thought." This book will develop the argument that the child's constitutional status is a key site for negotiating the meaning of citizenship in both senses: the judicial opinions related to children alter the legal meanings of important constitutional rights and also "constitute" the citizen by creating legal identities through their discourse. The judicial opinions are expressions of citizenship in the broader, second sense because the marginal case of the child requires judges to negotiate tensions in the meaning of citizenship for all in order to decide these cases. The book demonstrates the claim through a rhetorical analysis of judicial opinions considering the free speech and due process rights of children and adolescents. It shows how judicial precedents, the judicial philosophy of the Supreme Court at a given point in time, and the unique facts that confront the judges in these cases shape a broader trajectory of the legal identity of the child and the citizen. The analysis tracks a recurring set of descriptions about the (in)capable child to show how those portrayals construct a constitutional narrative of all citizens structured by their ability to form judgments.

The implications of this argument illuminate the meaning of citizenship for children, the meanings of citizenship for all in the American political order, and our understanding of "sound judgment" as it relates to both citizens and the judges issuing these pivotal opinions. First, the study highlights cognitive capabilities as an important aspect of the way we think about producing future citizens. The judicial opinions rhetorically construct these capabilities by framing the children involved in the cases as more or less capable of making decisions. The study identifies a trajectory of cognitive capabilities that comprises sound judgment, the presence of which determines who is included as a citizen and who is excluded.

Second, judicial opinions addressing the marginal case of the child alter the legal understanding of the social contract between the state and its citizens. The rhetorical development of the child's legal identity in the opinions has reconfigured the state's obligation to its citizens: if early cases addressed the child as an incapable individual who needed discipline to develop virtue, the evolution—or devolution—of this relationship between the state and citizen now posits a categorically equal child of whom much is expected but to whom little is promised.[11] This relationship reveals a state with authority over its citizens, without the concomitant responsibility to develop their capabilities. This "asymmetrical social contract" raises questions of its sustainability.

Finally, the study has important implications for understanding the role of judges in legitimating our legal order. The rhetorical analysis of the opinions studied here reveals that how an opinion conceives of the proper "role of the judge" influences (but does not determine) the outcomes of the cases. The study identifies repertoires for expressing the role of the judge in terms of temporality, distance, and reach in legitimating judgments. The rhetorical strategy from the early cases articulated this as "judicial distance" from the particular parties to a controversy; later cases showed that being a good judge also involved appreciating the fullness of time to scrutinize risks to democratic order (immediate/remote) and discover neglected traditions. Today, the sound judge must demonstrate interpretive command—this means the ability to synthesize multiple and oft-times contradictory timelines into a coherent, consistent whole. Practically, these implications mean two things: (1) the shape of citizenship is determined by how judges express their role and (2) that putting political or judicial ideology first in evaluating constitutional decision-making means missing an important element. To discuss legal change in terms of "strict construction," "judicial restraint," "originalism," or belief in a "living Constitution" is to oversimplify the judicial role. We should be suspicious when judges, scholars, politicians, and others suggest these labels as *the only way* to be a good judge. This study suggests that assessing the quality of a judge should include a consideration of the cognitive capabilities that judges display themselves and the capabilities that they expect of those subject to their decisions.

These judicial opinions articulate public meanings of citizenship rights. They set the parameters of who qualifies as a citizen premised on cognitive signs of judgment. The opinions inject new life into the public sphere by expanding or contracting citizenship status: they craft stock stories of public life, create characters, and relate them to certain democratic principles and civic practices. Finally, the opinions' displays of interpretive command lent authority to their appeals to a shared constitutional narrative. For each of these reasons, judicial opinions about the constitutional status of the child are a vital place of public discourse about important political concepts. Their significance for the study of citizenship includes not only the rules of law that they generate but also the tropes of cognition, capability, judgment, and civic life that are reinvented in each case.

The case of the child is a representative anecdote for the capable citizen. The child is "in between" citizenship, which means that they are explicitly considered a citizen in some respects while being simultaneously excluded from full citizenship rights and privileges in others. The child's status indexes a broader problem of political representation: children are affected by political decisions but lack the ability to voice their interests. The child's exclusion is temporary in nature, which means that this status is something that they pass through on the way to full citizenship. The state justifies this temporary exclusion so that children may develop the requisite capabilities of citizenship. The nature of the exclusion makes the case of the child a fertile ground for understanding citizenship for all, because these cases construct the core of citizenship capabilities that the excluded child does not yet display. For these reasons, youth activism frequently involves the child's assertion of voice and choice in contexts where children have been left out. These claims are constitutional in nature, because they seek inclusion in a shared social and political world. To fully grasp the significance of the child's importance to citizenship capabilities for all of us, we need to understand their claims under the law.

Court cases that address the child's rights to free speech and due process matter for this study because they are sites of discourse where courts explicitly negotiate the child's exclusion. These judicial opinions reinvent our shared constitutional narrative through the ways that they decide the child's claims to constitutional citizenship. To reveal how they accomplish this work requires rhetorical analysis, including of their manipulation of generic conventions and techniques of argument. The analysis demonstrates that judicial opinions resolve conflicts over the child's citizenship status by *novelizing* the public sphere. I use the term *novelization* to refer to the way that genres take on the distinctive characteristics of the novel—creating narrative through the placement of a variety of discourses alongside each other in a dialogic relationship. This study argues that judicial opinions legitimate the child's inclusion partially by creating new characters and themes, maintaining tension between competing discourses, and articulating idioms of democracy, judgment, and civic practice. Tending to this process of novelization shows how, by addressing the civic status of the child to constitute the citizen, these judicial opinions create norms of political participation and judgment.

The implications of the argument are significant for those concerned with political judgment and its relationship to shared civic practices. The judicial opinions studied here figure judgment as the display of cognition. This standard, which is found neither in the Constitution nor in statutory law, is the implicit core of citizen judgment in these opinions. Judges use that core to articulate the contextual factors for including the child as a citizen. As judicial opinions have included the child as a citizen by recognizing their rights to free speech and due process, the social contract has evolved. The state, which judicial opinions previously figured as a responsible entity with the duty to develop citizens, eventually has become a manager of risks. The child is treated at arm's length, and the state's primary concern has become preserving itself in a world in which it is increasingly detached from the habits and virtues of its citizens.

As the social contract has evolved, so has the role of judges in legitimating it. This study views judges as experts in constitutional interpretation whose written opinions perpetually *authorize* their expertise. This authorization function justifies their power as unelected officials to make decisions with the force of democratic law. Historically, as the child was gradually included as a citizen, the role of the judge became more pronounced and controversial. At first, the controversy revolved around the need for the judge to defer to more democratic decision-making mechanisms, such as the local school and the state legislature. The concern was that progressive judges were putting their personal feelings into the decisions, which was unsuitable for a judge's place in a broader democratic system. As the cases progressed, the argument for judicial restraint became less democratic, invoking deference to bureaucratic rules, student handbooks, and the like. At the same time, progressive judges less inclined to seek restraint were caught up in the demand to articulate limits to the expansion of rights. As a result, the very opinions that include the child as a full citizen contain the principles and techniques for the limitation of that inclusion.

To reveal how court cases about the rights of children inform the meaning of citizenship, I will outline the significance of the child to the problem of democratic citizenship. I will explain that the problem is inextricably constitutional, because these opinions create meanings for core citizenship rights. I will then demonstrate why reading them rhetorically helps explain how judicial opinions have created, adapted, and criticized a constitutional citizenship narrative, or an ongoing story about who belongs as an American citizen with rights and responsibilities. The law is more than an elite discourse removed from the people. Its performances make critical participation available to people bound by the constitutional narrative. The need to claim citizenship through a display of cognitive ability is not surprising, because the malleable and ambiguous character of citizenship points to its performative character.[12] Theorists seeking normative solutions to the problem of exclusion overlook this problem, but grasping it is crucial for an understanding of ideologies of exclusion and the available resources for political change.

Paying attention to the judicial opinions as rhetorical performances can reveal a shared tradition that describes citizenship's competent display. As citizenship rights became more available to the child, an understanding of cognitive ability emerged as a barrier to claiming full citizenship status.[13] The nature of the state's commitment to its citizens has also been altered. Where before the state was obligated to develop citizenship habits in the child, it now relies on a new vocabulary to articulate its role—to "manage risks" as a constitutional governing imperative. This risk management has denied state obligations—the need to protect the state from costly and time-consuming lawsuits, the acknowledgment that the state has limited fiscal resources, the clear textual commitments made by the state in its handbooks, and so on. The state made these arguments to avoid constitutional accountability and limit its constitutional obligations to its citizens. These insights have important implications for the role of the law in addressing problems of underrepresentation in our liberal democracy.

The Child as a Representative Anecdote for Defining Citizen Capabilities

The book draws inspiration from Kenneth Burke's notion of a "representative anecdote" in considering the case of the child, who occupies a subject position that is in between noncitizen and full citizen. For Burke, the representative anecdote functions as a method for analyzing discourse for its dramatic elements. In positing that literature was a kind of "equipment for living," Burke argued that the vocabularies that people use serve bonding and dissociative social functions.[14] Those working in the field of rhetorical studies have argued that "types, components, or structures of [discourse] recur as appropriate responses to recurring types of situations [and] there are ways of speaking about war, victory, civil unrest, marital problems, etc., which will reliably equip us to live through those situations."[15] As a methodology, the representative anecdote locates the particular characters, narratives, and vocabularies used to cope with situations. The ensuing selections, reflections, and deflections of reality emerge to create certain ideal types—abstractions that reveal aspects of the world by accentuating certain elements.

To study the figure of the child as a representative anecdote for the problem of citizenship understands the gulf between the child and the adult citizen as a recurring situation and calls on rhetorical resources for its resolution. On the one hand, children function as citizens because they possess "autonomous rights."[16] Children born in America are American citizens by law. They have access to education and healthcare, and their physical safety is a priority. But children's citizenship is less meaningful than adults'.[17] Children's opinions have traditionally been discounted and children lack the legal ability to determine their own lives.[18] They cannot work until they reach a certain age, cannot legally enter into contracts, or consent to most medical treatments. Children also enjoy fewer civil rights than the typical adult. They cannot vote and face restrictions on their free speech. A variety of restrictions circumscribe their freedom of movement—they are subject to the custody of their parents or guardians and cannot drive until they reach a certain age. Finally, their identities as citizens are weak, prompting the need for a variety of civic and religious institutions (and compulsory education) to inculcate in them the habits, values, and practices of good citizenship.[19]

The child's citizenship status has a broad impact because it indexes a gulf in political representation. Parents, guardians, policy makers, educators, and others represent children in politics. This raises problems of nonrepresentation, including the possibility that children's issues are given low priority, or that those who claim to be representing children's interests are representing their own interests instead.[20] Even if those who claimed to represent "children" acted solely for children's interests, "child" as a political category would require differentiation to account for variations in race, class, gender, ability and other intersectional identities.[21] But paradoxically, perhaps because of their nonrepresentation in public, children and youth occupy the center of many debates about justice. This situation persists precisely because the differential treatment of children demands justification.

Judgment in Public Discourse and in Law

The three controversies mentioned at the beginning of this book revolved in some way around the crisis of political representation. Each of the children in those cases lacked meaningful choice. The Never Again MSD students were compelled to attend public school, risking their safety; migrant children suffered traumatic consequences for accompanying their parents on a journey; Greta Thunberg had to endure an environmental crisis foisted upon her. Each of them was caught in a complex public problem that political elites have failed to resolve because of dysfunctional political processes. Each case mobilized public attention because society had failed in its obligation to care for these children. In each of the controversies, events have altered these children's life paths and limited their future options.

The case of the child reveals much about the core of citizenship because of the temporal character of the child's exclusion. The child eventually passes on to full adulthood.[22] Children earn their inclusion as citizens by developing their faculties to judge and make decisions. Studying the social institutional practices and assumptions that justify, negotiate, and amend their initial exclusion will also identify the evolving interests in maintaining these practices. If children's exclusion is premised on their lack of maturity, what, precisely do they lack, and what is the state's interest in developing it? If their correction is justified for a greater good, what kinds of corrections are legitimate, and for what kind of greater good? Is it a value or policy that benefits others, or is it for the direct benefit of the children? Frequently, courts justify the exclusion or limitation because the child is not capable of assuming the rights and responsibilities of citizenship.[23] The family, the state (through education), and a variety of institutions and civic organizations (churches, sports leagues, community centers) are entrusted with guiding children toward full citizenship status.[24]

The examples that opened the book demonstrate how exceptional youth were engaging in what Engin F. Isin and Greg M. Nielsen have termed "acts of citizenship."[25] Political voice and judgment are at the forefront of the discussion. Greta Thunberg's public speeches identified failures of judgment that converted a manageable problem into a near-term existential crisis. Adults did not discharge their obligations, compelling the young to act. Thunberg referred to adults' collective decision to "look away and come here saying that you're doing enough, when the politics and the solutions are still nowhere in sight. . . . You are still not mature enough to tell it like it is."[26] One commentator attributes her power to her wisdom: she is an "old soul" who "brushed off . . . talking points and . . . flattery," performing "much more seriously than most grown-ups."[27] Her politically disruptive speeches "take a shaming, authoritative tone that is . . . unusual for a child" and she benefits from the "unique moral position of being a teenager. She can see the world through an 'adult' moral lens. . . . But unlike an actual adult, she bears almost no conscious blame for this dismal state."[28] Thunberg's citizenship on display presents a paradox—we can see what is required of sound judgment, but the quality is most on display in a speaker who is not fully qualified to exercise it.

The Never Again MSD students likewise referred to adult inaction (on gun regulation), arguing that their own exemplary action was necessary to bring change. Their public performances were lauded: "articulate, witty, and digitally native, the survivors of the school shooting in Parkland, Florida, are using social media to . . . amplify their voices in a way the world hasn't seen before."[29] Strategic, specific, and calculated toward a clear end, they were a necessary corrective to an intractable political crisis: "Those young people are just extraordinary . . . You've had now a year of adults acting like children. And now the children are acting like adults and trying to get something done."[30]

The migrant children detained at the border represent the obverse of the exemplary child speaking in public—the innocent, passive, and helpless victim of the state's cruel machinery. One ProPublica report detailed the "squalor, the stench of unwashed bodies, and the poor health and vacant eyes of the hundreds of children" held in one detention facility.[31] Another report detailed the alleged molestation of a girl in detention: "As the days passed, she began urinating on herself and seemed unable to eat or drink. . . . 'She's so small for something like that to happen,' said her father . . . . 'I felt like I couldn't do anything to help her.'"[32] The migrant child's status as noncitizen serves as the impetus for a conversation about the minimal commitments that the state should make to extend basic dignity and personhood to migrant children in spite of their status.

The suffering of each of these young figures represents a "lost childhood," a moral failing pointing to the irretrievable loss of opportunities that children should have. In addressing the climate crisis, Greta Thunberg lamented that she "shouldn't be up here. [She] should be back in school. . . . [The adults] have stolen [her] dreams and [her] childhood with [their] empty words."[33] In the case of Never Again MSD, the "innocence lost" trope highlighted the depths to which democracy had sunk due to policy paralysis. Shooting survivor Ryan Deitsch lamented that he has had to prepare for active shooters in school "for as long as [he] can remember. . . . [During the shooting he was] in a closet with 19 other kids, waiting, fearing for [his] own life. . . . Why do we have to be the ones to do this? . . . Why do we have to march on Washington, just to save innocent lives?"[34] And in the case of migrant children separated from their parents, there was worry of emotional harm and cognitive damage, which would permanently limit children's future potential. A petition signed by over twelve thousand mental health professionals argued that the "only way to justify this policy is to completely disconnect from either one or both of the following realities: that these are children; and that children are affected by what happens to them. . . . There is a strong likelihood that these children's behavioral, psychological, interpersonal, and cognitive trajectories will be affected. . . . To pretend [otherwise] . . . is to disregard everything we know about child development, the brain, and trauma."[35] Children are a guide to democracy's failures. They have lived in fear of worsening crises and have been cognitively disrupted because they are grappling with problems that block the normal development of their capabilities. This is beyond the pale of what a child should have to endure to move through life.

These youth make claims about the meanings of fundamental citizenship rights of voice and process. The claims of Never Again MSD, Thunberg, and the migrant child detainees are not merely about substantive conditions—they are about the right to be heard and the right to be counted. And it is perhaps no coincidence that these claims are proliferating in the public sphere. High school students wish to express themselves by wearing T-shirts with political messages. Individual students seek recognition of nonconforming gender identities and equally secure access to public-school restrooms. African American students are challenging racially disparate treatment in schools and in broader public spaces.[36] These cases do not confine themselves to voice and expression. They extend to fair process as well. Controversies surrounding issues of discipline, abuse, and neglect bring the state's future interest in the child and the child's lack of cognitive capability into stark relief. The migrant child detainee cases are one example, but these claims are not limited to cases of children who are victims of others' actions. These claims also can include protecting children from their own choices. Consider the case of Cassie C., a sixteen-year-old with cancer who sought the right to refuse chemotherapy—but was denied that option on the grounds that she was not competent to make that choice on her own. The Connecticut Supreme Court in that case referred to her "compulsive and risky actions," and noted "that she was unable or unwilling to speak her true mind to those in authority, and that she was reluctant to hold opinions that her mother did not share."[37]

These claims are constitutional in nature, because they are appeals for inclusion in a larger narrative about who we are as a people. Our ideas about equality, voice, and fair procedure are bound up in canonical constitutional principles and cases. *Brown v. Board of Education* is a touchstone for the idea that "separate but equal" was unacceptable. It also observed that "education is . . . the most important function of state and local governments. . . . It is the very foundation of citizenship. Today it is a principal instrument in awakening the child to cultural values, in preparing him for later professional training, and in helping him to adjust normally to his environment."[38] The youth activism of today likewise appeals to inclusion into a shared identity and a reformulation of who counts so that we may act together. Whether these appeals succeed or fail, they create a new understanding about the rights citizens hold, and when they should attach. This means that in order to grasp the significance of the case of the child-citizen, one must account for the language of the law.

Constitutional Narratives of the Judging Citizen: The Child's Claims to Free Speech and Fair Treatment

Court cases that address the child's right to free speech and the child's right to due process of law—the cases that form the focus of this book—are particularly important to study the problem of the judging citizen, because they are topically relevant to the question of the child's citizenship. Legal scholars have identified models of childhood operating in key cases, have questioned laws that do not conform to the latest scientific understandings about cognitive development, and have noted the importance of liberal democratic ideas that shape the treatment of children.[39] These studies have been primarily normative in nature. They have developed a rich understanding of the abstract norms of liberal citizenship, demonstrated the challenge posed by the child's case, and have criticized policies and decisions for their unjust results.

But legal practices change the constitutional narrative as well. Cases involving the child's citizenship rights constitute a ground on which the courts negotiate the in-between position of the child. Norms matter in these decisions, but they are not the starting point. Because the child is on the periphery of citizenship, cases that address the child's constitutional status must articulate the core of citizenship capabilities to justify the decision to include the child in a given case. Court cases in this area constitute the nation in a specific way that both resolves the particular controversy but also keeps aspects of that controversy alive for the future. To study the related opinions as communicating a narrative involves more than evaluating a claim's propositional content. It involves the legal context for the particular cases—the places where democratic ideals and civic practices emerge in the texts themselves. Understanding how judicial opinions produce public meanings of these core citizenship rights yields insight into the identities that we claim to share as citizens. To grasp exactly how this is so requires attending to the opinions not merely as the application of a given doctrine or rule but as rhetorical performances that negotiate the principles, facts, values, and precedents for the child's inclusion and exclusion as a full citizen.

Judicial Opinions and Their Readers

To whom do these opinions speak? Audiences for judicial opinions may be vast, due to their contemporary political importance (*Roe v. Wade, Bush v. Gore,* and *Obergefell v. Hodges* come to mind). Others may have a smaller audience, comprising the lawyers and litigants involved. Still other cases in the middle range decide issues that affect broader populations, such as a Fourth Amendment case that decides police officers' abilities to search a suspect (which then requires police officers to conform to the new rules). Publics for each of these types of cases likely have grown with the advent of digital communication technologies, which have made it easier to follow, circulate, and publicly comment on them.[40]

But the study of judicial opinions need not depend on demonstrating their effects on a particular literal readership. Reading the opinions with a sensitivity to the distinctive form helps to reveal the "deep and dynamic interplay" between the opinions as texts: "the stories they tell, and the themes in terms of which we conduct our most persistent national conversations."[41] Culturally and politically, opinions constitute a genre, forming "peculiar kinds of statement[s]" that appeal to a democratic community bound by the rule of law."[42] As formal responses to periodic conflicts, judicial opinions resolve the tensions implicit in delegating conflict resolution to unaccountable judges. The courts write judicial opinions for imagined audiences to follow even where there is disagreement about the substantive result. To accomplish this task, judicial interpretations must produce their own authority, understood as unique insight, expertise, or experience that qualifies the judge to make the decision; and they must also produce legitimacy, understood as the acceptance of the outcome by those who may reasonably disagree with a decision.[43]

The "condensed quarrels" of judicial opinions establish their legitimacy with reference to the fundamental structure of the conflict.[44] The constitutional narrative is thus inherently contextual, dependent on factors that exceed the application of abstract norms. Judicial opinions define who we are by interpreting clauses, statutes, and past opinions. They mediate shared beliefs, common values, and factual disputes. They sketch a public culture replete with ideas and relationships, the type of citizen at home in such a culture, and a way of getting there.

Rhetorical Strategies of Legitimation

Judicial opinions have a variety of rhetorical tools at their disposal to balance these tensions. Courts frequently "speak as one," control a dispute by framing the "proper legal question presented," use a "declarative tone" to limit resistance to contested facts and law, and appeal to certainty and tradition.[45] Courts also will make a host of arguments referring to precedent. Precedential reasoning opens up a realm of choices about which precedents are analogous, how they should be interpreted, and whether they are relevant in contemporary times.[46] Courts define key terms and make fine distinctions in meanings;[47] those distinctions are used to derive principles to decide a case. Judicial opinions cultivate legitimate authority through the rhetorical display of exemplary character, which produces trust through the display of consistency, even-handedness, ethical commitments, respect for tradition and difference, and the like.[48] And courts make "public arguments" insofar as their forms invite acceptance, rejection, resistance, critique, and questioning.[49] Perhaps only lawyers could competently digest a nuanced argument about equitable estoppel, the doctrine of laches, or the byzantine rules of jurisdiction. But anyone can argue (in theory) about what is fair, why a policy is in place and whether to continue it, whether radical or incremental change is wise, the significance of widely known historical events, and so on. Finally, opinions cultivate an appearance of neutrality as a virtue whose fair procedures reflect the public interest.[50]

The point is not that each of these elements is present in each opinion, but that they in part resolve the problem of the child's citizenship by novelizing the public sphere.[51] The narrative's stock characters, common themes, tropic structures, and reversals comprise a forum through which deep social conflicts are staged and resolved because of the novel's ability to maintain a relationship with contemporary times. No single discourse predominates and even the narrative itself can break down. As a sociopolitical practice, novelization maintains a connection to democratization.[52] Its flexibility as a form means that the novel can adapt to new social realities. Its techniques are pluralistic, because it incorporates a multitude of discourses, characters, and themes in dialogue with one another.[53] It suspends authority without eliminating it entirely.

Novelization posits a link between rhetorical technique and sociopolitical function. Its presence in judicial opinions is significant because it counters the conventional wisdom that legal discourse involves elite judges applying technical rules according to canons of interpretation.[54] The judicial opinions that grapple with the problem of the child as citizen take on novelistic features. These opinions display a derivative quality, transposing stock stories of childhood, adolescence, democratic character, and the like, into constitutionally legitimate form. The child may be elevated in one opinion as a paragon of civic virtue. Another opinion may denigrate the child's impulsive tendencies. Still other opinions invoke imagined children who either need our protection or from whom we need protection. This novelization extends beyond characters toward idioms of judgment and democracy. Democracy is alternately a system, a way of life, a location, a moment in time. Judges are alternatingly rational, technical, emotional, conciliatory, and oracular. The opinions perform the meanings they claim; those meanings prefigure a new constitutional imagination. When an opinion passes on the constitutionality of a state's act to confine a child, it doesn't merely side with "state interests" or "parental liberty"; it uses the characters, themes, and legal materials at its disposal to inform and then alter the meanings of those terms.[55] These changed meanings shape the shared understandings of our community.

The book demonstrates how judicial opinions create norms of political participation and judgment by addressing the civic status of the child. The opinions craft characters, themes, and ideas that conform to legal discursive conventions. They are also subject to critique, reframing, reversal, relegation, and so on. This process of novelization highlights the importance of cognitive judgment capabilities to inclusion as a full citizen. Because the judicial opinions justify the child's inclusion within or exclusion from full citizenship based on their performance of vital citizenship capabilities, the meanings of the child's constitutional rights implicate the core of citizenship for all of us. These meanings have consequences for a shared constitutional narrative. Judicial opinions emphasize certain characters and themes and downplay others. As a consequence, they disclose competing visions of citizenship, judgment, expertise, and the social contract.

The Constitutional Status of the Child as a Civic Controversy: Implications for Inclusion and the Role of Judicial Expertise

This argument—that judicial opinions about the constitutional status of the child are a species of important public discourse about citizenship—has implications for the broader study of citizenship, judgment, and law. As these opinions have grappled with legal controversies, they have also described individuals as stock character types: the rogue/rascal, the innocent rube, the dissenter, the anonymous bureaucrat, the loving parent, the law-abiding victim, the quick-thinking manager. In doing so, they have thematized the functioning of democracy, its varied publics, and the place of communication and judges in that democracy.

Focusing on these judicial opinions suggests that citizenship depends in part on the display of cognitive capabilities of judgment. This knowledge is significant for problems of justice such as inclusion/exclusion and citizen voice. These capabilities comprise sound judgment: identifying properly political topics, setting strategic goals, planning the timing and form of public speech, predicting its reception, and facilitating the understanding (and practical assimilation) of bureaucratic procedure. On the one hand, this bundle of capabilities appears as an uncontestable core of citizenship, an impenetrable barrier to entry for the child. The cases present this core with agreed-upon legal principles, supported by past precedents, and validated by the actions of key players in the social controversies that gave rise to the cases. But on the other hand, their novelization makes them contested—they are time-and-fact-bound and they are subject to criticism through dissents. In drawing out the dialogic relationship among these characters and themes, the book presents a complicated picture of citizenship that is more than merely participation, or belonging, or status. More to the point, the nature of inclusion itself is altered. It is not merely that opinions decide who is "in" and who is "out." It is that the contextual factors involved in these decisions open up alternate paths (and close off others) for including or excluding the child. This characteristic makes them ripe for particular rhetorical strategies of description, constitution, and legitimation.

As the judicial opinions evolve to gradually include the child as a citizen, they also alter the social contract: the state now retains authority over citizens but without the responsibility it traditionally had to develop shared citizenship habits. This "authority without responsibility" highlights the role that rhetoric has played in developing risk management tools for the state to minimize its obligations to its citizens. Early cases presented an explicit concern for hierarchy as order. The characters of the children in those cases were aberrant and posed a threat to smooth functioning order. The state's authority was corrective, justifying benevolent discipline to maintain order. As the child was permitted to achieve status through a display of capabilities, the judicial techniques evolved to protect the state's power. Thematically, it shifted from punishment, to pedagogy, then to contractual management. This insight is broader than the standard critique of neoliberalism (which holds that a minimal state offloads responsibility on individuals to self-manage and compete in the market). The state has expanded its power to control the citizen in a flexible way. This shift is significant for those concerned with the justice of governing norms and the social contract. It also represents a potentially unsustainable condition that threatens the liberal democratic order.

Finally, the role of the judge as constitutional expert evolved as the increasingly complicated cases of the child became subject to novelization. Because characters and themes took on greater weight in justifying decisions, there were understandably more opportunities for resistance, dissent, and objection. As contestation over decisions grew, a shadow discourse about the judge's role emerged—the temperament, habits, and practices suited to constitutional application were now at issue. At first, the contestation centered around the judge's *distance* from a controversy—a traditional argument that judges should be deferential because they make decisions based on a cold paper record and do not fully understand local community norms and values. There was a dialectical relationship between judicial deference on the one hand and individual rights on the other hand. But as later cases adapted the same arguments in changed circumstances, judicial fidelity to these pure principles became untenable. Judges throughout the cases performed the structure of judgment in their opinions, meaning that they were not merely deciding the winner of a particular case but were simultaneously grounding that decision in a principle of judgment. This recurring element in the opinions suggests an inevitable doubling in the field of judgment: the judgment principles that the judge rhetorically performs also authorize the legal decision that articulates the field of judgment expected of the child.

This feature also led to two ironies of judgment, one conservative and the other progressive. The conservative irony is that the original argument for judicial restraint—that noninvolvement helps maintain respect for liberty, organic institutions, and local variations of democracy—has been inverted. For the last fifty-plus years, arguments for judicial restraint have deferred to arcane administrative procedures, minutiae, and complexity that require interpretive skill increasingly detached from and unaccountable to the average citizen. And rather than justifying conservative restraint in the name of local governing diversity, decisions have tended to justify these outcomes through monolithic constitutional interpretations.

The irony of progressive expert judgment is that it argues for the expansion of individual rights in an idiom of strict conditions and limits. Although progressive judges have included the child broadly (opening citizenship to increasing numbers) and deeply (expanding the number of rights), the relevant opinions have rooted these outcomes in certain received conventions—a hierarchy of texts, reference to common values, and arguments that expanding rights would not disrupt local governing life. Judges thereby can stay in their confined area of expertise because they have only expanded rights to exceptional plaintiffs in exceptional circumstances. The decisions have been justified with reference to the quasi-scientific process of judicial expertise. As a result, progressive judgment has created the ground for its own undoing, by embroiling itself in controversies that require these judges to depart from their own stated principles and goals for rights expansion.

The book follows the cases in chronological order, but they are better understood as expressions of distinctive strategies for constituting the child as citizen. The citizen relates to the liberal state, and so at times the child has been a passive ward, an active beneficiary (child as categorical equal), an object of traditional reform, and a contractual citizen of that state. The book follows that trajectory because the cases typify a generalized approach for addressing the problem of the child as citizen. They have produced distinctive strategies, which form a repertoire from which judges (and, by implication, the larger public culture) can draw in resolving the problem. The early cases are primarily state court cases because the Supreme Court simply was not involved in this area as much as the states. Being examples of early efforts to negotiate the child's partial citizenship through the law, they remain influential for their general propositions that the state may take custody of the child and may punish the child for improper conduct and speech. Later cases focus almost exclusively on the Supreme Court, due to its significant activity in construing rights of citizenship in the twentieth century. In one sense, the trajectory of the cases shows progress, because the child today has rights that were unthinkable in the cases mentioned in the early chapters. But in another sense, the results of the early cases have remained remarkably relevant. What is significant for the study of citizenship is that the opinions considered here reconstitute the citizen through their uses of a certain repertoire in reaching constitutional decisions.

The book is divided into parts and their accompanying chapters. Part 1 ("The Child as Ward") examines cases from the nineteenth century that treated the child as a ward. The cases selected in these early chapters (1 and 2) survey nineteenth- and early twentieth-century cases that address the question, "How does the state justify exercising sovereignty over the child?" Substantively, these cases cover two pivotal conflicts: (1) the state's power to compel children to attend certain schools or commit them to reformatories and (2) the state's power (as teachers' authority) to discipline students for inappropriate speech and conduct. These cases set the general terms of the constitutional narrative. The child could not be a full citizen because the child could not consent. State power was justified because the state was discharging a twofold obligation: it was protecting the public sphere from the threat the child posed and it was shaping future citizens. These were the state's interests in guiding these claimants through childhood.

These early opinions novelized the public sphere by emphasizing the child's lack of capabilities. Variations included the wayward or lost soul in need of benevolent guidance and the insolent and disruptive pupil. The state exercised authority to guide the child in a spirit of benevolence, as represented through well-intentioned teachers and administrators who themselves displayed outward signs of reasoned reflection, limited by a definitive goal. These characters did well because they meant well. Their authority over the child was justified to mold the child into a productive citizen who would respect economic rights. The judicial opinions claimed authority primarily through dualistic status distinctions and grants from foundational texts. These opinions invited little resistance and critique, except those based on the scope and accuracy of the metaphorical contracts and the specific case facts. The closing chapter of part 1 studies two key cases, *Meyer v. Nebraska* and *Pierce v. Society of Sisters*, which introduced an idiom of parental liberty to raise the child at the Supreme Court level and scrutinized an impulsive and fearful state as a civic value. These maneuvers disrupted earlier judicial dualisms and provided a language for expanding citizens' freedoms. Yet because these judicial opinions did not ground their conclusions in a principle of inclusion for children's citizenship rights, the performance strategies that the judges used to authorize these decisions were not available to the child in the public world writ large.

Part 2 focuses on the ways that the child gained access to performances of citizenship—the "Child as Categorical Equal." Chapters 3, 4, and 5 study three canonical Supreme Court cases of the mid-twentieth century: *West Virginia State Board of Education v. Barnette*, *In re Gault*, and *Tinker v. Des Moines Independent Community School District*. These three decisions made free speech and due process rights available to the child, placing them at the heart of citizenship. The majority opinions tended to erase distinctions between child and adult as a matter of doctrine but implicitly emphasized cognitive abilities as the mode through which the child earned citizenship. The opinions connected individual thought, strategic planning, critique, and the ability to make meaningful choices to civic notions of democracy as persuasive communication, free thought, and fair procedures. Although this shift appeared as an unbridled expansion of rights to citizens, this inclusion narrative was tempered by qualifications in the majority opinions themselves, as well as existing dissent. The latter questioned the child's cognitive ability to choose. It worried that including incapable citizens would pose intolerable risks to the political order and hierarchy necessary for our constitutional democracy. Dissenters also argued that the project of inclusion could produce injustice, because children should be treated with solicitude and care instead of being forced to strike out on their own. Finally, the dissenting opinions also questioned the authority of the judges themselves by raising poor judicial temperament as an argument for opposing constitutional change. This last factor was a key aspect of novelization, not a mere philosophical objection. Judges placed each other in the unfolding stories of these cases in ways that disrupted the traditional judicial role.

A more conservative Supreme Court expressed a desire to return to traditions to recover what was lost. Part 3 follows the "Child as Reform Object." Its chapters (6 through 8) study cases from the 1970s and early 1980s. These transitional cases—*Ingraham v. Wright* (corporal punishment in schools), *Parham v. J. R.* (indefinite civil commitment of minors), and *Bethel School District v. Fraser* (suspension for a ribald student government endorsement)—exploited the conditions of inclusive citizenship that the opinions in the cases from part 2 had articulated. Although these cases were decided by a conservative Supreme Court, the justices were constrained by the language and rhetorical strategies of their predecessors. The decisions limited the availability of full citizenship rights for the sake of shared traditions. And because cognitive capabilities structured the rationales for the opinions that expanded citizenship rights in prior cases, these transitional cases introduced new characters to illustrate poor judgment through their behaviors. The incorrigible and unruly child returned, and adults as prudent risk managers appeared as guardians of democratic order. The cases were bound by their affinity for judicial deference and appealed to a range of publics as justifications for this vision of civic life—a general public tasked with holding officials accountable, a public of benevolent parents and professionals, and a public of impressionable adolescent rubes who needed protection from certain speech in order to become citizens. Judgment in this version of the constitutional narrative becomes increasingly specialized, bureaucratized, and situational. The commitment to civic life was guaranteed by a beneficent, mannered state, but the legal narratives that justified the decisions described a fractured and complex state at a level of remove from everyday citizens.

These attempts to return to a time of tradition, protection, civility, and paternal care could not survive the pressures of increasingly fragmented and bureaucratic life. Part 4 studies the contours of that downfall for the "Child as Contractual Citizen." The chapters (9 through 11) investigate cases from end of the twentieth century (along with one from the twenty-first). *Hazelwood v. Kuhlmeier* permitted censorship of offensive newspaper articles. *DeShaney v. Winnebago County* declined to hold social workers accountable for the severe abuse of a young child. *Morse v. Frederick* suppressed student expression at a civic event. The judgment on display here is contractual—limited by the four corners of a text. The importance of cognition shifts to virtuoso performance backed by interpretive acumen. New characters are the vehicle for the change: the swift-acting administrator, the role-disciplined bureaucrat, and the synthetic interpreter were each used to justify a vision of democracy in the image of a contract. On the other side of the equation were characters at the margins of public life. The unprofessional teen who used the public sphere to settle scores and breach taboos, the victim of bad luck who never had a chance, and the fame-seeking slacker. The picture of democracy that emerged was one of a limited state managing risks. This conceptual shift altered the social contract between the state and the citizen. From one perspective, this is the privilege of success, a liberal democracy that, having already advanced individual rights and participation, was now merely defining its outer limits. But another perspective might see cruel neglect, a slothful state absolved from the responsibility of developing citizens' capabilities while devaluing critical questioning, diversity, and freedom of thought in the public sphere. That state is obliged only to implement consistently its own written commitments, which would essentially protect itself at the expense of its people.

That observation brings us back to the student activism and migrant children that opened the introduction. These examples point to specific instances of liberal democratic failure to make good on its commitments to security, dignity, and an open future. The case of the child as citizen may be a symptom of the larger crises that liberal democracy faces. A constitutional narrative can only succeed insofar as "We, the People" can see ourselves in its stories and themes. It may be tempting to write off constitutional commitment as a naïve appeal to an idyllic time that covers over a now-crumbling liberal democracy. The conclusion to this volume evaluates these questions with reference to influential attempts to rehabilitate liberal critique. The broader question of the fate of liberal democracy is beyond the scope of the book and the case studies. Resolving the crisis will necessitate a wide approach at a variety of institutional sites. Nevertheless, the book tries to demonstrate that cases involving the constitutional status of the child are an important site of study, because they resolve a recurring crisis of citizenship. Their provisional resolutions contain relationships between civic practices and democratic ideals, submitted for consideration to be discarded, retained, or rehabilitated as we remake a constitutional order anew.

PART I

THE CHILD AS WARD

In the nineteenth and early twentieth centuries, the United States was struggling with the question of state sovereignty over the child and its limits. The controversies—whether the state could commit the child to a reformatory over a parent's objection, whether a teacher could use corporal punishment for misbehavior in school, whether a teacher could use corporal punishment for speech off campus, and whether legislation could prohibit attending certain schools or receiving specific instruction in schools—illustrate the significance of the child to general understandings of citizenship. The opinions use the child's status as future citizen to justify state sovereignty, define citizenship virtues, and mark characteristics of sound judgment.

These cases constituted the child as a ward of the state. This strategy was a foundational approach for articulating broader themes of constitutional citizenship. The state's authority was justified in order to instill virtue in the child. The opinions argued that good citizens possessed specific virtues. They recognized sound judgment through the display of cognitive signs. These signs demonstrated how reason disciplined passion. Citizenship and judgment themes emerged in these cases as a complex mixture of persuasive public authorities, legal precedents, and shared community values. Reference to broad principles alone would not explain how these opinions constructed their legitimacy. Specific characters and their interaction with these themes embodied the principles at issue in the opinions. At the same time, the opinions authorized themselves through appeals to stock stories, ideas, and themes without much evidence. In these ways, they resolved disputes through novelistic contestations, adaptations, and applications. Put simply, the *how* matters as much as the *what,* and can only be discovered with careful attention to each opinion's details.

The child in these cases was rendered as passive or incapable. Read in our own time, the children in these opinions were far different from student activists like Greta Thunberg, Zyhana Bryant (the student who first petitioned the City of Charlottesville to remove a statue of Robert E. Lee from a public park), and the NeverAgain student movement in favor of stricter regulations on gun ownership. The child's actions in these early cases were generally not significant; when courts did focus on the child's behavior, the opinions described it as impulsive, destructive, or incorrigible. Because of these traits, the child's behavior was a threat to a liberal order that respected private rights of property ownership and a commitment to economic activity. This understanding of citizenship was static: the state guaranteed the citizen's natural rights. The opinions wedded state authority for that guarantee to the regime of property ownership it served. Citizens were virtuous by nature. They possessed these virtues (rather than performed them), and families and state institutions were tasked with a near-religious mission to instill them as character traits in the children who did not have them. As a result, the opinions constructed a model of the citizen as a worker-producer and not primarily a political participant tasked with making judgments.

Judgment mattered when agents exercised sovereignty over the child. These latter included the parents, teachers, and legislators charged with implanting virtue in the wayward child. How would the judicial opinions considered here authorize sound judgment? The cases made rhetorical choices that constructed judgment ideals for citizens and experts alike. Benevolence justified sovereignty. In assessing benevolent intention, judges marked its display as the presence of contextual markers—time, place, setting, sequenced process—from which one could infer the capacity to be reasonable. It prized the display of cognitive control, meaning the discipline of emotion so that an authority could accomplish a greater good. As the cases that conclude the chapter demonstrate, emotional discipline also opened up a longer time horizon, because good judges were not beholden to fear of immediate circumstances. For judges similarly needing to establish their constitutional authority, expert judgment meant the display of distinction through dissociative categories. Judges performed their authority by showing their ability to classify and discipline the intentions of those they judged. Because these acts of judgment stimulated anxiety about judicial overreach, the judges also introduced a discourse of limits—expert judges needed to maintain critical distance (and humility), root their decisions in deeply held traditions, and tolerate periodic injustices as the price of constitutional expertise.

Chapter 1 begins with *Ex parte Crouse* (Pennsylvania, 1839) the pivotal case that established the legality of juvenile reform houses as a response to the public problem of wayward children. This case was the first to justify state authority to take control of children from parents in order to reform their character. *Ex parte Crouse* constructed state constitutional power over the child under a model of delegated authority to address the child's character shortfalls.

The chapter then studies two cases that examined the bounds of teachers' disciplinary authority. *Pendergrass v. North Carolina* (North Carolina, 1837) involved a teacher who allegedly used excessive physical punishment and *Lander v. Seaver* (Vermont, 1857) dealt with a teacher exercising his authority off of school grounds. Each case considered in this chapter extended the logic of zones of public officials' legitimate competence, defining sound judgment as the control of dangerous speech (and action) through the management of time, space, and topic.

Chapter 2 studies three cases (one state case and two landmark Supreme Court opinions) that opened the door to considering the child's liberty. The first, *People v. Turner* (1870), was an Illinois case that reached a contrary conclusion to *Ex parte Crouse,* holding that Illinois could not indefinitely hold a juvenile without violating his or her natural liberty. The second and third cases, *Meyer v. Nebraska* (1923) and *Pierce v. Society of Sisters* (1925), considered the constitutionality of statutes that regulated who may instruct children and in what manner. *Meyer* and *Pierce* retained the figure of the child as a future citizen, as well as the economic focus of citizenship and the political order. But these cases explicitly cast the question in terms of liberty—the freedom to raise one's children as one sees fit, and the freedom of teachers and schools to educate them accordingly. These latter cases conceived of constitutional injury in private terms. As they expanded the bounds of liberty for a modern society, they limited the state's ability to develop public civic virtues. This posture would form the ground for extending (and, eventually, limiting) the child's citizenship rights and in fact for expanding the liberties of all citizens. It would also inform the bounds of reasonable judgment.

The set of rhetorical strategies that the chapter highlights constitutes one model for addressing the problem of the incapable citizen in constitutional discourse. The model emerges from the rhetorical reconstruction of the characters and themes present in the relevant judicial opinions. The model does not claim to be authoritative in a particular legal case. The cluster of arguments, tropes, and commonplaces that form it also implicitly structures a constitutional understanding of the citizen in the ways noted in the introduction—by filling out the meaning of values, virtues, and rights of citizenship, and by connecting those meanings to the performance of judgment. Like any culture-variant model, its utility has a lifespan and its influence can wax and wane with shifting political and social conditions. Nevertheless, the model's themes and discourses appear in cases that explicitly expanded liberal rights, as well as more recent disputes that have limited those rights. These early cases identify the role of cognitive performance in the evolving constitutional narrative.

1

VIRTUOUS CHARACTER

Nineteenth-Century Controversies

THE ESTABLISHMENT OF THE NEW YORK HOUSE OF REFUGE IN 1825 marks a watershed moment in making child welfare a public concern in the United States.[1] Addressing the needs of children who were begging and allegedly committing crimes in the city, it was spearheaded by "Quaker reformers who had gained prominence through earlier works of charity and reform."[2] Quaker advocates for the House of Refuge argued for rehabilitation and reformation instead of retributive and punitive ends. They associated tropes of character reformation with moral blamelessness and appealed to crime prevention and Christian obligation. The public spectacle of these vagrant children was repulsive: "Every person . . . must be forcibly struck with the ragged . . . appearance, the vile language, and the idle and miserable habits of great numbers of children, most of whom are of an age suitable for schools, or for some useful employment."[3] The Quaker argument was a combination of altruistic striving and an anxiety about techniques to manage and discipline these potential citizens.

Reform advocates believed that the wayward child's lack of moral culpability meant that the child could be saved. This idea justified a separate institutional arrangement and method for reform. The vagrant child did not stray because of selfish or evil choices, but rather because of failures in the family. Parents were "too poor, or too degenerate" to provide for basic needs of clothing and schooling. These same parents encouraged their children to beg, lie, and speak in indecorous ways. The child did not freely choose these threatening and antisocial behaviors. As a consequence, to treat the child as a hardened adult criminal was unjustified and immoral. All of these arguments came to the fore in the landmark Pennsylvania case *Ex parte Crouse*, which considered the legality of the enabling legislation for the state's ability to take custody of these children. *Ex parte Crouse* began a long-term legal engagement with the problem of the child as a nascent citizen—not yet capable of citizenship because their capacities must be developed. This chapter investigates the response to that problem in the *Crouse* opinion itself and in two cases that applied some of the rhetorical strategies of *Crouse* to the different context of situational school discipline (*North Carolina v. Pendergrass* and *Lander v. Seaver*).

What were some of the background conditions that shaped the category of the child as a constitutional problem? The Constitution relies on a type of refined political participation that filters the worst passions of the mob and finds voice in representation. "A republic, if you can keep it" was Benjamin Franklin's expression of the sentiment that the Constitution was worth ratifying, even though it was an imperfect document, because it was the best hope for stable democratic rule. The complicated story of the founding has returned time and again to an idyllic picture of reasonable deliberation, decision-making informed by reason, and procedures that support freedom of thought and speech. But from the earliest days of the United States, not everybody was given access to these freedoms, nor were they charged with the responsibility to "keep" the republic. The country maintained the system of slavery, a cruel, ruinous, racist institution that explicitly denied citizenship to enslaved people. Many states also restricted voting, denying the franchise to women and to men who did not own property. These basic exclusions served as painful reminders that America's new democratic ideals were supported by unjust categorical exclusions.

Nor was the child charged with keeping the republic, because the child could not participate in the sites of discussion and democratic decision-making necessary for political life. Education would become an important aspect of preparing children for this kind of participation. Horace Mann argued for a collective responsibility to develop the "liberal education of youth, especially of the lower class of people."[4] The public school served as the touchstone for a professionalized education made available to all. It would provide a shared experience to introduce republican values and to disseminate them widely, in no small part to discipline threats to this still-emerging order.[5] Public education in America advanced republican virtues by also pushing religious practices into the sphere of private choice and by emphasizing the public goal of shared work and economic activity. All of this meant that from the child's treatment in the cradle, to the selection of work, to the cultivation of sentiments, education was a key site to produce liberal citizens with the requisite capabilities and civic attitudes.[6]

Legal controversies in the British colonies and early American contexts worked through the question of childhood and meaningful consent: "Political theorists, ministers, judges, legislators, and lawyers, ordinary men and women, and even children themselves fought over the meaning of consent . . . because major questions of political power and the fundamental ordering of society hinged on the meaning of consent."[7] Legal practice guides and common law decisions carried these conflicts forward as the state was refining its governing project grounded in the equal capacity for consent. Changes to legal rules reflected shifts in the liberal democratic theory of consent, influenced by the Lockean concern that children "learn to reason to obtain training for future consent" to be governed.[8] Age replaced birth status as the proxy for capable judgment.[9] Questions concerning competent child testimony, culpability for crimes, and consent to marriage, among other areas, all show that at the time of America's founding, children were held to be contextually incapable of meaningful consent until they matured into citizens. These exclusions were byproducts of gradual political struggle, and legal discourse reflected their evolution.[10] By the mid-nineteenth century, John Stuart Mill took the child's exclusion to be *constitutive*, relating to liberalism's central axioms to an extent that historical and situational restrictions did not.[11]

Children became the focus of an intense investment whose goal was to preserve an industrializing and urbanizing democracy dedicated to liberal principles. The wayward child's flawed decisions violated the liberty of others, reflecting the state's failure to guide the child to develop the capabilities of judgment necessary for citizenship. Organic institutions such as the family, the school, and the church managed the problem. Pedagogy in America in the late eighteenth and early nineteenth centuries "order[ed] the principles of action and thus tame[d] and regularize[d] the uncertainties of the world of individual liberty and freedom."[12] An emerging genre of imaginative literature aimed at children expressed moralistic and virtuous themes in an effort to move children from dependency toward autonomy.[13] Because the child's threat to social order was a failure of individual character, the state began to instruct in virtues to correct character flaws.

This activity pushed the boundaries of state authority in a democracy founded on the liberal ideal of limited government. The judiciary played a significant role: from its early forays into family law answering questions regarding the legitimacy of children, a child's competency to testify, and custody disputes concerning the best interests of the child, the judiciary established its own legitimacy as a governing institution in part by crafting legal authority over the child.[14] Early judicial approaches to the child reveal an attitude towards the latter as a nascent citizen. Judicial opinions that assessed the legality of state custody and discipline over the child demonstrated important early liberal values in their rhetorical justifications. They figured children as incapable because they lacked the requisite skills for citizenship in a liberal society. These early decisions held that the child was not capable of consent, embedding a theory of character formation that equated judgment with sound decision-making. The relevant opinions justified these decisions with reference to liberal values related to industry, property ownership, and productivity. Embracing these values became the sign of one's good character, evidence that one had the self-discipline to act as a liberal citizen.

The Incapable Child, the House of Refuge, and *Ex parte Crouse*

Mary Crouse had committed her daughter, Mary Ann Crouse, to the House of Refuge in Philadelphia (which had been founded following New York's lead). Mary Ann was committed for "vicious conduct" that "rendered her control beyond [her mother's] power."[15] Mary Ann's father did not agree with this decision. He filed a writ of habeas corpus to release his daughter, challenging the constitutionality of the act and arguing that his parental right and her right to liberty were being violated by her continued confinement. The House of Refuge claimed the authority to retain custody of Mary Ann through its enabling legislation. The original 1826 law "declared that the managers should, 'at their discretion, receive into the said House of Refuge, such children who shall be taken up or committed as vagrants, or upon any criminal charge, or duly convicted of criminal offences, as may be in the judgment . . . of any alderman or justice of the peace, or of the managers of the almshouse and house of employment, be deemed proper objects.'"[16]

An 1835 supplement broadened this authority, enabling House of Refuge managers "to receive into their care and guardianship, infants, males under the age of twenty-one years, and females under the age of eighteen years committed to their custody" if they fit into one of the following categories: (1) a child who, "by reason of incorrigible or vicious conduct" is "beyond the power" of the parent, making commitment necessary "for the morals and future welfare" of the child; (2) a child who, for reason of "vagrancy, or of incorrigible or vicious conduct" coupled with the parent's "moral depravity . . . or otherwise" faced a situation that rendered the parent "incapable or unwilling" to properly care for the child; or (3) a child committed under the procedures of the original 1826 act.[17]

The Supreme Court of Pennsylvania rejected Mary Ann's father's petition in a per curiam opinion.[18] *Ex parte Crouse* justified state control over the incapable child as an exercise of parens patriae authority.[19] The rhetorical decision to ground the state's authority in this doctrine legitimized character reformation as an acceptable goal of the state. Furthermore, the doctrine embodies a long tradition that managed incapacities through possession. Latin for "parent of the nation," it dates back millennia in both the Judaic tradition and in Roman law.[20] This tradition found its way into English rule and common law, which inflected the practice with a notion of responsibility. Its early manifestations asserted authority over the disadvantaged: Edward I's rule in the thirteenth and fourteenth centuries claimed wardship over "fools and idiots," put into law by the Statute Prerogativa Regis of 1324.[21] The ruler's sovereignty was at its strongest when the individual's capabilities were at their weakest.

The *Ex parte Crouse* opinion is extremely short—under a thousand words. Yet the opinion is influential because of its legal result in applying parens patriae to the case of the child. *Ex parte Crouse* justified this decision by classifying the House of Refuge as more akin to a school than a prison. Because its purpose was to reform (and not punish) the child, the statute overrode the parental right to custody, because "the public has a paramount interest in the virtue and knowledge of its members."[22] The opinion was unconcerned about Mary Anne's loss of liberty.

The opinion here demonstrates that the problem of citizenship is partially one of rhetorical management: how could judges justify state intervention with the natural rights of citizens (in this case, Mary Ann's father)? Did Mary herself have these rights? These questions presented an emerging liberal constitutional order with the problem of balancing ideological commitments to natural rights with the need to produce citizens who embraced these commitments and the public policy of violating the natural parental rights of citizens in order to do so.

Character Reformation, Benevolent Management, and Citizenship: Unfit Parents and Incorrigible Children

Ex parte Crouse resolved the constitutional problem rhetorically, with reference to the characteristics and virtues of the parties. It presented the state statute and the House of Refuge as a benevolent cure. The opinion made four significant rhetorical choices to shape the meaning of citizenship. It described the child with tropes of incapacity, which removed natural right claims from the child and justified abrogating the natural rights of the parent. The opinion then articulated a meaning of citizenship as the possession of virtues oriented toward industry and the economic production of private goods. As it did this, it created an image of the wayward child in a liminal state—alive, but not possessing natural rights; incorrigible, but salvageable; doing wrong, but not culpable. The state's intervention was acceptable because of its benevolent intention and its method of character reformation. These novelizations justified the legal outcome. The opinion reserved the practice of judgment for the court because the parents were incapable and the child was corrupted. The opinion understood civic practices as displays of virtue rather than performances of participation: a citizen's display of character instead of their expressions of preference and critique of the political order, or social bonding through shared practices. Being primarily about expertise, the opinion displayed sound judgment by aligning legal distinctions with a hierarchical model for decision-making thematically and stylistically: judges authorized opinions by evaluating acceptable intentions, valid goals, and character assessments. These distinctions permitted the opinion to introduce terms of higher legal abstraction. Like the expression of citizenship as virtue, this rhetorical style deflected attention from concrete practices and toward appropriate legal categories.

The opinion framed the child as incapable and therefore not entitled to robust citizenship rights. This incapable child was an "infant," a standard legal term that nevertheless signaled the child's diminished capacities, as well as their diminished rights. The opinion relied on references to Mary Ann Crouse's inability to conform to liberal society—she was fortunate that the House of Refuge "snatched [her] from a course which must have ended in confirmed depravity."[23] Although the short opinion did not address her status as a citizen, her categorization meant that she did not have the same rights that her parents had. She had no "natural right to exemption from restraints which conduce to [her] welfare."[24] These diminishments of the incapable child shifted the legal question from one of discretionary authority to moral command. Mary Ann's confinement was "not only . . . lawful, but it would be an act of extreme cruelty to release her from it."[25] Couched in the rhetoric of inevitability, the opinion claimed that because the incapable child threatens liberal order, the state's authority to curb liberty was not merely justified but compelled.

Second, the opinion used the child's (and parents') lack of capabilities to articulate citizenship as the possession of virtue. Mary Ann's descent into depravity was a public threat because she would not be trained (at home) to respect commonly shared values of economic production. The opinion validated the House of Refuge's control over the child because of its dedication to instilling these virtues of economic productivity and devotion to morality. The House of Refuge "train[ed] its inmates to industry . . . imbuing their minds with principles of morality and religion . . . [and] furnish[ed] them with means to earn a living."[26] *Ex parte Crouse* identified liberal citizens as productive workers guided by a religious zeal, traits the wayward child lacked. Without them, the child could not work to maintain a liberal order that valued private rights. At the same time, Mary Ann's parents were "incompetent or corrupt," implying that they caused her delinquency by failing to instruct her properly.[27] Their parental rights were "natural, but not inalienable."[28] The opinion argued that parens patriae authority could override parental authority where parents are "unequal to the task of education, or unworthy of it,"[29] because of the public's "paramount interest in the virtue and knowledge of its members."[30] The public interest in the higher virtues of property ownership, work, and industry outweigh individual parental custody rights.

The House of Refuge embodied the discourse of benevolent savior of the child through a particular mode of character reformation. The historical record has already established these motives;[31] their connection between the state's intention and the end goal lies in their importance for citizenship. Benevolence signaled a key strategy for grappling with those who lacked the requisite character—where they were morally blameless, they were subjects for reform through isolation. The House of Refuge was "not a prison, but a school."[32] A school reformed character, while a prison punished people. The proper pedagogy was isolation: the House of Refuge worked by "separating [its inhabitants] from the corrupting influence of improper associates."[33] The wayward child was unfit because of habits created by immoral routines. Isolation promised character reformation by disrupting these routines. By replacing poor imitative influences with habits of industriousness, the House of Refuge would cultivate citizens attached to liberal values. This frame also contextualized the state's restriction of Mary's freedom. Because she experienced "no more than what is borne, to a greater or less extent, in every school,"[34] the public's interest outweighed her claim to liberty.

Finally, the opinion made a statement about sound judgment as the cognitive ability to make fine distinctions. Although this ability is an aspect of all judicial opinions—to distinguish one case from another, to divide a concept in terms of its better and worse applications, to interpret a fact based on contextual information, etc.—the distinctions in *Ex parte Crouse* matter because of their role in the process of novelization. Their use reinforced the judgment of the opinion through linguistic performance. This ability to display judgment through making material distinctions was present in the opinion but was unavailable to Mary Ann Crouse or her parents. The latter were mere possessors of rights, whereas the opinion could perform authority through command of these distinctions. The opinion used distinguishing tactics, such as dissociation, definition, and abstraction, to legitimate Mary Ann's commitment. The opinion claimed its authority through abstract categories, a sparse style, and plain, compelled conclusions. This expert judgment prefigured the legal answer by focusing on public purpose (not means). Liberty was natural, government restrictions artificial. The House of Refuge claimed authority over Mary Ann through delegation, which expressed shared agreements on status and preference (a contract that excluded the child). The parent held primary authority over the child and the state was a second-best substitute. Tropes of categorization and sorting drove the legal narrative, and these techniques performed the idea of hierarchical authority over the child. In so doing, they did more than exclude the child: they signaled that the gulf between citizen and noncitizen was the gap between those capable of making these distinctions and those who were incapable of so doing. Mary Ann was an infant, not an adult citizen. The House of Refuge was like a school, not a prison. Prisons punished inmates and schools reformed children. Expertise in separation and alienation produced common bonds. The House of Refuge *separated* the child offender from adults and *isolated* these children from each other to reform character.

Ideologically, the discourse of judgment in *Ex parte Crouse* focused on intentions, rather than the means of permissible state action. This discourse valued what legal actors wanted to accomplish and their reasons for wanting to accomplish it. If you meant well, you did well: the House of Refuge's benevolence was taken as a constitutional mandate. This choice ignored institutional practices and Mary Ann's specific conditions of confinement. "Isolation" and "reformation, not punishment" may have been the stated purposes, but they were inaccurate descriptions of child experiences at places such as the House of Refuge—abuse was common.[35] The opinion's mode of judgment rendered this issue irrelevant. In making its legal determination according to purpose, it limited its analysis to the state's own descriptions and arguments about that purpose. Much like the opinion itself, the House of Refuge's declaration of intent proved its own legitimacy. This intention justified controlling the child as an object invested with the possibilities of future citizenship.

Ex parte Crouse "set a trend" for the expansion of juvenile commitment processes focused on rehabilitation (but less concerned with due process).[36] More importantly for citizenship, it exemplified an approach to the problem of the incapable child as a problem that well-meaning state institutions were authorized to correct. Its creation of characters—the child who lacked virtue and threatened liberal order, the corrupted parents, and the benevolent reformers—connected to a discourse of character formation that was permitted precisely because of the state's declarations of its own good intentions. Although the opinion presented the ruling as an obvious declaration, the creation of the characters and themes left space for imaginative resistance, as well as open questions for future resolution. *Ex parte Crouse* suggests that Mary Ann's mother had chosen to commit her because Mary Ann's behavior was "beyond [her mother's] control."[37] Mary Ann's primary caregiver had attested to her own incapability, and the state stepped in to the rescue. The opinion authorized the state's action through larger abstractions, which left open key questions: If Mary Ann's commitment to the House of Refuge's was permissible because of its nonpunitive nature, what about punishment in schools? Did conditions of abuse in reformatories matter, and if not, why not? What about contrary discourses of character reform? And what cases, precisely, were appropriate for character reform? These types of questions addressed situations that called for quick decisions by guardians. But these situations also had the same stakes for civic life: if the delinquent child turned loose in public posed a threat to public order, then potential future wayward children were present in schools as well. Physical discipline and correction in schools, presumably to neutralize the threat, was common. *Ex parte Crouse* did not address the issue, but it could not go unaddressed for long. Its answers began, however deliberately, to articulate images of public judgment through the masters and teachers whose disciplinary actions to control the child received scrutiny.

Judgment as Temporary Delegation: Justifications of Authority in School

Episodic physical punishment in school implicated questions of individual judgment because it involved a momentary decision to respond to a child's behavior. By the mid-nineteenth century, the American public school bore increasing responsibilities for producing future citizens of the republic.[38] This mission, reflected in school committee advice and pedagogical plans, set itself the goal to "shape children into industrious, frugal, temperate, subordinate, trustworthy, brave, clean, and reverent adults."[39] This shift brought about conflict between parents and schools over who had the authority to discipline children as a way to influence their character.[40] Corporal punishment was an obvious lightning rod, displayed in the attitude of compromise between parents and school committees whereby it was "considered a last resort, [but] was generally defended . . . in the face of parental challenges."[41] The constitutional controversy over a school's ability to inflict corporal punishment implicated the scope of citizen judgment, because it foregrounded individual judgments of students (nascent citizens) and teachers (tasked with developing citizenship capabilities) alike. Two cases in particular—*North Carolina v. Pendergrass* and *Lander v. Seaver*—served as paradigmatic examples of an approach that asserted state authority over the child.[42] These cases displaced parental prerogative and legitimated the state's authority over the child according to developing norms of judgment. The resulting judicial opinions framed judgment as the manifestation of cognitive signs and temporal distinctions that legitimates the abrogation of natural rights.

Judgment as Reasoned Reflection: *North Carolina v. Pendergrass*

Rachel Pendergrass was a teacher who "kept a school for small children" in North Carolina.[43] One day, "after mild treatment towards a little girl, of six or seven years of age, had failed, [Pendergrass] whipped her with a switch."[44] The beating left physical marks on the girl's body. Two other marks (on her arm and neck) were made with something bigger than the switch. All of the marks "disappeared in a few days."[45] The state brought a criminal case for assault against Pendergrass. The trial judge instructed the jury that Pendergrass's right to "chastise the child was coextensive with that of a parent," but that because the child was young, the jury should convict Pendergrass if it found that her punishment produced the physical marks. The jury convicted Pendergrass, who then appealed.[46]

The Supreme Court of North Carolina reversed the decision in a per curiam opinion. According to the opinion, a conviction required more evidence than the marks alone, because the child's injuries were temporary: "Any correction . . . which produces temporary pain only . . . cannot be so pronounced, since it may have been necessary for the reformation of the child. . . . Teachers exceed the limits of their authority when they cause lasting mischief; but act within the limits of it, when they inflict temporary pain."[47] The jury could only convict her if it believed that Pendergrass was "gratifying [her] malice."[48]

Like *Ex parte Crouse*, *Pendergrass* related the figure of the child to a mature citizen, contrasting the child's incapabilities with the citizen's virtues. Its narrative focused primarily on the desired outcomes in order to justify state power. Relying on parens patriae authority, the opinion presumed that the child lacked citizenship capabilities and justified restrictions on liberty as acceptable discipline to reform the child. First, the *Pendergrass* opinion described the state's authority to train children for citizenship as a delegation of (natural) parental authority, which functioned as a limiting principle for individual judgment. It explained that the state's power over the child "is analogous to that which belongs to parents, and the authority of the teacher is regarded as a delegation of parental authority."[49] Creating virtuous citizens was a mission that qualified parental rights to raise a child with the "sacred duty" to produce liberal citizens and defined judgment as the ability to "train up and qualify their children, for becoming useful and virtuous members of society."[50] This language did not describe the kinds of virtues that were necessary, or the uses to which they would be put. These omissions demonstrate the value of reading opinions for their novelistic properties—the court was not legally compelled to introduce such elements, but its choice to do so necessarily shaped the relationship between individual citizen and state as a contract. The important question was the authority of the teacher, and by shifting away from the specifics of the end goals of a citizen's character, the opinion took on the perspective of the teacher, which privileged the time horizon of the school (not the long-term product of the citizen). The delegation metaphor filled out a story of citizenship values containing a natural preference for private (parental authority) over public (teacher authority). The latter was accountable to the former, and the child deferred to both authorities. Delegation functioned at a level of generality, because no teacher possessed complete information about how each parent of every child would react in every conceivable situation.

Couched in the language of individual character, the opinion framed the bounds of a teacher's authority with the goal to instill habits of citizenship. What mattered most was to establish immediate control. For this reason a teacher, like a parent, needed the "ability to command obedience, to control stubbornness, to quicken diligence, and to reform bad habits; and to enable him to exercise this salutary sway, he is armed with the power to administer moderate correction."[51] By telling this story from the perspective of the teacher pursuing a goal, *Pendergrass* endowed the journey toward full citizenship with the sense of an almost religious mission the state must earnestly pursue. *Pendergrass* reinforced the importance of public institutions for recognizing private rights through training and discipline. The short opinion justified this approach with a discourse of power in military terms ("command," "control," "armed with the power"). Those who lacked capabilities were subject to this power so that they could become useful citizens able to habituate their movement between the private and public spheres.

Judgment in *Pendergrass* required the display of proper motives. The decision in this instance was more complicated than the one that faced the *Ex parte Crouse* court, because unlike the question of committing a child to a reformatory (yes or no), the abstract power to discipline a schoolchild did not necessarily include its extreme application. *Pendergrass* limited these extreme applications by articulating signs of judgment—the teacher who exercised poor judgment exceeded her authority. In doing so, the opinion once again limited its analysis to the teacher's perspective—the actions she undertook and the immediate results of those actions.

Dissociative categories specified a sense of proportionality for individual judgment. The law will only tolerate "moderate correction," distinguished from "immoderate punishment."[52] Moderate correction was defined through a second dissociation—if it produced permanent injury, it was immoderate, but if it "produce[d] temporary pain only," then "it may have been necessary for the reformation of the child, and does not injuriously affect future welfare."[53]

These dissociations understood bodily integrity, a key liberal right, as a marker of proportional decision-making. Temporary physical pain was allowed, as was shame to produce virtuous citizens. The dissociations marked sound judgment as the periodic power—the proper time and measure—to limit accepted liberal rights.

Pendergrass also addressed the anxiety of expert judgment in a democracy—the reluctance to put the court in the story by passing judgment on the actions of another. As noted in the introduction, legal discourse conceals the role of novelization because of the need for judicial opinions to impose discipline, finality, and their own authority. Courts typically end the story through their own judgments. *Pendergrass* shows how the problem of judgment in legal opinions is doubled—it assessed the judgment of another while legitimating its own credibility to judge. *Pendergrass* established its authority with a discourse of legal judgment as analytical declension, proceeding first from generally accepted principles to the gray zone of judgment. These principles guided but did not resolve the case. The opinion performed judgment first as procedure and later as practical wisdom. This style explains the elevated roles assigned to definition and dissociation, because those tactics propelled the opinion through the gray zones where practical wisdom might otherwise pertain. The tactics appeared to maximize private liberty by categorically limiting judicial review and tying public institutional incursions to goals around which there was an unquestionable public consensus. These strategies relate to citizen judgment and civic virtue because they established the lingua franca necessary to "talk back" to the opinion in the proper form.

Finally, *Pendergrass* signaled the importance for legitimate expertise to acknowledge its own limits. Articulating a general principle of deference when assessing individual intentions, the opinion framed standards that reserved judicial intervention for exceptional and extreme cases. When dealing with moderate correction, the legality of a teacher's actions "must depend entirely . . . on the *quo animo* with which it was administered. . . . The master is the judge when correction is required, and of the degree . . . he cannot be made penally responsible for error of judgment, but only for wickedness of purpose."[54] It reversed the lower court jury's verdict because temporary physical marks were insufficient evidence for a conviction. Without signs of "wickedness of purpose," these temporary marks could not be considered traces of an assault. Pendergrass was within her zone of permissible judgment in hitting the child.

Pendergrass structured expert judgment with rules of presumption to guide inferences based on signs. Its own performance articulated a limit for expertise: a liberal society must tolerate injustice and have faith in alternate sources of redress. Separating judgment from justice, *Pendergrass* aligned sound judgment with democracy for its function within the political system. If producing the virtuous citizen sometimes resulted in abuses, "these indiscretions [would] probably find their check and correction, in parental affection, and in public opinion."[55] This tactic reproduced the principle of delegation that the decision had applied to the teacher-parent relationship. Because the judiciary lacked the institutional tools, parents and public opinion were a more democratic means to judge whether a teacher's conduct related to civic purposes. This expression of institutional humility implied the toleration of periodic injustice. The teacher behaving badly was simply the price of democratic life, to be "tolerated as a part of those imperfections and inconveniences, which no human laws can wholly remove or redress."[56] Reaffirming state sovereignty over the child to produce good citizens, *Pendergrass* emphasized the power that parents and teachers had over the child in order to instill the virtues necessary for public life, tempered by the judgment to accomplish these ends. Like the style of *Ex parte Crouse*, the *Pendergrass* opinion performed sound judgment with linguistic distinctions that connected content to form—the distinctions elevated a particular set of signs that signaled higher cognitive ability. This cognitive ability, as much as any doctrine or precedent, legitimated Pendergrass's decision to punish the child. The criteria—whether the punishment left a mark, and whether the decision maker communicated limits to their authority—supported an inference that the individual acted with moderation and permissible intention.

Pendergrass merely reversed a conviction because it was grounded in insufficient evidence. The opinion set general parameters for parens patriae authority but did not apply these parameters to a specific act of school conduct. As schools and parents continued to clash over this issue, these conflicts would produce jurisprudence that scrutinized the contextual facts of on-the-spot discipline decisions. A child's public speech could easily provoke disciplinary action. This development marked the initial acknowledgment of the child's own capabilities. The next case, *Lander v. Seaver*, typified the state's evolving authority over the child in terms of explicit punishment for public speech.

Public Criticism as Threat: Dangerous Speech and Authority in *Lander v. Seaver* (1859)

Peter Lander Jr. was an eleven-year-old student in A. B. Seaver's classroom in Burlington, Vermont. One day after school, while "driving his father's cow" past Seaver's house, Lander called his teacher "Old Jack Seaver" in front of Seaver and some of his other students.[57] The next day, Seaver "reprimand[ed] [Lander]" for the insult and "whipped him with a small rawhide."[58] Lander brought a claim for assault and battery. Seaver argued that the discipline was justified because Lander had disrespected Seaver, damaging Seaver's authority with the other students. Seaver claimed that "his ordinary management of his school had always been mild and moderate," and that Lander's punishment was a part of "the usage and custom of the teachers in other schools in Burlington."[59]

The trial court had to decide whether Seaver's decision to punish Lander was justified, and if so, whether the punishment was excessive. It instructed the jury that Seaver's punishment was justified if Lander had used "contemptuous language . . . and the tendency of this conduct, if unpunished, would be to . . . lessen . . . [Seaver's] control over the school as a teacher."[60] The trial court also instructed the jury that it was "reasonable and proper" that Lander understand what he was being punished for; the jury could infer this understanding even "without any formal communication from the master."[61] In deciding whether using the rawhide whip was excessive, the trial court instructed the jury to consider the instrument of discipline's relation to the character of punishment, and Seaver's motives in using it.[62]

The trial court included statements of law in its instructions that referred to the in loco parentis doctrine: "the authority of a schoolmaster over his pupils was nearly related to that of a parent over his child, and . . . its exercise rested in a measure in discretion, and that . . . the schoolmaster acts in a judicial capacity in administering correction."[63] The jury was instructed to enter a verdict for Seaver if "he acted with proper motives and in good faith, and in his judgment for the best interests of the school," even if the jury believed the punishment "too severe . . . and beyond what they would have gone [*sic*] in a similar case."[64] The trial court also instructed the jury to consider Seaver's "temper of mind" and the prevalence of rawhide whips in nearby schools in making its decision.[65] After deliberations, the jury found for Seaver.

The Vermont Supreme Court upheld the jury's verdict. It stated that schoolmasters have the authority to punish misconduct off of school grounds and after school hours and applied a general standard of "reasonable judgment" to review Seaver's authority, which they located in a zone between public officers and parents. *Lander* novelized the public problem of citizenship in both the characters that it created and in associated discourses of virtue and judgment. Like earlier cases that addressed the state's authority over the child, *Lander* described the child as an incapable proto-citizen lacking the discipline—and values—necessary for full participation in society. The antidote to the problem of the incapable child was the authoritative master, who protected political order through compliance with commands. Discourses of judgment constituted the relationship between incapable proto-citizen and authoritative master—a "reasonable judgment" standard emerged for Seaver (analogous to that which a citizen should possess) in parallel to an expert judgment that the court itself displayed through rhetorical form. *Lander* advanced a discourse of judgment as a management technique that mediated the transition between the private and public realms through the performance of wisdom and sensitivity to context. This discourse included the calibration of incommensurable factors limited by the contexts of space, time, and topic.

Lander specified the incapable citizen's threat to liberal stability—critical speech that upended status hierarchies. In contrast to the child in *Ex parte Crouse* (who was described as "incorrigible") and the child in *Pendergrass* (whose conduct and dispositions received no attention), *Lander* marked the conduct for which the child was punished. Lander's utterance threatened prevailing beliefs related to respect, honor, and exalted status.[66] The child in *Lander* was in between immaturity and citizenship because of his capacity for critical speech. Neither passive (or invisible) like the children in earlier cases nor a mature adult, Lander embodied the impetuous child at play. His speech reflected a failure of judgment: he knew his own audience but risked too much, taunting his teacher within the latter's earshot. In this way, *Lander* novelized a public sphere in which the capacity for play and subversion—when not tempered by judgment—could threaten the prevailing order.

The incapable citizen's subversive resistance required a management strategy. Seaver's character embodied this strategy through his function as the protector of order. Lander's speech threatened Seaver's authority because it was uttered in the presence of Seaver and his other students. Seaver's judgment was legitimate because it corrected a status injury. This rationale carried a theory of character formation as rule-following and mimicry. Seaver had to punish Lander's off-grounds speech so that Seaver could keep order during school hours. *Ex parte Crouse* had argued that wayward children grow into low-character adults because they imitate poor examples of behavior—their parents at home, and later adult criminals in jails. Similarly, *Lander* argued that schoolchildren imitate poor behavior of classmates, even if off school grounds and after school hours. Discipline conditioned the child's expectations in the present and shaped their character in the future. And just as the House of Refuge was almost compelled to confine Mary Ann for her own benefit, the justification for Seaver's authority implied that he had disciplined Lander for the sake of the entire class. This uncomplicated perspective focused on a small number of elements—the way that Lander's words might later shape learning in Seaver's classroom because of their effects on their hearers if the words went unpunished. Seaver secured order through compliance, which depended on respect for his authority. For all of these reasons, *Lander* developed an extended discourse relating Lander's playful, resistive, critical speech to its effects on Seaver's authority.

The discourse in *Lander* was a discourse of *reasonable* judgment. Indeed, Lander and Seaver were divided by judgment: Lander demonstrated that he lacked good judgment with his indecorous after-school utterance. *Lander* described the general practice of judgment and related it to a purpose, placing Seaver in-between the role of the parent and the public official.[67] A parent's actions would be justified by the natural right to control a child, and Seaver had argued that he was not liable for "errors in judgment" because he was "invested with public authority, with discretionary powers, and acts in a judicial capacity."[68] Rejecting both of these extremes, *Lander* measured the teacher's judgment by a general standard of reasonableness.

Reasonable judgment had important cognitive dimensions, each one introducing a different discourse. As was the case in both *Ex parte Crouse* and *Pendergrass*, judgment implied virtue. It maintained order through its control of unruly resisters. Moving from the known of common law cases to the unknown threat of Lander's off-campus speech, the opinion associated that threat with destroying property, denigrating reputation for authority, and corrupting fellow students' industry. This maneuver reconstituted liberal ideological commitments through justifications for Lander's punishment. It likened Lander's insult to a host of behaviors for which the common law authorizes punishment, including "acts done to deface or injure the schoolroom, to destroy the books of scholars, or the books or apparatus for instruction, or the instruments of punishment of the master; language used to other scholars to stir up disorder and insubordination, or to heap odium and disgrace upon the master; writings and pictures placed so as to suggest evil and corrupt language, images and thoughts to the youth who must frequent the school; all such or similar acts tend directly to impair the usefulness of the school, the welfare of the scholars and the authority of the master."[69] Seaver's authority to discipline Lander was the next logical step in a progression that held that reasonable judgment maintained order by enforcing fealty to commonly held virtues.

Lander also introduced a temporal dimension to sound judgment. Like *Pendergrass* (which permitted physical punishment whose material traces faded over time), *Lander* used temporality as a sign of wisdom. Seaver's decision to punish could only be justified if there were a temporal connection between Lander's critical speech and Seaver's work in the classroom. This approach repurposed the rationale for control found in *Ex parte Crouse* and *Pendergrass* from their focus on general character dispositions to Lander's particular speech, and from the school grounds to broader public situations. Closing time and space between the utterance and the classroom, the court posited a "direct and immediate tendency to injure the school, to subvert the master's authority, and to beget disorder and insubordination."[70] Temporal dissociations created an outer limit for judgment—the master can punish immediate threats but not remote ones. This temporal understanding ensured liberty because it would prevent judgment's overreach. At the same time, it also pointed to the need to consider additional contextual signs: because "it will often be difficult to distinguish between acts which have such an immediate and those which have such a remote tendency. . . . Each case must be determined by its peculiar circumstances."[71]

In this way, *Lander* articulated sound judgment as the cognitive assessment and calibration of signs. These included "the nature of the offense, the apparent motive and disposition of the offender, the influence of his example and conduct upon others, and the age, sex, age, size, and strength of the pupil."[72] Because reasonable people could diverge on how to calibrate the factors involved, individual judgment was entitled to deference. It was more important that individuals assessed the factors than that they would reach the same results. The master was "on the spot," in the best position to "know all the circumstances, the manner, look, tone, gestures and language of the offender."[73] Because these circumstances were "not always easily described," the master should be "protect[ed] in the exercise of his discretion."[74] The master's authority over the incapable child was only illegal if punishment was "clearly excessive," and in this the master "should have the benefit of the doubt."[75]

Finally, *Lander* performed expert judgment by using ordering strategies to display a proper hierarchy of principles. The opinion used quasi-deductive distinctions that identified the relevant legal questions. Two legal questions structured the inquiry: whether Seaver had the authority to discipline Lander for events off school grounds and after school hours, and, if he did have this authority, whether the punishment he meted out was excessive. *Lander* claimed expertise by staging the inquiry incrementally—first answering the general question and then applying the principle derived from the answer to the first question to answer the specific one. The opinion conceived of legitimate authority as an indispensable precursor to expert judgment—in order to exercise it properly, one had to exercise it in one's legitimate field.

The opinion's ordering techniques also claimed expertise to mediate a shared tradition of natural rights. A rhetorical order moved from known principles to their unknown application. Seaver's authority "extends to school hours, and there seems to be no reasonable doubt that the supervision and control of the master over the scholar extends from the time he leaves home to go to school till he returns home from school."[76] Familiar roles defined authority in master-scholar relations marked by tropes of place and routine. These places and routines justified control, which shifted back to the parent alone when the child returned home. Doctrinally, Seaver's ability to discipline Lander began with the (known) tradition of parental authority, but settled on a standard of reasonable judgment that grounded the decision in natural right (parental control) while creating a vocabulary of objective judgment standards.

The opinion justified the punishment of critical speech with a similar movement. Beginning with the (known) punishable conduct of property destruction, *Lander* moved through a progression of examples of conduct that threatened citizen virtues, inferring that punishment for an off-campus joke ("Old Jack Seaver") was naturally connected to other affronts to authority. Like the techniques that moved from parental control to reasonableness, the ordering sequence progressed from clear cases (for which the common law authorized discipline) to the case at hand. The rhetorical strategy of *Lander* thus performed expertise as the exemplary performance of tradition. It is not merely that these techniques were present in the opinion; their performance moved from common to tenuous ground under a unifying sign of civic virtues.

Incapable Children Justify State Control

These three cases—*Ex parte Crouse, Pendergrass,* and *Lander*—represent the earliest approach in judicial opinions to the problem of the child's citizenship. They posited that the child was fundamentally incapable, and the threat that the child posed to liberal citizenship justified state control. These opinions used the child's incapabilities—their incorrigible character and critical speech—to articulate citizenship values. The wayward child was neither a capable citizen nor a good judge. These children threatened core values and virtues of industry, property ownership, and productivity. Simultaneously, the state's power over these nascent citizens implied a theory of character reformation as a corrective. That corrective relied on authority, isolation, and separation in order to reshape the incapable child in the image of an ideal liberal citizen.

At the same time, judgment was exercised by benevolent institutions and their representatives (teachers). Judgment was a response to the problem of the child. Judicial opinions identified sound judgment as the faculty of decision that restored respect for liberal order and virtues. Sound judgment had its own temporality, understood as the display of a cognitive understanding that reflected reason. The *Pendergrass* court understood judgment because of the temporary nature of the marks left by corporal punishment. The *Lander* court grasped the time of judgment by distinguishing between remote and immediate threats. *Lander* introduced a more complex set of contextual signs under a rubric of reasonableness. That one agree with how a particular person arrived at an act of judgment was of secondary importance. What mattered was that they had assessed the relevant factors before taking their decision.

Finally, these cases presented the problem of judicial expertise. If these decisions justified state authority over the incapable child because teachers (or state institutions) were circumstantially authorized to restrain natural rights, this necessarily raised the issue of how judges claimed their own opinions as authoritative. By and large, these cases performed such authority rhetorically, demonstrating a symmetry with their jurisprudential content. Where they endorsed decisions that shored up the state's authority to separate children from their corrupting influences, their rhetorical strategies likewise relied on distinction, dissociation, and hierarchical ordering. As noted earlier in this chapter, the mere presence of these features is not as remarkable (they are features of most judicial opinions) as their functions in connecting the problem of the child to the capacity of citizens to judge. Because the challenge of judicial authority also involved the question of constitutional expertise (which knew no obvious limits), the opinions introduced a discourse of deference to counterbalance the antidemocratic tendencies of expertise. These limits were most clearly embodied in *Pendergrass* when the court acknowledged that alternate public institutions and parents should check extreme abuse, and in *Lander* when the court observed that courts should be reluctant to severely scrutinize a teacher's "on the spot" decisions.

The characters and themes that these opinions created were held together by a discourse of natural rights. The incapable child was naturally controlled by parents, who had a sort of ownership interest in the child. Parents forfeited these rights only by incompetently exercising them, threatening political order. When teachers exercised authority over the child, they did so as second-best actors. They were justified because of a theory of implied delegation. Parents had consented to a teacher's authority. This formulation created conceptual space for resistance to the state's authority, raising the question of its limits. What virtues was a state empowered to instill in the child? Under what circumstances, if any, could the state act where the parents' consent and delegated authority was in question? And what were the possible examples of state actors displaying poor judgment?

2

NATURAL LIBERTY

Turner, Meyer, and *Pierce*

THE TROPES, ARGUMENTS, AND DISCOURSES FOUND IN THE CASES examined in chapter 1 constitute a management strategy for the nascent citizen's inability to consent and judge. This strategy legitimated the state's efforts to restrict citizenship rights in the name of developing these citizenship virtues and capabilities. These opinions presumed the child's lack of capabilities, and the failure of families and schools to remedy this lack justified constitutional authority. State actors were authorized to restrict natural rights because of the mission to instill virtue in citizens. This discourse recast the question of state power from an area of questionable judgment to one of impending necessity.

In resolving these cases about specific children, the related opinions were declaring parameters for citizens more broadly. They legitimated sovereignty over the child by filling out the content of judgment for citizens, even if that discourse remained largely implicit. The judges simultaneously performed their own authority to bind the parties (and state entities tasked with complying with the decisions). Judgment maintained order aligned with liberal values of industry and property ownership. The end of judgment was primarily the reformation of character. And perhaps most importantly, because judgment was an antidote to its incapable performance, understanding whether a decision was an exercise of good judgment entailed signs of cognition—the ability to read for the appropriate time, measure, and other specified targets (critical speech and behavior disruptive to order).

The opinions performed their own expertise with a series of abstract categorical classifications, themselves markers of rarefied judgment to make principle-driven distinctions. These techniques complemented an ideological preference for the private over the public, and negative liberty over state power. The opinions presented state power as an exception to the general rule by deploying legal categories. Family authority was preferable to state authority.

School/prison marked the permissible purposes of confinement. Moderate/immoderate limited the kinds of correction a teacher could enact. Temporary/permanent created the line for judging the motives of a teacher's correction. And immediate/remote limited the kinds of threats to which a teacher could respond. In this way, judicial rhetoric supported the kind of hierarchical liberal order that state action was meant to maintain. Declarations of operative legal categories supported declarations of fact and outcome.

Although this management strategy introduced the general terms of the disputes, it did not guarantee case outcomes. For practical purposes, the state-level decisions legally bound neither the federal courts nor other state courts addressing similar issues. Further, the management strategy itself had embedded rhetorically certain preferences amid the arguments for a wardship model of childhood. A restrained state was a second-best measure for extreme cases because of strong presumptions in favor of natural liberty. Finally, as with legal discourse generally, legal justifications rarely remain static. In spite of the insistence from some originalists that judges should interpret the law based on the principles of "original public meaning," "original intent," or "strict construction," the cases themselves presented new circumstances. For these reasons, the management strategy admitted of the possibility that cases with differing contexts could be resolved differently.

The present chapter looks at three such cases, each one an important paradigmatic example for the evolving character of the "child as ward" approach to managing these controversies. The cases in this chapter altered the repertoire for addressing the child as ward in the following ways. They introduced explicit concerns for the natural liberty of parent and child, which limited the extent to which a state may dictate the terms of a child's upbringing. They connected liberty rhetorically to a narrative about the freedom of economic production. They contrasted the modern democratic project with its Ancient Greek forerunner, arguing that the democratic state was terminally limited in the lengths it could go to instill virtue in citizens. Contrary to an understanding of the child as the beneficiary of wardship, these cases introduced the possibility that the child is, in certain respects, a free individual.

From Ward to Free Individual? *People v. Turner* and the Limits of State Sovereignty

In the late nineteenth century, the juvenile court movement in Illinois provided an example of a drive to apply to the child the kinds of natural right principles enjoyed by parents. This movement, which in 1899 established the first separate juvenile court system in the United States, established due process protections for children. The new court system was significant not merely for its safeguards against state power but also for the ways in which it "guarantee[d] at risk children . . . the positive rights of social citizenship. . . . This creative moment for thinking about children as persons with both negative and positive liberty occurred . . . when lawmakers began developing liberal constitutionalism."[1] The cases leading up to the creation of the juvenile court (including *The People v. Turner*, *Petition of Ferrier*, and *County of McLean v. Laura B. Humphreys*) laid a foundation for both the treatment of the child as a liberal individual citizen *and* an expanded state role in protecting juveniles from older, regressive patriarchal structures.[2] *Turner*, in particular, was remarkable for the way it used the figure of the child to expand individual liberty and complicate the relationship between judgment and authority.

Novelizing the public sphere can provoke discourses of resistance and change from within the law. *Turner* illustrates this principle in its decision ordering the release of a teenager who had been held in a reformatory (without having been convicted of a crime) to the custody of his father. Like the Pennsylvania House of Refuge at issue in *Ex parte Crouse*, Illinois had a statute that provided for the commitment of children "within the ages of six and sixteen years, who [a justice of the peace or police magistrate] has reason to believe is a vagrant, or is destitute of proper parental care, or is growing up in mendicancy, ignorance, idleness or vice."[3] But unlike *Ex parte Crouse*, the Illinois Supreme Court reached almost the exact opposite conclusion, ordering Turner's release.[4]

The Illinois Supreme Court's opinion mobilized the resources first identified in earlier child custody cases in order to justify its decision. Beginning with the parent's right to custody, the opinion turned from that departure point to reach a conclusion premised in pluralism as to how natural rights are exercised: "The best and kindest parents would differ [on the question of proper parental care] . . . and when we consider the watchful supervision, which is so unremitting over the domestic affairs of others . . . there is not a child in the land who could not be proved, by two or more witnesses, to be in this sad condition."[5] *Turner* rejected the character reformation theory of *Ex parte Crouse*: "If the child perform all its duties to the parent and to society, the State has no right to compel it to labor. . . . What . . . degree of virtue . . . will save from the threatened imprisonment? In our solicitude to form you for the duties of civil life, we should not forget the rights which inhere both in parents and children."[6] Parents enjoyed a right "to the care, custody, and assistance of [their] child" and a "duty to maintain and protect [the child]" as a "principle of natural law."[7] But even this right was limited in a modern liberal republic: "we are not governed by the twelve tables [of Roman law] . . . If a father confined or imprisoned his child for one year, the majesty of the law would frown upon the unnatural act."[8] *Turner* argued analogically that the lesser included the greater—if the parent could exceed natural rights with excessive treatment, the state confining a child who had not committed a crime was intolerable: "Such a restraint upon natural liberty is tyranny and oppression."[9]

Turner recognized the child's liberty. This recognition acknowledged that, despite lacking certain capabilities, the child possessed citizenship rights: "The disability of minors does not make slaves or criminals of them. . . . The only act which they are under a legal incapacity to perform, is the appointment of an attorney. They are liable for torts, and punishable for crime."[10] Citizenship rights guaranteed in the Constitution applied to the child, because its language "is not restrictive; it is broad and comprehensive, and declares a grand truth."[11] Although judges needed to tread lightly before invalidating laws, *Turner* was exercising its "solemn duty . . . to adjudge the law, and guard, where assailed, the liberty of the citizen."[12]

Turner demonstrated that the modes of novelization present in judicial opinions are subject to resistance, contestation, and reversal in negotiating the meaning of citizenship. The *Turner* court grounded its opinion in the discourses from *Ex parte Crouse*, reaching a very different result. First, *Turner* participated in a discourse of benevolence, maintaining the concern for the child's virtue while implying that the state could not instill virtue at liberty's expense. Second, *Turner* used the discourse of delegated authority to bolster the liberty of the child (and, by implication, all citizens). When *Ex parte Crouse*, *Pendergrass*, and *Lander* each ruled that the state (or teachers) could claim authority over the child, they appealed to delegation. The parent's natural right to authority over the child was delegated to the teacher, or else given up because of its incompetent exercise. The discursive innovation in *Turner* is that the parent cannot delegate what the parent never possessed. Because the modern citizen had a right to liberty, the state could not claim any kind of delegation of parental authority to confine a citizen without the latter being convicted of a crime.

These novelizations opened possibilities for expanding those eligible for citizenship in spite of their perceived "disabilities." Children were individuals insofar as they were entitled to treatment befitting their unique circumstances, and yet that individuality counseled in favor of a separate approach from similarly situated adults.[13] Although benevolence was used to justify a mode of judicial correction concerning the child, sovereign authority to discipline perceived threats remained a constant.[14] By the early twentieth century, America was in the midst of sociopolitical conflicts the likes of which had not been seen since the Civil War and Reconstruction. America's contested involvement in World War I acted as an extreme stress test for the health of constitutional liberties. It presented crises requiring difficult decisions to balance protection of the individual with the maintenance of secure order, much like historical forerunners like the Alien and Sedition Acts and Lincoln's suspension of habeas corpus rights. The case of the child's liberties amplified these concerns because of the friction between the power of the state and the organic ordering traditions of the family. The public and private were in direct conflict.

Civic Unity Against Liberty: *Meyer v. Nebraska* and *Pierce v. Society of Sisters*

Two cases from the early twentieth century, *Meyer v. Nebraska* and *Pierce v. Society of Sisters,* addressed governmental efforts to strike the proper balance between these conflicting goals. Both of these cases reviewed state laws that sought to regulate the child's instruction in schools, one in Nebraska and one in Oregon. These seemingly xenophobic laws constituted a public response to the conditions of mass migration, the increasingly alienating character of the American economy, and the geopolitical chaos and trauma of World War I: "War and international unrest intensified the demand for a more tightly knit nation. Patriotic societies and politicians joined with settlement houses and educators . . . . Large segments of the public and prominent educators viewed Americanization as a responsible answer to a serious sociological challenge."[15] Nebraska's law, passed in 1918, prohibited the teaching of foreign languages to students below eighth grade. Oregon's 1922 law made public education compulsory (as opposed to private or parochial school), subjecting parents to fines and/or jail time for each day the parents' child was not in public school. The Supreme Court struck down both laws because it violated the fundamental right to raise one's children.

Legal commentators have treated the outcomes of these cases as classic liberal statements against cultural homogeneity, and for the protection of individual rights.[16] Laurence Tribe highlighted the legacy of *Meyer* and *Pierce* for the law of substantive due process, observing that they "described what they were protecting from the standardizing hand of the state in language that spoke of the family as a center of value-formation and value-transmission . . . the authority of parents to make basic choices."[17] The child was the oft-forgotten center of the dispute, which resolved the question whether the child was the private property of parents or a public resource.[18]

These opinions were consequential for citizenship, judgment, and civic practice. The opinions add to the character of the teacher, supplementing the teacher's need for authority with dignity as a professional economic actor. The opinions cultivated an attachment to economic values by grounding constitutional injury in contract—investment, expectation, and return. This is significant for the kinds of legal vocabularies for constitutional injury as well as the avenues for resistance and development they opened for future cases. The child in these opinions remained largely passive—the object of education and the vindication of rights exercised by other citizens (parents and teachers). This passive child marks the cases' transitional status—the respective opinions shaped a rhetorical conflict between state-enforced civic practices and the private individual citizen.

These cases embodied public judgment through state legislation. The citizens of *Meyer* and *Pierce* understood themselves as modern because modern citizens' values and practices supported private lives, from which pluralism sprang. To support such a culture, public judgment needed to be reflective, which meant that it could articulate legitimate threats to political order (and not merely respond to immediate emotional fears). The opinions repurposed the temporal arguments of *Pendergrass* and *Lander* for collective acts of legislation. Finally, *Meyer* and *Pierce* marked an important shift in the performance of expert judgment. Expressing an affinity between content and form, the opinions developed factual narratives and detailed descriptions of the parties. These narratives in turn supported a cluster of new expert justifications. Where earlier cases mined common law tradition, *Meyer* and *Pierce* relied on foundational texts—the Fourteenth Amendment and the Northwest Ordinance. Relying on these texts led to practices of textual interpretation that enforce contractually guaranteed constitutional liberties. The opinions also reflected anxieties about the reach of expertise, giving rise to a counterfactual discourse—aspects of state power that the decisions did *not* address—which set the terms for future constitutional conflicts over permissible state actions to mandate civic practices.

Private Rights of Citizenship

Driven by patriotic anxieties, Nebraska passed a law that prohibited teachers from teaching subjects in languages other than English to students who had not passed the eighth grade. The law applied to private, religious, and public schools. A group of churches that operated parochial schools challenged the law, arguing that the state could not prohibit instruction in specific subjects, and that instruction in specific non-English languages "enable[d parents] to participate in the same religious services and exercises in the home and in the church."[19] The Nebraska Supreme Court viewed the law as necessary for "an intelligent American citizenship . . . to imbue the alien child with the tradition of our past . . . and to teach him love for his country, and hatred of dictatorship, whether by autocrats, by the proletariat, or by any man, or class of men."[20]

Some schools moved the afternoon school session to 1:30 pm to give teachers a 1:00 to 1:30 pm slot to teach in a non-English language at a time where there was no "official school control" of students.[21] One day, the county district attorney stepped into a one-room schoolhouse in Hampton, Nebraska, and observed Robert T. Meyer teaching the Bible story of Jacob's Ladder, with ten-year-old Raymond Parpat reading it in his native German. Meyer was arrested, convicted, and fined (the jury found the argument that school was not in session to be a pretext for violating the law). The Nebraska Supreme Court's opinion upheld Meyer's conviction, relating the education of children to community cohesion.[22] The majority opinion argued that the statute maintained public order by assimilating immigrants. It deferred to the legislature's determination that education in a non-native language raised risks to community safety. Justice Charles Letton dissented, believing that this interpretation could "destroy both the God-given and constitutional right of a parent to have some voice in the bringing up and education of his children."[23]

The Supreme Court reversed the Nebraska Supreme Court decision on the grounds that the statute restricted liberty guaranteed by the Fourteenth Amendment. A state could not curb liberty "by legislative action which is arbitrary or without reasonable relation to some purpose within the competency of the state to effect."[24] The Nebraska statute infringed on Meyer's liberty "to teach and the right of parents to engage him so to instruct their children."[25] The court found Nebraska's interest in civic unity unpersuasive, because there was "no emergency . . . which render[ed] knowledge by a child of [a non-English language] so clearly harmful."[26]

Modern Economic Liberty and Reciprocal Values

The *Meyer* majority decision limited state-sponsored attempts to instill civic virtue, using contractual interpretation techniques and authoritative sources to legitimate its preferred vision of modern liberty.[27] These techniques thereby became signs of sound expert judgment. The opinion articulated standards of public judgment through its evaluation of the Nebraska public that passed the law. Finally, its projection of counterfactual situations legitimated its decision in two ways—by confining its reach and making liberal values appear mutually entailing.

First, the opinion appealed to the character of the teacher as a professional exercising an economic "liberty" to ply a trade. Creating this character connected the decision to natural freedoms with textual mandates. It also placed state-mandated civic practices in conflict with the natural freedoms that the Constitution guarantees to citizens. A textual argument limited an investigation of the state's responsibility to develop liberal habits or civic practices in its future citizens: "Corresponding to the right of control, it is the natural duty of the parent to give his children education suitable to their station in life, and nearly all the States, including Nebraska, enforce this obligation by compulsory laws."[28] Citizenship conferred both the parental freedom to educate the child and Meyer's liberty to ply his trade; this commitment formed the deep social contractual foundations of American democratic government. Civic practices were addressed through natural order first, and then sovereignty. State power could only curtail liberty to protect this natural (private) order—work, striving, family. The *Meyer* opinion created a tension between rights and responsibilities through the figures of the parent and teacher. It imbued that tension with substantive content, limiting the responsibilities side of the equation to private economic industry and self-actualization.

The constitutional injury addressed in *Meyer* was the law's interference with teaching as a profession. Conceiving the injury in this way imagined professionalism as the natural private provision of a public good. Education was "only possible in schools conducted by especially qualified persons. . . . The calling always has been regarded as useful and honorable, essential, indeed, to the public welfare."[29] Meyer "taught this language in school as a part of his occupation. His right thus to teach and the right of parents to engage him so to instruct their children . . . are within the liberty of the Amendment."[30] Economic virtues formed the common ground to reconcile conflicting values.

By emphasizing economic liberty as the core of citizenship, *Meyer* transcended the conflict between parents, children, schools, and a state law designed to produce civic values through the curriculum. It downplayed any ethnic hostility underlying the law, the religious implications, and the law's substantive curricular content. Instead, it argued that striking the law down enhanced individual choice for the benefit of all parties. The shared status of the teacher, the parents, and the pupils as private persons was the common principle (and legal injury) that produced a community of citizens. This approach reshaped the common civic mission around the pursuit of individual rights: the parents' right to educate children and the educator's right to ply a trade.

In this rendering of public life, the child was invisible. Neither an incorrigible youth nor a purveyor of critical and subversive speech, the child in *Meyer* is scarcely mentioned. As a result, *Meyer* implicitly excluded the child from its vision of natural rights-holding citizens, an object of parental control. Partially for these reasons, public judgment in *Meyer* was embodied by collective legislative action. Invalidating Nebraska's law, the court implied that sound judgment was marked by cognitive signs of reflection and the ability to grasp a longer time horizon. The failure of Nebraska's people was the failure to recognize the American constitutional order's distinct modern emphasis on individual rights, in contrast to the ancient world's Spartan/Platonic focus on serving the state. The opinion highlighted the law's effect on "modern language teachers."[31] A modern liberal public should be grounded in the rights of the individual, the court held: "The State may do much . . . in order to improve the quality of its citizens . . . . But the individual has certain fundamental rights. . . . The protection of the Constitution extends to all, to those who speak other languages as well as to those born with English on the tongue."[32] American citizens rejected the Platonic educational ideal, where "children are to be common, and no parent is to know his own child. . . . take the offspring of the good parents to the pen or fold . . . but the offspring of the inferior, or of the better when they chance to be deformed, will be put away in some mysterious, unknown place, as they should be."[33] This practice severed the organic ties of families "in order to submerge the individual, and develop ideal citizens."[34] These ideas "were wholly different from those upon which our institutions rest."[35] Modern constitutionalism required citizens who could control their desires and act as a monolithic population that adhered to a single mode of virtue. *Meyer* protected a kind of pluralism that flowed from the diversity of parental rights and choices to pursue remunerative work.

This mode of judgment relied on the proper display of cognitive reflection to guard against emotional impulse. Good judgment involved reflective and reasoned decisions untainted by passion. Americans, like the ancients, may have wanted to "foster a homogenous people with American ideals prepared readily to understand current discussions of civic matters."[36] Citizens, in contrast, needed to reflect and accommodate multiple perspectives: rather than allowing "unfortunate experiences during the late war and aversion toward every characteristic of truculent adversaries" to "quicken [the] aspiration" for homogeneity and civic commonality, the Constitution appealed to the common desire to work and make a living.[37]

The Nebraska law was an impulsive effort to respond to an exceptional (and exaggerated) threat. Implicitly, the *Meyer* opinion expected citizens to exercise judgment informed by tradition. This was not merely the enlarged perspective of seeing a situation in a different light;[38] it was, rather, a conservative counterpart to this form of judgment, which viewed ruptures to the social fabric in the light of a longer stable tradition. Temporally, this implied a long horizon, recalling public values. Reactive legislation to guard against threats to the community misdiagnosed these values. The threat was an exception to a longer and more secure American identity, found in the rule of family, school, and work. With a textual performance that mirrored its interpretive instincts, the *Meyer* opinion called forth traditional liberal constitutional principles to prefigure its decision.

The *Meyer* opinion derived expertise in judgment from authoritative texts supplemented by governing precedent. This strategy introduced a contractual element to the court's expertise as the enforcer of constitutional promises. The opinion framed the legal question as follows: "whether the statute . . . unreasonably infringes the liberty guaranteed to [Meyer] by the Fourteenth Amendment. 'No State shall . . . deprive any person of life, liberty, or property, without due process of law.'"[39] This rhetorical choice began with the canonical text and derived its authority through divining that text's meaning.

Precedent supplied details that the text left ambiguous. This maneuver cast expertise as the construction of a hierarchy of interpretive protocols—precedent supplements authoritative texts. The opinion cited a series of cases to broadly construe liberty, summarizing them as the declaration that the amendment ensured "not merely freedom from bodily restraint, but also the right of the individual to contract, to engage in any of the common occupations of life, to acquire useful knowledge, to marry, establish a home and bring up children, to worship God according to the dictates of his own conscience, and generally to enjoy those privileges long recognized at common law as essential to the orderly pursuit of happiness by free men."[40] This broad construction of liberty clustered around a traditional focus of the private sphere—religious, familial, and economic activities.

Textual precedent demonstrated the privileged place of *economic* liberty. Beginning with the *Slaughterhouse Cases*, the opinion cited cases that expanded a general right to contract.[41] This technique helped to frame the law as a labor regulation, as the court cited the infamous *Lochner v. New York* (which struck down labor laws for bakers) and supporting cases. The tactic also restrained expert judgment by narrowing the decision's own precedential reach. Going only so far as was necessary to justify an ideology of private economic freedom (and not elaborating on its more ambiguous definition of liberty), the opinion's use of precedent contained a movement from doctrine to principled application. This style performed the habits of mind for expert judgment in a manner similar to the opinion's expectations of state legislators—just as a judge must issue limited opinions with a small range of authoritative materials, so must state legislative authority be limited in scope and practice to the bare necessities of community order.

The opinion's use of foundational sources displayed its expertise through a discourse of contract: the court redeemed promises made by authoritative sources through its interpretive practice. Unable to locate enough guidance in the Fourteenth Amendment, the opinion connected civic education and economic liberty through the Northwest Ordinance of 1787:[42] "The American people have always regarded education and acquisition of knowledge as matters of supreme importance which should be diligently promoted."[43] The ordinance declared that "religion, morality and knowledge being necessary to good government and the happiness of mankind, schools and the means of education shall be forever encouraged."[44] According to *Meyer*, the ordinance reconciled conflicting values through a quid pro quo. It expressed a prior commitment to restricting the federal government's reach. Nebraska's law violated that promise.

Finally, the opinion imagined counterfactual situations about the case's precedential impact. Because these counterfactuals did not rely on facts or arguments of the parties, they permitted the court to interpret its own opinion. This tactic performed sound expert judgment by limiting its application in space and time. In expressing what the case was *not* about, it defined the bounds of acceptable state legislative action: "The power of the State to compel attendance . . . and to make reasonable regulations . . . is not questioned. Nor has challenge been made of the State's power to prescribe a curriculum . . . . No emergency has arisen which renders knowledge by a child of some language other than English so clearly harmful as to justify its inhibition."[45] Nebraska's statute only prohibited instruction in "a modern language," and "experience shows that this is not injurious to the health, morals or understanding of the ordinary child."[46]

This mode of expert judgment signaled a preference for mandates over prohibitions and security against immediate (rather than remote) threats. The range of counterfactuals narrowed the dispute. Deferring questions for a later day imagined potential variations that could cause the case to resolve otherwise. This style "allow[s] leeway to expediency without abandoning principle,"[47] cueing future cases by leaving the state's legislative authority subject to future litigation. This maneuver created time for a longer democratic conversation to develop outside the courts, a "partial or reversible solution . . . that bespeaks its own uncertainty . . . invites the other branches of government, and the public, to rise to a consideration of principle and address the problem in the same spirit."[48]

The opinion's last hypothetical alternative would also prove to be its most prescient management technique. By emphasizing what the statute did not regulate, the court imagined statutes that would act as legitimate exercises of state authority. "Prohibition of a trade" was disfavored, and "language instruction" did not injure to a child's health, morals, or understanding. But what about other potentially dangerous ideas? What if their threat to core values was direct and immediate? Was the child capable of asserting core citizenship rights? And what happened when educators and parents were not aligned in schooling? *Meyer* opened the door to these kinds of questions concerning the appropriate limits to the state's authority. It carried forward a deep association between legitimate state power and a pedagogical theory that protects a child's well-being (and the community's) by limiting the child's thoughts expressed in dangerous speech. It signaled that a different regulation of a different liberty responsive to a more immediate threat may produce a different result.

Deepening the Connection between Economic Liberty and Liberal Order

Two years after *Meyer*, the Supreme Court extended the influence of economic liberty over the shape of the citizen in *Pierce v. Society of Sisters*. This time, the court rejected an Oregon law that required all parents or guardians to send their children to public schools in the district in which they reside (effectively outlawing parochial schools). Oregon had passed the Compulsory Education Act, which mandated that parents send their children "'to a public school for the period of time a public school shall be held during the current year' in the district where the child resides."[49] The Society of Sisters, an organization of Catholic nuns, ran a school in Oregon that risked closure should the law take effect (another school, Hill Military Academy, also filed suit). The court's opinion described the "manifest purpose" of the law as "to compel general attendance at public schools."[50]

Pierce deepened the connection between liberal economic rights and civic order. Where *Meyer* struck down Nebraska's Americanization law because the immigrants' threat to social cohesion was exaggerated, *Pierce* cast the Oregon law itself as the threat to liberal values—without investigating the racial and ethnic hostility influencing its adoption.[51] Here, the Supreme Court advanced a model of citizenship as the right to reap the rewards of one's economic investment, identifying such freedom to pursue economic returns as a ground for liberal pluralism, and counseling that economic virtue pays off over time. *Pierce* further subordinated public civic practices to private liberties; meanwhile, the child remained an invisible and inactive figure with an obscure pathway to developing citizenship capabilities. Finally, *Pierce* deployed techniques similar to *Meyer* concerning expert judgment, relying on counterfactuals to assuage fears of judicial overreach.

First, *Pierce* reinforced private economic activity as a core citizenship right. Where *Meyer* chastised the Nebraska legislature for exaggerating the threat immigrants posed to community cohesion, *Pierce* framed regulation of economic activity itself as a serious threat, anxiously observing that the law could "seriously impair, perhaps destroy, the profitable features of appellees' business and greatly diminish the value of their property."[52] It activated tropes of corporate power and self-governance: the Society of Sisters was "an Oregon corporation, organized in 1880, with power to care for orphans, educate and instruct the youth, establish and maintain academies or schools, and acquire necessary real and personal property. It has long devoted its property and effort to the secular and religious education and care of children, and has acquired the valuable good will of many parents and guardians."[53] Aligning efficiency, economic profit, and social value with constitutional tradition extolled long-standing investment as a virtue. It implied that this virtue should be paid off, that is, that the Society of Sisters' hard work in educating children entitled the organization to reap the fruits of its labor.

Like *Meyer*, this approach advanced a contract model of liberal citizenship by framing constitutional rights as a narrative of promise, reciprocation, and return on investment. In noting the date and purpose for which the corporation was established, the opinion's quotidian description of the school's activities created a temporality for that narrative. Per the court, the school's courses "contemplate continuity of training under [its] charge; the primary schools are essential to the system and the most profitable. It owns valuable buildings. . . . The business is remunerative."[54] Because the school was profitable, the contested law's economic impact constituted a significant legal injury: "The Compulsory Education Act . . . has already caused the withdrawal from its schools of children who would otherwise continue, and their income has steadily declined."[55] The legislation interfered with the school's liberty to pursue a return on its substantial investment.

Second, the opinion grounded citizenship in individual economic pursuit at the expense of civic virtue: "Under the doctrine of *Meyer* . . . we think it entirely plain that the Act . . . unreasonably interferes with the liberty of parents and guardians to direct the upbringing and education of children under their control."[56] This declaration recast *Meyer* as a ruling for strong parental rights to raise children under their control, downplaying the substantial influence in that decision of the teacher's ability to ply a trade. *Pierce* imagined the child as an object of parental ownership enshrined as a constitutional right. This preference for parental liberty to develop the child into a citizen rejected the liberal state's power to instill civic virtue: "The fundamental theory of liberty upon which all governments in this Union repose excludes any general power of the State to standardize its children by forcing them to accept instruction from public teachers only. The child is not the mere creature of the State; those who nurture him and direct his destiny have the right, coupled with the high duty, to recognize and prepare him for additional obligations."[57] The opinion treated the child as a beneficiary of parental rights. The strategy in *Pierce* framed a core of citizenship based on property ownership and a profitable investment in the child. It related this core to a durable political order based in pluralistic individual economic activity.

Finally, the opinion legitimated its authority with a counterfactual rhetorical tactic similar to the one advanced in *Meyer*. Seeking to quell fears of an overreaching judiciary, the justices wrote, "No question is raised concerning the power of the State reasonably to regulate all schools . . . to require that all children of proper age attend some school, that teachers shall be of good moral character and patriotic disposition, that certain studies plainly essential to good citizenship must be taught, and that nothing must be taught which is manifestly inimical to the public welfare."[58] This prudential tactic activated a set of common values as noncontroversial assertions of state authority. It authorized state action in the area of morals and welfare and its power to establish uniform requirements for the child's development as a citizen. The opinion appealed to a civic imagination that sought to instill virtue through instruction by teacher-patriots who lodged in students a reverence for a moral order guaranteed by the state.

The Catholic and military schools that challenged the Oregon law embodied this moral order. The *Pierce* opinion legitimated liberal values by performing judgment as the procedural enforcement of a contract. The opinion blocked the state from acting here because it lacked an original grant of authority. Morality, patriotism, family, and even the citizen were framed as natural, predating the history of the liberal state. Oregon's law would "destr[oy] . . . appellees' primary schools, and perhaps all other private primary schools for normal children within the State of Oregon. These parties are engaged in a kind of undertaking . . . long regarded as useful and meritorious."[59] The declarative tone posited judgment as a balance of relative equities. This conservative approach prefigured the answer with the weight of tradition and consensus. The private schools protesting against the Oregon law fulfilled "their obligations to patrons, students [and] the State. And there are no . . . present emergencies which demand extraordinary measures relative to primary education."[60] Imagining a community of private obligation, the opinion reserved state authority for emergencies only.

Citizenship as Virtue, Judgment as Cognitive Performance

Meyer and *Pierce* reshaped the constitutional approach to citizenship and judgment through controversies surrounding the child. They framed influential terms for the development of citizenship, while carrying forward the substantive tensions and judgment strategies of the earlier nineteenth-century cases.

These opinions mediated a shared sensibility of the state's obligations to develop citizens and a concept of expert and public judgment necessary for these latter to exercise their freedom on the one hand while replicating a virtuous democratic political order on the other. In considering these cases along with their nineteenth-century predecessors, we can see how a composite strategy for addressing the problems of citizenship and judgment emerged through these legal controversies about the child.

First, the cases studied here and in the previous chapter utilized particular characters to novelize the public sphere as a paradox of liberty. Liberty was natural, but the cases expressed a concern that people left to mature naturally would not develop the requisite habits for the maintenance of social order. The judicial opinions sometimes treated the children in the disputes as invisible (*Meyer* and *Pierce*), choosing to focus on their parents or teachers as rights holders. Where children's actions mattered, the opinions assigned threatening characteristics to their incapable exercise of voice and choice. They were incorrigible (*Ex parte Crouse* and *Pendergrass*) or disobedient (*Lander*). In other words, the passivity and incapability of the child discursively demarcated the image of a typical citizen with the necessary habits for liberal society. These typical citizens required virtue as a prerequisite for participating in civic life. The narratives in these opinions valued industry, economic activity, and respect for property and authority. Children displayed their lack of these capacities when they spoke critically, playfully, or subversively (*Lander*). They thereby demonstrated their unreadiness for citizenship because the latter concerned the judicious exercise of one's natural rights to control and produce.

The character of the child thus required a discourse of judgment and authority. The latter were embodied by actors—teachers, parents, and state legislators—whose decisions to control and discipline the child were subject to scrutiny. These actors dramatized the exercise of judgment as a cognitive practice manifested through communicative signs; this sound judgment in turn legitimated state sovereignty. They established legitimacy because they responded to a threat to order, were close in time to that threat, and were related to character reformation. For their part, communicative signs involved a notion of temporality. Earlier opinions used markers of time to infer the exercise of reason rather than emotional retribution, including the characterization of the House of Refuge as a project to reform the child's character in *Ex parte Crouse* and the lack of permanent marks from a teacher's physical discipline in *Pendergrass*. *Meyer* and *Pierce* imported this judgment characteristic into threat assessment. The former chastised the Nebraska legislature for failing to distinguish between short- and long-term threats to political order in its Americanization law, while the latter framed Oregon's legislative act as the threat because it interfered with virtuous economic actors who worked hard and were entitled to reap long-term rewards. In all instances, the opinions returned to the embodiment of shared virtues—their judgments were in each case benevolent and productive.

Recalling the examples from the introduction, these are precisely the kinds of capabilities that adults supposedly lack. Greta Thunberg criticized the lack of adult leadership manifested in contemporary adults' almost nihilistic focus on present politics at the expense of the future. The NeverAgain students took on a position of leadership precisely because of their atypicality: compelled to speak, they expressed their reluctance to be forced into proposing solutions to a problem that adult legislators had neglected for so long. And of course the incapable children who had been separated from their families at the border echoed the passive child, with public discourse fixated on the state actions to seize them and the rupture of the seemingly sacred liberty of the parent-child bond.

As the introduction noted, these cases double the problem of judgment because the role of the judge matters, in that judicial opinions must legitimate their own authority through novelization. The cases examined so far performed this authority with rhetorical strategies that textually related constitutional concepts to judicial performance. Early strategies began with distinction, definition, and dissociation, thereby authorizing judges as expert mediators of a common law tradition. Rights were natural, restrictions unnatural. Threats were immediate or distant. Discipline was reasoned or extreme. At the same time, the cases grappled with the anxieties of expertise—namely, that the "better" one was at exercising judgment, the more it threatened American democratic practices. For these reasons, expertise grounded in distinction required a limiting supplement. Early cases found these supplements in practices that observed the need for deference to those "on the spot," because judgment from a distance—while able to claim the authority of tradition and the long view—also ran the risk of doing injustice to specific contexts. In other words, the detachment of expertise could tend to be antidemocratic if the experts were "bad readers."

Meyer and *Pierce* performed with even more nuance. Here, judicial acumen relied on more sophisticated modes of representation. By way of summary, three techniques were particularly significant: the reliance on sophisticated factual narratives, the invocation of foundational texts, and the use of counterfactuals. The kind of authority these rhetorical choices produced was thoroughly contractual. Narratives connected characters and relevant legal facts to specific discourses of value and judgment. Foundational texts limited the state in general (and judges in particular) to specific grants of authority. This interpretive practice marked a good judge as one who follows original grants of sovereignty and does not "read in" meaning where it does not plainly exist. This tactic shaped an ideology of citizenship that ties economic liberty to a particular interpretive practice for the sake of protecting one's expectations. Counterfactuals also served as a prudential management technique to assuage fears of judicial overreach, providing a mode of self-interpretation that sought to guide democratic deliberation while also signaling to those citizens and legislatures affected by a decision about the court's likely attitude toward considering particular future cases.

The Child as Ward: Beneficiary or Individual?

As argued earlier, these judicial opinions introduced particular discourses to justify their decisions with reference to imagined truths, characters, and theories about public life. The cases in chapters 1 and 2 have detailed a particular strategy of addressing citizenship through these controversies about the child. Each case framed the child as an incapable citizen who was the beneficiary of sound judgment by a state entity—a reformatory, a teacher, a parent. Each case justified authority over the child in order to supply it with virtues. Each case implied a particular method of character formation premised on the opinions' understandings of the incapable child: lacking cognitive ability, children were best saved through benevolent caretakers who isolated them from bad influences in order to impress upon them new virtuous habits.

Yet these discourses also involved points of resistance, some of which later opinions raised in subtle inflections of previous themes, while other aspects of these discourses awaited contestation. For example: in *Pendergrass* and *Lander*, teachers claimed authority as the means to virtuous ends by instilling respect for industry and property. In *Meyer* and *Pierce*, the educators embodied these virtues themselves. Instead of performing authority by enacting violence on the incapable citizen, they performed their virtue by making investments and working. This discursive transfiguration appeared as an expansion of liberty. But it also raised questions about the limits of authority. Would Pendergrass's or Seaver's actions be considered virtuous in this light?

This is but one example of a question that the model of the "child as ward" raised. The natural status of liberty did not explicitly extend to the child yet. But did this mean that the child had no rights? There were limits to how one could treat the child. Those limits were expressed through the trope of delegated authority: teachers could use judgment to discipline as long as it was reasonable, because they were proxies of parental authority. Yet the question remained: if liberty was fundamentally expansive, what prevented the child from claiming core rights? If children had liberties, what were they, and how did they relate to civic virtue? And would a child's liberties restrict acceptable modes of character formation? These questions raised more than the issue of who is entitled to citizenship. They related to the core meanings of citizenship rights for everyone. As part 2 will show, they gave rise to new discourses about the child and citizenship and a distinctive alternative to the beneficiary model as a management strategy for the incapable citizen.

PART II

THE CHILD AS CATEGORICAL EQUAL

REFLECTING YEARS LATER ON HER ROLE IN ONE OF THE LANDMARK constitutional cases of the twentieth century, Gathie Barnett Edmonds recounted the historical accidents of her life that brought her case to the Supreme Court in 1943. As the United States was fighting World War II, Gathie was at the center of an intense community conflict over a school routine that required all pupils to say the Pledge of Allegiance at school. Gathie's comments provide a glimpse into her refusal to pledge allegiance to the flag. Two opposing forces—the individual's right to worship and the state's insistence on compulsory routines for the sake of unity—produced tension here between the individual and the community:

> Q. Had your parents alerted you to this issue of flag salute as you were beginning your school years?
>
> A. Well, they just taught us the purpose of our faith, which is to give our devotion and worship to Jehovah God, not to any image of any sort, and we were taught that the bowing down to the flag, saluting it, was like bowing down and giving reverence to it—it was like an idol. So we believe definitely not to worship idols. . . . We respect the flag and what it stands for. We don't have anything against that. We just don't believe in worshipping or saluting it.[1]

The tension between individual belief and the state's insistence on ritual constructed a model of citizenship as performance. It implied a connection between thought, speech, and democratic participation, with a strong emphasis on individual judgment. The capacity to decide what to say and when to say it for strategic and ethical effect would become a core mode of a citizen's self-understanding. But Gathie's response also revealed another wrinkle: only eleven years old when asked to salute the flag, her status as individual dissenter was not at all clear. Her parents were the source of her religious faith. Was she a free thinker or a conformist? Was she expressing her individual belief, or following the mandate of parental authority?

The wider global context of the 1930s and 1940s demonstrates the importance of controversies involving the child's civic identity and democratic citizenship. America was struggling through the gravest economic crisis of the century. Germany was waging war across Europe, and the sickening details of Hitler's rise to power were circulating in the public sphere. In the throes of these domestic and international conflicts, America's status as a liberal bastion was being tested, in part through the tension between a centralized organization dedicated to preparation for war and the liberal pluralism that seemed to distinguish America from the Axis powers.

Barnette symbolized America's answer to the tension between the free individual and a social order grounded in common habits. The case was a rarity—a quick overruling of a recent landmark precedent (*Minersville v. Gobitis*). It marked a new phase in the rise of the child as a liberal individual. Whereas nineteenth-century legal cases had treated the child as an object of sovereign control, *Barnette* freed the child. It marked a trajectory of sustained judicial reflection on the question of the kind of public that distinguished American political society, its core capabilities for citizenship, and the best implicit approach to instilling those capabilities as habits and practices. Each of these areas shaped a new understanding of judgment for the individual as well as the expert judge.

Part 2 analyzes four landmark Supreme Court cases: *Minersville v. Gobitis, West Virginia v. Barnette, In re Gault,* and *Tinker v. Des Moines*. It argues that the judicial opinions in these cases shifted the constitutional vision of citizenship through a new model that addressed the child as a categorical equal. In these cases, the Supreme Court treated the child as a rights-bearing individual, in contrast to the "child as ward" model introduced in part 1. Elevating the child's status in this way influenced core meanings of citizenship. Including the child meant that performances of capability were available to them. This development brought with it a subtle discourse of cognition, related to the discourse that part 1 identified as the display of sound judgment. Here, the court included the child because of the latter's ability to form beliefs (*Barnette*), use those beliefs to engage in political speech for strategic effect (*Tinker*), and to participate in adversarial process (*Gault*). At the same time, the court used the teacher-student relationship to define the civic habits and sentiments required for a stable order. Concerning expert judgment, an explicit oppositional discourse about the role of a judge emerged in the majority and dissenting opinions. Majorities that elevated the child to the status of individual argued that the expert judge's role was to protect the core of individual constitutional rights from state encroachment. Dissenters in these cases appealed to a different judicial role, privileging a detached assessment of their own place in an ordered democratic system. These dissenters argued that the justices whose opinions were broadening the scope of citizenship status lacked the requisite judicial temperament, because they were merely using their personal beliefs to decide these controversies.

This distinct model of addressing citizenship capabilities nevertheless relied on elements of the "child as ward" model to ground its justifying discourses. Justices made use of argument threads, democratic themes, and interpretive styles similar to those that were used in the cases discussed in the previous chapter. The question of how to produce civic unity remained. Where the wardship model posited the need for authority to instill industrious virtues, the cases in part 2 addressed communication as a way to produce (and challenge) such authority. This adaptation of earlier themes focused on how civic values are mediated, and that shift meant that the role of communication—its types, styles, times, topics, and publics—would take on a greater role. Concerning expertise, the justices continued the discourse of authority, which in the cases from the previous chapter was marked by carrying forward traditions through distinction, definition, and dissociation. Here, these performances of judgment emerged as explicit themes in the opinions via exercises in self-reflection. Disagreement about constitutional citizenship was now framed in terms of differences between experts' views of their institutional role. The opinions produced nuanced meditations on interpretive practices in an effort to prevent judicial abuse—these included privileging evidence above belief and emphasizing the role of procedures as textual guardrails. Both of these expert judgment practices inscribed the intentions of state actors and left traces for evaluation by others in potential future cases.

Part 2 begins with *Gobitis* and *Barnette*, two cases about compelling pupils to say the Pledge of Allegiance in schools. *Gobitis* allowed this practice. *Barnette* reversed it a few years later, beginning a series of cases that broadened the scope of the meaning of citizenship rights. *Barnette* emphasized the child's status as a categorically equal individual and connected that individual with persuasion as the favored mode of liberal communication. *In re Gault* held that the parens patriae doctrine that had justified juvenile reformatories in the previous century ran afoul of a citizen's right to due process of law. The court's indictment of parens patriae implicitly denigrated care and compassion as disfavored purposes of the liberal state and linked justifications of state authority to achieving pragmatic ends. Finally, *Tinker* upheld the free speech right of students in school to protest the Vietnam War. In doing so, *Tinker* complicated the model of citizen communication, privileging a particular kind of speech, a particular cognitive capability to deploy that speech, and a particular public habit of mind.

These opinions are exemplars of judicial style. Their authors are among the most renowned Supreme Court justices of the twentieth century: Robert Jackson, Felix Frankfurter, Abe Fortas, Hugo Black, and William Douglas. Their opinions, written under maximal pressure, generated real-world effects both for the litigants and for the law's development. Inventing with the tools of technical legal analysis, the creative application of precedent, and the characterization of facts and evidence, these opinions imagined a public world that altered shared legal commitments and articulated principles for decision-making.[2] These new commitments and principles emerged in the midst of political (and constitutional) turmoil of the 1930s and 1940s, and developed further with the Warren Court's constitutional jurisprudence of the 1960s.

The cases considered here introduced a new vocabulary for understanding judgment. For individual citizens, they highlighted the importance of performing signs of consent through persuasion instead of compulsion, as well as the cognitive abilities to analyze public-speaking situations strategically. While the need to speak strategically in terms of time, topic, and form mattered, the cases also highlighted the importance of textual practices as demonstrations of intention. All of these aspects now factored into the evaluation of individual judgments. For expert judgment, the opinions increasingly emphasized the temperament necessary for expertise and the bounds of its claim on authority to judge. That topic became an explicit controversy among the justices, prefiguring their perspectives on the constitutional issues. Through contrasting visions of the ideal judge, the opinions authorized themselves with reference to the institutional limits and responsibilities of judges, as well as with interpretive practices that were homologous with those limits and responsibilities. As a result, the zone of performance available to judicial opinions occurred in the space between the judges' self-understanding of their proper role and the constitutional themes that justified the outcomes in each case.

Each of these cases addressed pivotal questions for citizenship with reference to a larger social and political world and a distinct civic vocabulary for figuring that world. The production of patriotism, freedom of thought and mind, the capabilities of citizens, and the place of procedure in safeguarding liberty took turns assuming prominence in the self-identification of constitutional citizenship. These topics structured citizenship's meaning by setting standards of performance, both in the sense of topical content and the display of cognitive thought capabilities.

3

PATRIOTISM AND POLITICS

Gobitis and *Barnette*

In 1935 in Minersville, Pennsylvania, ten-year-old William Gobitas refused to salute the flag during his fifth-grade class's daily Pledge of Allegiance.[1] His older sister Lillian did the same the next day, explaining to her teacher that she "can't salute the flag anymore. The Bible says at Exodus chapter 20 that we can't have any other gods before Jehovah God."[2] These refusals appeared to be part of a broader strategy of conscientious objection practiced by Jehovah's Witnesses, to whom the Gobitas family belonged. It was a "grassroots movement . . . [that] had emerged almost accidentally. Judge George Rutherford, one of the national leaders of the Witnesses, had given a speech earlier in 1935 denouncing the Nazi 'Heil Hitler' salute: 'All people who have faith in God,' he said, should hail 'Jehovah and Christ Jesus,' not Hitler 'or any other creature.' After the speech, young Witnesses around the country applied its logic to the flag salute, which at the time closely resembled the straight-arm Nazi salute. . . . Rutherford then gave a radio address praising the students who were standing up for their faith. Lillian and William had heard that speech and had decided as a matter of conscience that they would not salute."[3]

The Minersville community interpreted the children's refusal to salute the flag as unpatriotic. The children reported being subject to violence at school and their parents were threatened with attacks and a boycott of their grocery store. Shortly after this, the school district enacted a regulation making the flag salute mandatory and expelled the Gobitas children when they refused to comply.[4] After their expulsion, the family sought protection from the courts, claiming that their freedom to practice their religion required a special exemption from participation in the ritual.

The Supreme Court agreed to hear *Gobitis* in 1940, within the unfolding global context of World War II: "To its proponents, the flag salute meant something different with a world war brewing and a draft in the offing. . . . A child's salute has special significance when there is the prospect that the nation may go to war behind the flag."[5] Compounding this matter was a popular characterization of the Witnesses' beliefs as "a strange mixture of several ancient heresies, a touch of fundamentalism, a dab of first century eschatology, and pacifism."[6] This context shaped the Witnesses' claim for religious liberty as a threat to the United States' national mission. Accordingly, the Supreme Court rejected the Gobitases's claim by a vote of eight to one. Arguing that community cohesion was the crucial support for the religious freedom that the plaintiffs claimed, Justice Frankfurter wrote that "the flag is a symbol of our national unity, transcending all internal differences, however large, within the framework of the Constitution."[7]

Justice Frankfurter's opinion in *Gobitis* subordinated the question of citizen judgment to a vision of expertise that prized system, function, and rank. This choice also implied that judicial expertise was derived from knowledge of democracy as a system, which contained a hierarchy of values and knowledge of the limits of expertise so that democracy could work. The opinion opposed individual conviction to public order, which derived its legitimacy through symbolism. The child plaintiffs of *Gobitis* were cognitively threatening to political order because their assertion to a right to opt out of democratically passed laws that conflicted with their beliefs could undermine the laws' collective effectiveness. That association between public order, liberty, and dominant symbolic interpretation counseled in favor of judicial deference, which respected the pluralism of local governing decisions.

In order to grasp the pressure that produced the opinions in both *Gobitis* and *Barnette*, it is important to understand the prevailing conventions of constitutional interpretation when the Supreme Court heard these cases. As the Great Depression gripped the United States in the 1930s, constitutional jurisprudence became a source of political and ideological conflict over the contours of judicial review. This conflict had its roots in the (now) infamous legacy of *Lochner v. New York*. *Lochner* protected fundamental economic rights through the judiciary, invaliding a law that restricted the number of hours bakery employees could work because it violated a constitutional freedom of contract.[8] Justice Holmes dissented, arguing that this substantive vision of liberty would frustrate the legislative will of the people: "The liberty of the citizen to do as he likes so long as he does not interfere with the liberty of others to do the same . . . has been interfered with by school laws, by the Post Office, by every state . . . which takes his money for purposes thought desirable."[9]

For the next few decades, Holmes's warning proved prescient, and the court blocked a stream of FDR's New Deal programs, partially justifying their decisions with reference to the *Lochner* precedent.[10] The Supreme Court struck down signature initiatives in a string of cases in 1935–36, including the National Industrial Recovery Act, the Agricultural Adjustment Act, and the Railroad Retirement Act.[11] Relying on *Lochner*, the Court also struck down a state law that regulated working hours for women and children.[12] Then, in 1937, after FDR won reelection and proposed to increase the number of Supreme Court justices to as many as fifteen, the court shifted course, paving the way for a stronger and more centralized federal government.[13]

This context shaped the constitutional backdrop in *Gobitis* and *Barnette*. These cases had to authorize their decisions with reference to the role of the judge in American constitutional democracy. An opinion that would invalidate state legislative action would have to answer objections that it was grounded on mere preference, and not constitutional principle. Thus these cases implicitly required judges to opine about the judging capabilities of citizens while simultaneously negotiating a controversy about their own expertise. This recurring structural conflict produced extensions of liberty through declarations of the child's capabilities. But the discourses in these cases also created the argumentative ground for their undoing via the retrenchment of state authority through alternate means.

Civic Unity: The Child, the Citizen, and the Expert

Justice Frankfurter identified the judge's constitutional expertise as a matter of conscience in deciding an irreconcilable conflict over values. This approach built on themes of hierarchy and ordered decision-making that appeared in the previous chapter, but it also added a connection to the judge's place in a larger system of democratic governance. The opinion noted the "grave responsibility [that] confronts this Court whenever . . . it must reconcile the conflicting claims of liberty and authority. But when the liberty invoked is liberty of conscience, and the authority is authority to safeguard the nation's fellowship, judicial conscience is put to the severest test."[14] Such an approach prefigured the outcome: no opinion would realistically side against safeguarding the nation's fellowship and civic bonds. The frame also created a distinct zone of expert judgment—an individual's "liberty of conscience" may threaten national unity, but a distinct "judicial conscience" separate from personal belief was required to evaluate the competing claims. This frame of expert judgment was distinct from those found in earlier cases about the child. Its explicit meditation on the role of the judge departed from the typical sequence that constituted authority by invoking tradition and precedent. Here, Justice Frankfurter's appeal to expert judgment as the product of reflection splits the self. The opinion built this judicial persona on the discourse of hierarchy and order from prior cases. Judicial conscience was a higher self because it could detach from personal conviction or belief. It recognized itself through a fidelity to the Constitution. Yet it is also introduced a new discourse of judicial temperament as a marker of authority. Judicial conscience was performed: acts of judicial self-control were linked explicitly to constitutional citizenship and civic unity.

The expert judge displayed the proper judicial temperament through expressions of neutrality. These conventions of performance were premised on an idea of democracy that prized legislative power. This argument strategy marched from premise to inevitable conclusion, deriving constitutional principle from shared history. Substantively, it valued a Burkean conservatism of limited actions in the face of uncertainty. Judicial fidelity to democracy subordinated religious conviction to a system designed to maintain a pluralism of beliefs. Even though individual conscience was protected, "the manifold character of man's [*sic*] relations may bring his conception of religious duty into conflict with the secular interests of his fellow men [*sic*]."[15] Siding with the plaintiff forced a choice that might "deny that very plurality of principles which, as a matter of history, underlies protection of religious toleration."[16] Historical and doctrinal arguments authorized expertise: "judicial enforcement of religious freedom . . . [is] concerned with a historic concept," which has "never excluded legislation of general scope . . . not directed against particular sects."[17] Referring to Justice Oliver Wendell Holmes's jurisprudential approach, Justice Frankfurter's judicial conscience necessarily subordinated the citizen's liberty to the popular legislative will.

This judicial approach connected to a discourse of the cognitive citizen. The opinion used the figure of the child as an example of a person who has the conviction of belief but lacks the cognitive wherewithal to make reasoned choices. Imbuing the frame with the weight of tradition, the opinion highlighted the Pledge of Allegiance's entrenched practice ("the ceremony is a familiar one") and the potential incapacities of the children to choose whether or not to say it. Noting their ages (ten and twelve), it marked that they "had been brought up conscientiously to believe that such a gesture of respect for the flag was forbidden by command of Scripture."[18] The description emphasized the sincerity of belief without any indication of rational choice to support it. Illustrating the ways that novelization of judicial opinions can lead to judicial invention, this maneuver used the virtue discourse of prior cases to justify its result. The opinion appealed to the need for general limits of freedom and the necessity to compel the incapable citizen. Doctrine supported curbs on the expression of belief when the latter "contradict[ed] the relevant concerns of a political society," and "relieve[d] the citizen from the discharge of political responsibilities."[19] Here, the court argued for sovereignty over the citizen to justify a political theory of civic unity—ironically enough, where *Meyer* had held the Constitution did not authorize civic unity when it interfered with private economic liberty, *Gobitis* held that it could indeed so authorize in the case of individual belief.

The sound judge displayed the cognitive ability that the child lacked. Judgment required detaching from personal belief in order to achieve neutrality in balancing competing values: "In all these cases, the general laws in question, upheld in their application to those who refused obedience from religious conviction, were manifestations of specific powers of government deemed by the legislature essential to secure and maintain that orderly, tranquil, and free society without which religious toleration itself is unattainable."[20] Precedent and tradition held that so long as laws did not target a specific group, they were permissible to further a function of the state. Because "national unity is the basis of national security,"[21] Justice Frankfurter framed the issue as a dilemma. Quoting Lincoln, he wrote, "'Must a government of necessity be too *strong* for the liberties of its people, or too *weak* to maintain its own existence?' No mere textual reading or logical talisman can solve the dilemma. And when the issue demands judicial determination, it is not the personal notion of judges of what wise adjustment requires which must prevail."[22] Here the interrogative mode articulated expert judgment as a distinct field grounded in a limited assessment of legislative action. A judge's role was not to independently assess whether legislation is likely to achieve its effect. Political wisdom cannot authorize a judge's expertise.

Gobitis introduced a discourse about the role of communication in producing civic unity. Symbolism supported the good citizen, because it was informed by a political psychology of hierarchy and conformity: "The ultimate foundation of a free society is the binding tie of cohesive sentiment. Such a sentiment is fostered by all those agencies of the mind and spirit which may serve to gather up the traditions of a people, transmit them from generation to generation, and thereby create that continuity of a treasured common life which constitutes a civilization. 'We live by symbols.' The flag is the symbol of our national unity, transcending all internal differences, however large, within the framework of the Constitution."[23] Abstraction from particularities permitted an argument from transcendence, which reproduced the opinion's hierarchical structure: national security was the basis of national unity, and national unity was the ground for freedom.

This unity was only achieved through a kind of communication that relied on symbols to produce an agreement about the continuity of common life. The opinion infused this symbol with meaning by referring to past precedent: "the flag is the symbol of the Nation's power, the emblem of freedom in its truest, best sense. . . . It signifies government resting on the consent of the governed; liberty regulated by law; the protection of the weak against the strong; security against the exercise of arbitrary power, and absolute safety for free institutions against foreign aggression."[24] Having first appealed to a psychology of repetitive exposure to symbols, Justice Frankfurter claimed judicial authority by referring to a unitary construction of the flag's symbolic meaning.

The opinion then connected its discourse of communication to the role of the judicial expert in considering pragmatic effects. A judgment for the child would not merely impact civic unity in the abstract sense, it would also invalidate legislation in the public interest: "The precise issue . . . is whether the legislatures of the various states and the authorities in a thousand counties and school districts of this country are barred from determining the appropriateness of various means to evoke that unifying sentiment without which there can be no liberties."[25] Here, judicial expertise counteracted the antimajoritarian risk by acknowledging the trappings of elitism. The plaintiffs' claim fell outside the court's expertise because it would "amount to . . . the pronouncement of pedagogical and psychological dogma in a field where courts possess no marked and certainly no controlling competence."[26] The uncertain effect provided a reason to focus on a familiar judicial test—whether the goals were appropriate. Because the policies to produce national unity were "manifold" and their effects were "unauthenticated by science," Justice Frankfurter argued that the court should not invalidate the law.[27]

Judicial expertise wedded a conservative skepticism of power with a liberal respect for diversity reflected in local governing institutions. Even if the justices disagreed with the outcome of the measure, "such belief would be no proof of its unconstitutionality," because "the courtroom is not the arena for debating issues of educational policy."[28] Because of the judiciary's method of expertise, it was an unsuitable venue to "choose among competing considerations" in the process of balancing the need to "secur[e] effective loyalty to the traditional ideals of democracy" and the need to respect "individual idiosyncrasies among a people so diversified in racial origins and religious allegiances. So to hold would . . . make us the school board for the country. That authority has not been given to the Court."[29] Emphasizing the distinct functions of these institutions, the opinion argued for a humble judicial expertise in the name of a freer and more democratic government.

This limited version of expert judgment connected the importance of symbolic communication with a theory of the incapable child. The child had low status and lacked capabilities, so liberty was best guaranteed by internalized habits manufactured through repetition. The opinion achieved this result through a rhetoric of inevitability—deference to schools was the only choice because these institutions best dealt with "the formative period in the development of citizenship."[30] To decide otherwise would risk public disorder. The opinion allowed for the possibility that "an exemption might introduce elements of difficulty into the school discipline, [and] might cast doubts in the minds of the other children which would themselves weaken the effect of the exercise."[31] Repeating the notion from *Ex parte Crouse* and *Lander v. Seaver* that the child mimicked behavior (rather than exercised independent thought), the opinion implied that repetitive traditions such as the Pledge of Allegiance ingrained habits by concealing their force: "Personal freedom is best maintained . . . when it is ingrained in a people's habits, and not enforced against popular policy by the coercion of adjudicated law."[32] This approach resonates with concerns evoked in the introduction to this book about the incapable child separated from their family at the border, whose stunted cognitive development would keep them stuck in a feedback loop of repetition and prevent the development of a sense of independent thought.

Justice Frankfurter's *Gobitis* opinion addressed the evolving pressure that the vocabulary of individual liberty had placed on controversies about the nascent citizen. In this context, individual belief appeared to pose a threat to national unity, with proper judgment as the antidote. Frankfurter's response to this tension simultaneously asserted judicial expertise and limited its scope. The opinion's argument for judicial restraint elevated experts who expressly acknowledged both the limitations of their authority and their own place in a larger liberal democratic system. Under this construction, a good expert judge owed a commitment to his place in the rank and function of the overall democratic system. Legislative power was the paradigmatic liberal democratic act. Practicing judicial expertise required knowledge of history and tradition; that tradition meant an aptitude and a reverence for neutrality. This cognitive ability pointed the way to a choice from a hierarchy of values. All of this served a pragmatism of systemic effects—Justice Frankfurter's opinion combined an argument about values (religious freedom depends on national unity) with a political psychology of repetitive development of habit to transcend the tension between the individual and the community. Judgment from individual conviction was uncertain, impulsive, and risky. Its systemic effects would confront everyone with a question that constitutional litigation was ill-suited to answer.[33]

Some members of the public received the *Gobitis* decision as a tacit approval for overt discrimination, which quickly escalated into violent persecution against Jehovah's Witnesses. Justice Frankfurter's opinion, which aimed to support community cohesion, may have encouraged community conflict instead. Many towns adopted statutes similar to the one originally brought before the court; reports of violence against Jehovah's Witnesses spiked.[34] Justice Frankfurter did not necessarily believe in the power of a particular symbol, but rather that judges were simply no good at second-guessing the legislature. Having underestimated the risks to minority rights, his faith in the wise judgment of the legislature led to social stigma, tension, and violence. The ensuing crisis precipitated a rare opportunity to quickly reconsider the controversy.

Judicial Conscience, Communication Capacities, and Citizenship: *West Virginia v. Barnette*

In 1942 the West Virginia Board of Education enacted a resolution that ordered educators to make the flag salute "a regular part of the program of activities in the public schools." All teachers and students had to participate in the pledge, and students who did not comply were to be expelled. The resolution considered any expelled child "unlawfully absent" and empowered the state to prosecute parents or guardians. Convictions could result in a fine not exceeding fifty dollars and a jail term not exceeding thirty days.[35] *Gobitis* appeared to permit precisely this sort of legislative action.

A group of citizens sought to enjoin the enforcement of these laws against Jehovah's Witnesses, on grounds similar to the *Gobitis* plaintiffs. Students adhering to this faith considered the flag an "image" to which they could not swear allegiance above God. Some of them were expelled, and some were threatened with criminal prosecutions.[36] The plaintiffs' claim was that the law violated the due process and equal protection clauses of the Fourteenth Amendment. A three-judge panel of a federal district court found for the plaintiffs, and the West Virginia Board of Education appealed directly to the Supreme Court.

The Supreme Court also sided with the plaintiffs. Justice Jackson's majority opinion held that the law violated the Fourteenth Amendment. The court overruled *Gobitis,* arguing that the *Gobitis* court had asked a different question: while *Gobitis* had assumed that the state had authority to compel speech, the *Barnette* plaintiffs questioned that power at its core.[37] Justice Jackson's opinion reasoned that the law compelled speech, dictating how citizens should think. It then asserted that the judiciary's primary role was to protect individual constitutional rights and argued that the statute was unconstitutional because the state was manufacturing consent to its positions.[38]

Justice Frankfurter dissented. He argued that the majority's approach injected the judge's personal opinion about the law's wisdom, rather than an analysis of its constitutional permissibility. In his view, the judge's role was to perform the latter task. He rejected the majority's description of the West Virginia law as compelled speech. According to the dissent, the state could require citizens to do much that is unwise, if the laws were passed democratically. He reasoned that the law was constitutional because it applied to all citizens—it didn't single out Jehovah's Witnesses and so could not be struck down because of its disproportionate impact on them.[39]

Barnette has earned near-sacred status for its discussion of civic duty and independence in the crucible of World War II, its emphasis on the dangers of state compulsion, and its concern for a liberal polity opposed to orthodoxy.[40] Justice Jackson's opinion has been called "one of the greatest statements on civil liberties ever written,"[41] and an "American . . . prayer" that "form[s] a central part of our civic constitution."[42] In the public imagination, it demonstrates the Supreme Court's mediating role with reference to civil rights, as well as a commitment to a role for federal courts in protecting individual rights from state and local legislative bodies.[43]

Form Follows Function: Pluralism, Persuasion, and the Citizen

Justice Jackson's opinion resolved a political and prudential crisis. Ostensibly motivated to limit the damage that *Gobitis* had inflicted on the political fabric, *Barnette* was in tension with the court's discursive conventions that derived authority from its apolitical modes of address and procedures for decision. Indeed, here the court was reconsidering an issue it had just decided a few years prior, which had contributed to an atmosphere of sectarian violence. Reversing a precedent was admitting error, which threatened the court's legitimacy.[44] But since the court does not confirm what it had already decided, the mere fact that it had granted certiorari to *Barnette* signaled that it was ready to reverse *Gobitis*.

The majority opinion performed expertise through its legal question. This tactic used the discourse about tradition to create a substantive vision of the expert judge's role in construing individual citizenship rights. It downplayed the radical nature of the overruling, describing the circumstances as part of a long institutional history. This maneuver grounded the decision in tradition and also connected it to the temporality that judicial discourse prized (taking the long view in recognizing traditions and genuine threats to democratic order). The language of judicial routine introduced the question: "this case calls upon us to reconsider a precedent decision, as the Court, throughout its history, often has been required to do."[45] "Reconsideration" calls forth the activity of judging as a natural process familiar to those with knowledge of the court's history. The language placed the opinion in dialogue with Justice Frankfurter's *Gobitis* opinion and his *Barnette* dissent when it posited that institutional conditions—

not the political preferences of the justices—compelled the court to act. The strategy managed institutional anxieties, describing *Barnette* as part of Supreme Court tradition. It propelled a vision of citizenship through the figure of the child with three significant maneuvers. First, it altered the question presented to focus on state coercion, imagining a new role of the judge as protector of the liberal individual. Second, it used the pedagogical practice—the Pledge of Allegiance—to express an idea about liberal communication that elevated persuasion over symbolism. Finally, as a result of the first two strategies, the opinion performed the role of the expert judge as a calibrator of competing interests to protect the core of rights, in contrast to the judge's function as a mere applier of original documents.

Justice Jackson's new question responded to the implicit demand that the judge perform expertise. It differentiated *Barnette* from *Gobitis* so that the court was not seen by others to be merely responding to political pressure. This new question centered on limits to sovereign authority instead of on individual exemptions (i.e., whether Jehovah's Witnesses could opt out of the ceremony). The question implied that children were liberal individuals, passing over any distinction between adults and children in terms of producing allegiance to the state. In a sense, this question built upon the discourse of belief in *Gobitis*: if a child had the capability to hold beliefs and convictions, the question of whether a state could be limited in how it shaped those beliefs became relevant. This new approach opened up an evaluation of state practices in terms of first principles of citizenship. It led directly to a question of appropriate communicative forms for citizens.

This new question connected citizen judgment to persuasive public communication. This communicative citizen (and state) differed from the type of ideal citizen that previous cases described. Ideologically, the citizen was now formed not by virtues instilled by authority figures but by individual communication practices. Rhetorically, the opinion instilled this new idea with familiar tactics of dissociation and distinction. Dividing favored and disfavored modes of education, it then extended that division to modes of address. Instruction and provision of information was permissible; compulsion was not. This pedagogical approach disavowed the justifications for discipline and corporal punishment of earlier cases and implied the child's individual rights. The state could require instruction in the American governmental tradition, but it could not compel the declaration of individual belief.

The opinion aligned citizenship with a civic unity derived from persuasive communication practices. Elevating persuasion over symbolism, it framed the issue about civic unity as a question of "whether this slow and easily neglected route to aroused loyalties constitutionally may be short-cut by substituting a compulsory salute and slogan."[46] The opinion employed tropes of regression and force to describe practices—like West Virginia's law—based on rank, compulsion, hierarchy, and status. This direct commentary on Justice Frankfurter's *Gobitis* opinion compared his idea of political participation by symbolic ritual with the performative requirements of Nazism. Symbolism conveyed little but the acceptance of authority—"a salute, a bowed or bared head, a bended knee," which embodied the worst of the Axis powers' militaristic society, which was limited to "gestures of acceptance and respect."[47] Similarly, West Virginia's communication techniques were outdated, illogical, and undemocratic.

Persuasion was necessary to produce civically united citizens because it valued individual thought and a pluralism of sentiments. The ability to differentiate among these sentiments shifted the discourse about pluralism from considerations grounded in economic pursuits (as was valued in *Meyer* and *Pierce*) to those grounded in critical thought. As a feature of citizen judgment, *Barnette* discerned this idea through contrast with symbolism. Persuasion permitted individual flourishing; compulsion might "strangle the free mind at its source."[48] The opinion then made a pragmatic appeal for the survival of the democratic state and its individuals. Unlike the supposed threat to cohesion in *Meyer* and *Pierce,* the threat to democratic government was suddenly real and palpable. This strategy demonstrated how *Barnette* participated in the discourse of threat and temporality characteristic of *Meyer* and *Pierce*. Equating the West Virginia effort to produce virtuous youth with the Romans' attempt to eradicate Christianity and the Axis countries' attempts to stamp out dissent, the opinion argued that all such wars over virtue concluded with the "unanimity of the graveyard."[49] Like *Gobitis,* the opinion transcended traditional practice with a more important value—one that also subsumed the state's interest in community cohesion. Like *Meyer* and *Pierce,* the decision validated modern democracy over ancient barbarism.

Finally, the opinion carved out a role for the expert judge as a protector of individual citizenship rights by calibrating the competing interests of the citizen and the state. This element fit with the opinion's vision of citizenship. The opinion's propositional content of citizenship—respect for noncompulsion—valued unforced choices. Its vision for judges as protectors of individual rights implied that judges should calibrate decisions not merely by picking sides among conflicting values but by articulating ordering principles that defuse the very choice. There was a symmetry here between this interpretive approach and the opinion's praise of pluralism and persuasion. Compulsion and symbolism were insufficient because they were impoverished modes of expression. Likewise, the expert judge should refuse forced choices and dilemmas—civic unity or individual liberty?—and discern the guiding principles of democracy to evaluate the choices presented before the court. Illustrating the point, the opinion legitimated its own expertise by locating those very principles.

The opinion deployed this logic to respond to the long-running discourse of the expert judge as deferring to democracy. Justice Jackson's argument against deference dislodged romantic images of the school board as local democracy-in-action. Performing the interest-balancing role, the opinion argued that the interest in deferring to smaller governing structures was tempered by the countervailing worry about abuses of discretion: "Small and local authority may feel less sense of responsibility to the Constitution. . . . There are village tyrants, as well as village Hampdens, but none who acts under color of law is beyond reach of the Constitution."[50] Emphasizing the Constitution's superiority to local law implied a dramatic reversal. Governing structure and professional competence compelled expert judges to review legislation that threatens individual rights. Jackson defused the seemingly irreconcilable conflict not with a forced choice but with a distinction—between instances where individual rights encroach on the rights of another and those which do not. The expert judge acts legitimately when she engages in the discernment necessary to recognize the difference between the two instances. Hearkening back to the criticism of the state in *Meyer* and *Pierce*, a general interest in community cohesion (like a general fear of social breakdown) would not justify restrictions except where individual rights were at stake.

The expert judge needed to be skeptical of democratic majorities and protect a set of rights that were exempt from democratic discussion. That is a vision that participates in the discourse of the social contract, while altering its focus to broaden citizenship rights. The Constitution removed "certain subjects from the vicissitudes of political controversy, to place them beyond the reach of majorities and officials, and to establish them as legal principles to be applied by the courts." These core rights "may not be submitted to vote; they depend on the outcome of no elections."[51] This argument created an autonomous function for the judiciary that justified its antidemocratic tendencies and defined its core. A declarative tone shaped the expert's function to safeguard against the manufacture of consent to political positions. These rhetorical strategies created the opinion's famous defense of free speech, where citizens exercising individual thought served as the organic structure of community: "To believe that patriotism will not flourish if patriotic ceremonies are voluntary and spontaneous . . . is to make an unflattering estimate of the appeal of our institutions to free minds. . . . If there is any fixed star in our constitutional constellation, it is that no official, high or petty, can prescribe what shall be orthodox in politics, nationalism, religion, or other matters of opinion, or force citizens to confess by word or act their faith therein."[52] This reversal of Supreme Court precedent ushered in a new era of constitutional liberalism grounded in the expansion of rights to include the free-thinking child.

The opinion's strategies also contained the grounds for a counterdiscourse. It used a general vocabulary of rights and state restrictions to discuss the child's status, moving away from the wardship language that justified external control (by parents or the state). Justice Jackson's formal constraints shaped the practical consequences of the opinion's rhetorical choices. For expert judgment, it created a new role for the judge as protector of individual thought and expounder of liberal first principles. For individual citizen judgment, the opinion articulated standards for the kind of communication worthy of inclusion in public discourse, and an idea about the organic force of the free mind that would develop judgment capabilities. What was previously produced with repetitive practices imposed by outside forces (and punishment and discipline when those failed) was now declared out of step with liberal values. In these respects, the opinion assumed that the child possessed core citizenship rights, but it failed to address differences in their performance. Justice Frankfurter's dissent resisted this vision, preserving an alternate possible future of committed citizens and restrained judges.

Performing Restraint, Detaching from Belief: Justice Frankfurter's Dissent

At various turns erudite, reflective, self-righteous, and angry, Frankfurter's dissent rehabilitated his case for liberal expert judgment as the exercise of restraint. If it were a matter of his own "personal attitude," he would endorse the court's decision, but "one's own opinion about the wisdom or evil of a law should be excluded altogether when one is doing one's duty on the bench."[53] The dissent's case for restraint included four important elements. First, it argued that the proper role of the expert judge required the cognitive detachment of personal belief from judicial role. Second, it reiterated the association found in *Gobitis* between this capability and its pragmatic fit with institutional design. Third, it developed facial neutrality as an interpretive practice that would express this mental capability. Finally, that interpretive practice furthered an idea about citizenship: consent was the display of committed choice. The dissent cast an argumentative template for opposing the categorical equality of the child as a citizen. To pursue this inclusion via judicial declaration would cause a crisis of ordered governance.

First, the dissent asserted that the majority opinion failed to separate belief from judicial role. In other words, the majority opinion lacked impulse control. Justice Frankfurter referred to his own Jewish minority status to perform this cognitive detachment. He belonged to "the most vilified and persecuted minority in history," but that did not absolve him of the duty to be "bound by . . . judicial obligations" and to resist the temptation to "writ[e] . . . private notions of policy into the Constitution."[54] This performance figured expert judgment as the capability to restrain the self, separating one's personal identity and feelings before engaging in constitutional decision-making. The majority's opinion signaled a type of hubris ill-suited to the role of a judge: "Judicial self-restraint is equally necessary whenever an exercise of political or legislative power is challenged."[55]

Second, the dissent connected such restrained expertise to a discourse about democratic functions. Following *Gobitis,* it held up legislation as the paradigmatic democratic form. Judges could only decide whether there is a reasonable justification for a law, not whether the law itself is wise.[56] This form of expert judgment aligns with an idea of democracy as a relationship between governing institutions and a mode of political participation—voting—suitable to the form. For Frankfurter, the Witnesses' claim was political, not constitutional, because it complained of a disproportionate burden from an otherwise neutral law. This argument embraced liberal individualism while disavowing the majority's principle of judgment. It also shifted focus from the state's coercive action back to the majority's practical effects on state functions.

The dissent used the distinction between legislation and judicial decision to limit the latter's field of inquiry. The judicial expert was ill-equipped to preserve pluralism in the public sphere. The legislature was "charged solely with civil concerns of society." Liberal pluralism and respect for the individual mattered, but expert judges could not will them into being: "Tact, respect, and generosity toward variant views will always commend themselves to those charged with the duties of legislation. . . . But the real question is, who is to make such accommodations, the courts or the legislature?"[57] Justice Frankfurter criticized the majority's preoccupation with coercion because it interfered with collective democratic practices.

The dissent emphasized the inherent institutional limitations of judicial expertise. Judges acted without nuance. They "can only strike down" and can neither "modify or qualify" nor "make exceptions to a general requirement."[58] To consider the wisdom of a statute detached from a disciplined judicial role would be counter to the structural and functional differences between the two branches found in the Constitution. The dissent's strategy recast the pivot point of the dispute, beginning with an ideal community of politically engaged citizens who correct their mistakes through the legislative process. The people decided how best to govern through legislation. Judges intervened only to correct grave process errors.

Third, the dissent performed expertise in its interpretive practice of neutrality. The West Virginia statute was permissible because it did not single Jehovah's Witnesses out for persecution, even if it affected them differentially: "The constitutional protection of religious freedom . . . gave religious equality, not civil immunity. Its essence is freedom from conformity to religious dogma, not freedom from conformity to law because of religious dogma."[59] This compact phrase progressed from distinction to chiasmus, performing expertise by ordering a hierarchy of liberal principles. The figural reversal of the plaintiffs' claim justified the dissent's interpretive practice. State neutrality was a goal preserved through committed interpretive practice, not a declaration to be defended. Because freedom of religion existed to preserve state neutrality, a statute's neutrality could establish its reasonableness.[60]

This practice of liberal neutrality became a distinguishing characteristic of a good expert judge, buffered by its practical consequences. The dissent authorized this practice through a counterfactual slippery slope that invoked public threats. If the judiciary could disregard a statute's neutrality, what other neutral statutes might be in danger? Compulsory vaccination, food inspection, conscription, civic testimony, and medical treatment are all examples of legislation that courts have upheld in the past, "even though the religious consciences of particular individuals rebelled at the exaction."[61] Here, the dissent posed neutrality as the guarantor of good public government. Embroidering this principle with the weight of tradition (each of Frankfurter's examples was a precedent case), the dissent argued that the majority would protect the individual at the expense of democratic governance.

Finally, the dissent appealed to an idea of consent as a type of committed choice to live with the unforeseen consequences of decisions. It observed that "law is concerned with external behavior, and not with the inner life of man."[62] Committed choice was the ground of the social contract, which was supported by understanding one's proper judicial role. Expert judges needed to maintain a distinction between obeying the law and believing in its worth: the dissent observed that Socrates died to vindicate "the conviction that duty of obedience to secular law does not presuppose consent to its enactment or belief in its virtue."[63] Like Socrates, the judge must separate personal conviction from duty to obey the law and cannot defend disobedience based on the mere fact of disagreement with the collective choice.

To what did the citizen consent? The dissent associated citizenship with consent to a democratic structure of decision-making. This structure emanated from legislation: "The consent upon which free government rests is the consent that comes from sharing in the process of making and unmaking laws. . . . The individual conscience . . . cannot . . . restrict community action through political organs in matters of community concern, so long as the action is not asserted in a discriminatory way."[64] Barnette could choose her faith, but once she had done so, could not use that faith to frustrate laws that aim to achieve community goals. The plaintiffs' compelled speech was a product of liberal consent. To think otherwise would potentially render the nation ungovernable.

This logic connected Justice Frankfurter's discourse of cognition, belief, and democratic system to the enduring discourse of prioritizing original commitments. This argument shifted the legal question from an impermissible state action to a practice that the state can neither legislate away nor declare unconstitutional. Because the child was a creature of belief—but not consent—persuasion could not be the mandatory mode of producing civic unity: "Symbolism is inescapable. . . . It is not for this Court to make psychological judgments as to the effectiveness of a particular symbol in inculcating supposedly indispensable feelings."[65] The use of symbols was simply one social fact of human communication that the legislature deployed for communitarian ends. The majority's argument "mock[ed] reason and denie[d] [America's] whole history," because it exaggerated one remote risk—deferential respect to a leader—to generate a liberal constitutional principle.

Aligning restraint, tradition, neutrality, and the necessity of each to upholding constitutional function, Frankfurter wrote that "saluting the flag suppresses no belief, nor curbs it. Children and their parents may believe what they please, avow their belief and practice it. . . . All channels of affirmative free expression are open to both children and parents."[66] Liberalism demanded the expert temperament to acknowledge the open-ended nature of divisive social questions. This attitude tapped into the weakness of Jackson's approach by marking its fundamental irony—an illiberal practice of judgment to protect rights-bearing citizens. The dissent's restraint called this "attitude . . . a great enemy of liberalism. . . . Much of which should offend a free-spirited society is constitutional. . . . Only a persistent positive translation of the faith of a free society into the convictions and habits and action of a community is the ultimate reliance against unabated temptations to fetter the human spirit."[67] Expert judges could not translate ideas about liberalism's moral force into practice, so they could not create and defend a particular liberal individualism.

The dissent's neutrality discourse nevertheless operated under the fiction of choice. Because the child had neither the choice nor the equal capabilities necessary for meaningful consent, children were not represented in the legislative process that symbolized America's democratic commitment. The dissent's mode of expert judgment claimed to preserve liberal pluralism by respecting the democratic process. It resolved the conflict between individual and community with reference to committed choice. But this maneuver disguised interpretive conflicts as constitutional mandates and posed deference to a majoritarian process as a compelled result. In concealing that contingency, the opinion's certainty about the judge's role in a constitutional democracy wished away the problem of individual capable choice (who can choose, and what communicative traits are taken as a sign of their competence).

The fissures of the *Barnette* opinions embedded significant tensions in its discourses about the child's constitutional status. First, the discourse of the communicative citizen embedded a tension about the relevance of the child's differential cognitive capabilities (different from adults as a category, and different from each other). Because *Barnette* was grounded in the effect of state power on individual citizens, it would become increasingly difficult to push questions of the child's performance of communication capabilities to the background. The majority's anticoercion principle constituted a new liberal identity and ordered future disputes around the contours of these capabilities. *Barnette* implied that the signs of persuasive communication (and standards for its judgment) were relevant places of contestation in future cases. Its basic idea—that a liberal community must persuade, and not compel allegiance—raised important questions concerning its limits. It left untouched consideration of symbolism's benefits, what place it had in democratic persuasion between individuals, and whether children could speak their differences of opinion in this world of persuasion. Each of these questions was placed on future cases, for the future parents, school boards, legislatures, and citizens to resolve. Finally, Frankfurter's dissent foregrounded expert judgment in the name of a pragmatic, role-and-function-based interpretive practice. The question of judicial expertise shifted the ground of dispute away from the facts of the case and onto the character of the judge. For Justice Frankfurter, a good judge must articulate a limiting principle for any extension of individual rights to conform to a circumscribed role in a larger system of democratic government. Concern for judgment as a capability that maintained the governing order took on increased importance, which entailed a question about material differences between the child and the prototypical adult citizen—their relative capabilities to speak and judge and the degree to which their interests are reflected in stock expressions of popular will.

4

PROCEDURE, CARE, AND LIBERTY

In re Gault

As part 1 discussed, state custody over the child was justified in part by the doctrine of parens patriae, which anointed the government with authority to protect the child. *Ex parte Crouse* had held that parens patriae allowed the state to commit juveniles to reformatories, for the sake of reshaping their character. By the 1960s the pieces were in place for a challenge to parens patriae relating to juveniles accused of crimes.[1] The Warren Court achieved distinction for its efforts to reshape the political order with a robust expansion of individual rights. Its forays into reapportioning representation ("one man [*sic*], one vote" of *Baker v. Carr* and *Reynolds v. Sims*), the law of criminal procedure (Miranda warnings, excluding evidence obtained in violation of the Fourth Amendment, guaranteeing a right to counsel for indigent criminal defendants in *Gideon v. Wainwright*, among others), and its landmark decision concerning the constitutional right to privacy (*Griswold v. Connecticut*) pointed to an assertive role for the judiciary in protecting the individual and regulating state practices. The court was expanding individual rights against the state. *Barnette* (and *Brown v. Board of Education*) served as bold examples where the child was the beneficiary of this new rights regime.

Reform or abolition of parens patriae was a possible next step in this progression. The Supreme Court sent a strong signal of this disposition in *Kent v. U.S.* (1966), in which it held that a juvenile court's transfer of a juvenile to a criminal court was arbitrary because it lacked notice to his counsel and parents, and because evidence was taken and used against him. Justice Fortas wrote that for the parens patriae system, "there is evidence that the child receives the worst of both worlds: that he [*sic*] gets neither the protections accorded to adults nor the solicitous care . . . postulated for children."[2] *Kent* opened an opportunity for a broader challenge to the longstanding juvenile justice system.

That opportunity came with the case of fifteen-year old Gerald Gault.

Gault was arrested on June 8, 1964, for making obscene phone calls to a neighbor, Mrs. Cook. He was already on probation for having been with a boy who had stolen a wallet. Gault's parents were not at home when he was arrested, and the arresting officer didn't notify them of his arrest. Gault's mother arrived at the Children's Detention Home in Gila County, Arizona, and was told that there was to be a hearing the next day. At the hearing, the arresting officer filed a petition with the court but did not serve Gault or his parents with it. The accusing witness was not present. The judge questioned Gault at the hearing, and there were conflicting reports about the contents of Gault's testimony. There was no transcript or recording of the hearing. Gault was held for a few more days before being released.

On June 15, Gault had a second hearing. Probation officers filed a report listing the charges as "lewd phone calls." Neither Gault nor his parents were served with the report. Again, Mrs. Cook was not present at this hearing, in spite of Gault's parents' request that she be there to identify which boy had made the calls (he was with a friend at the time of the alleged incident). Again, there was no recording or transcript, and there was disagreement about Gault's testimony. After this hearing, the judge committed Gault to juvenile detention for six years (by which point Gault would turn twenty-one). Under Arizona law at the time, an adult who had been convicted of a similar offense would have received a maximum sentence of two months in jail and a fifty-dollar fine.[3]

The case was an ideal vehicle to challenge the parens patriae system, and the ACLU filed suit.[4] Arizona law did not provide for appeals in juvenile court proceedings, so Gault filed a habeas petition in the Arizona Supreme Court, which referred it for a hearing to the Arizona Superior Court. The Arizona Superior Court dismissed the petition, and the Arizona Supreme Court affirmed that ruling. The United States Supreme Court took the case in order to rule on the scope of a juvenile's procedural rights in delinquency proceedings.

Gault argued that parens patriae was unconstitutional because it placed all crucial decisions about who was prosecuted and how the law would be applied in the hands of judges and probation officers.[5] Criminologists criticized these proceedings because they were not subject to systematic review frustrated policy goals due to their arbitrariness. Justice Fortas issued the majority opinion, holding that the Due Process Clause of the Constitution applied to adversarial proceedings at which incarceration was a possible outcome. Due process meant adequate notice to the child and his or her parents or guardians. The notice should inform them of "the specific issues that they must meet," and must be given "at the earliest practicable time, and . . . sufficiently in advance of the hearing to permit preparation."[6] The opinion held that Gault had the right to counsel (and the state had to so inform him) and the right against self-incrimination.[7] Applying these standards to the facts of the case, the court held that Gault's statements should not have been admitted as evidence against him, and that he had the right to confront witnesses.[8]

Justice Stewart dissented, predicting that to "impose the Court's long catalog of requirements upon juvenile proceedings in every area of the country is to invite a long step backwards into the nineteenth century."[9] He would have deferred to the Arizona courts' rulings that found that due process requirements were satisfied, and he thought that the Supreme Court's broad uniform requirements on juvenile proceedings would result in injustice.[10]

In re Gault is one of the integral symbols of the Warren Court's rights revolution, which substantially altered the landscape of constitutional interpretation and the liberal self-understanding of rights as entitlements. By the end of the 1960s, the Supreme Court had reshaped the constitutional governing relationship in the areas of education, criminal procedure, free speech, and voting rights. Chief Justice Warren himself had opined that *In re Gault* would be considered as "the Magna Carta for juveniles";[11] Gault's lawyer argued that it "convert[ed] juvenile courts from 'no law' areas, with the attendant dangers of judicial arbitrariness, into tribunals functioning with procedural regularity."[12] Its opinions used the passive—but constitutionally free—child as a vehicle for their dispute about the connection between the cognitive application of procedure and free citizens.

Expert Judgment as Clear and Pragmatic Procedure

Justice Fortas identified procedure as the pragmatic way to maximize constitutional liberty, framing expert judgment as the application of adversarial procedure to make decisions. Its narrative about the decline and fall of parens patriae provided a powerful contrast with the virtues of fair procedures. These virtues included categorical equality, accurate deliberation and assessment of fact, and the mutual entailment of liberty and efficient policy. The opinion implied that individual differentiation, passionate belief, and caring relationships were incompatible with expert liberal judgment. Concerning the individual citizen, the opinion replicated the rhetorical strategy of *Barnette*. It elevated the child to equal status as other individuals, but it retained the child's passive characteristics as a site of great public investment, justifying state power. The narrative of lost childhood innocence authorized the child's procedural rights.

The opinion justified procedural rights based on the categorical equality of individuals. The parens patriae system was incompatible with a free citizenry because it relied on individual differentiation and made decisions grounded in passionate conviction. Defenders of the juvenile court system had "tolerated—

indeed insisted upon" differences "between the procedural rights accorded to adults and those of juveniles."[13] They were "profoundly convinced" of their purpose, they "believed" it extended beyond determinations of guilt or innocence to get to the essence of the child's person, "to save [the child] from a downward career."[14] Parens patriae was opposed to categorical equality, the latter implying a strict boundary that the state should not cross. This portion of the opinion built on the discourse of mere belief and intention as an outmoded or primitive judgment mode. This disposition was similar to the attitude expressed in *Meyer* and *Pierce* (mere belief in a threat to civic unity was insufficient and antimodern), as well as the denigration of belief and conviction that lurked in the flag salute cases. In contrast, expert judgment looked beyond the stated intentions of action to test its actual results. Parens patriae was a failed experiment out of step with constitutional requirements. Although the system was created to avoid the harshness of adult penalties and the undesirable social consequences of "mix[ing children] in jails with hardened criminals," its presumed duty to the child was at odds with liberal justice.[15]

To make this discursive shift, the opinion contrasted parens patriae with expert judicial procedure. Procedure was indispensable to expert judgment because it accounted for the practical consequences of decisions to grasp whether results matched intentions. This attitude contrasted with the well-intentioned parens patriae reformers, who were moral crusaders expressing deep convictions born of optimism about human nature: "The child—essentially good, as they saw it—was to be made 'to feel that he is the object of [the state's] care and solicitude,' not that he was under arrest or on trial."[16] The motive of action stood in for the fact of individuated judgment, which was indifferent to just results.

Expert procedural judgment advanced liberty because it knew its limits: binary determinations on narrow questions of guilt or innocence. Ironically, Justice Fortas's opinion relied on the discourses from both *Barnette* and *Gobitis*. From *Barnette*, it drew on the notion that there was a core of individual rights to which the citizen was entitled, that the judiciary must protect, and for which the distinction between child and adult was immaterial. From *Gobitis*, the opinion adapted arguments about the distinctive nature of judicial expertise, and the need to limit the judge's power. Parens patriae was a form of individualized judgment that violated these precepts. Care, solicitude, and a desire to rehabilitate had no place in judicial analysis. The individualized care of parens patriae was suspicious because it served as a pretext to disregard rules of criminal procedure for their "apparent rigidities, technicalities, and harshness."[17]

Individualized judgment deprived citizens of liberty for the sake of their improvement. The beneficent motives of the state concealed a malign desire to control individuals and expand power. Rehabilitation was a result "to be achieved, without coming to conceptual and constitutional grief, by insisting that the proceedings were not adversary, but that the state was proceeding as *parens patriae*."[18] The opinion assailed this choice because of its misuse of language and tradition. Its doctrine "rationalize[d] the exclusion of juveniles from the constitutional scheme; but its meaning is murky, and its historic credentials are of dubious relevance."[19] Stylistically, this maneuver extended its suspicion of judgment practices to modes of description. Expert judicial procedures were the antidote. The language of the opinion opposed parens patriae—Latin shorthand—to a common vernacular. The former obscured bad constitutional practice under the moniker of tradition.

Parens patriae failed because it departed from its original intentions. Originally used in chancery practice, it was limited to "protecting the property interests and the person of the child."[20] Yet, the opinion ignored two crucial rationales: the public motivations of nineteenth-century reformers and the differences in capabilities among children and adults. Instead, it noted the doctrine's absence "in the history of criminal jurisprudence. . . . In these old days, the state was not deemed to have authority to accord [children at least seven years old] fewer procedural rights than adults."[21] According to this logic, expert judicial procedure responded to the arbitrary errors of chancery courts. This maneuver discredited individualized distinctions, installing categorical equality as the highest liberal value. Judicial procedure maximized liberty for all equally. Decisions authorized by mere conscience were illiberal because they could not be tested empirically as an exercise of objective reason.

Citizenship of Efficiency and Open Futures

In contrast to the vague and arbitrary standards of individual conscience, the opinion introduced a discourse of clarity and transparency in language as a relevant marker of expert judgment that advanced citizens' liberty. Clarity was rigorous, and progress was achieved by applying standards of relevance and unambiguous legal concepts. This practice of ideal judgment expanded liberty while managing risks. The narrative associated procedure with efficiency, and efficiency with pragmatism and liberty. Parens patriae was an emblem of a bygone era of elites ruling by conscience. This was irreconcilable with constitutional ideals: "the highest motives and most enlightened impulses led to a peculiar system for juveniles, unknown to our law in any comparable context."[22] Paradoxically, expedience justified the principle: "unbridled discretion, however benevolently motivated, is frequently a poor substitute for principle and procedure. . . . The absence of substantive standards has not necessarily meant that children receive careful, compassionate, individualized treatment. . . . Departures from established principles of due process have frequently resulted not in enlightened procedure, but in arbitrariness."[23] The opinion's argumentative structure illustrated the procedural judgment it valued: objective measure of outcomes, not intention, was the gold standard of constitutional fairness. Due process was the presumptive rule; parens patriae was the exception that bore the burden of articulating success on its own terms.[24]

The opinion described the general textual practices that made expert judgment a safeguard of citizens' liberty. It focused on relevant facts, where parens patriae lacked a rigorous fact-finding method: "Failure to observe the fundamental requirements of due process has resulted in . . . unfairness to individuals and inadequate or inaccurate findings."[25] When judges got the facts wrong, they could not provide proper care and guidance. Expert judgment grounded a constitutional community and set of practical tools for its realization: "The procedural rules which have been fashioned from the generality of due process are our best instruments for the distillation and evaluation of essential facts from the conflicting welter of data that life and our adversary methods present. . . . These instruments of due process . . . enhance the possibility that truth will emerge from the confrontation of opposing versions and conflicting data. 'Procedure' is to law what 'scientific method' is to science."[26] Liberty was preserved best when the state got it right. Determining the relative truth and importance of contextual facts and maintaining proper procedure were the best ways to prevent biased judgment.

Expert judgment formed the external criteria for this project, furthering both liberty *and* individualized justice, because it favored relevance and probability. This argument contrasted facts and procedural method on the one hand with mere belief on the other hand (associated with emotion and care). The standard for evaluation was pragmatic because "neither sentiment nor folklore should cause us to shut our eyes" to the recidivism rates of juveniles; indeed, Fortas referred to a Stanford Research Institute report finding that "66 percent of the 16- and 17-year-old juveniles referred to the court by the Youth Aid Division had been before the court previously."[27] The contrast continued: "the early conception of the Juvenile Court proceeding was one in which a fatherly judge touched the conscience of the erring youth by talking over his problems," but "recent studies . . . suggest that the appearance as well as the actuality of fairness, impartiality and orderliness—in short, the essentials of due process—may be a more impressive and more therapeutic attitude so far as the juvenile is concerned."[28]

This discourse supported a civic unity premised on fair treatment. Outcomes flowing from proper procedure produced trust. Forms of evidence performed this judgmental mode. Statistical proof enforced the theme of "proper method, proper result." Rigorous peer-reviewed studies demonstrated a new nontraditional insight about human psychology. The individual feeling of fair treatment replaced the feeling that somebody cares. The opinion implied that juveniles have the cognitive ability to recognize fair procedures and that cooperation is induced through trust. The consistent application of procedures produced trust because it guaranteed that the facts were disclosed.

The opinion then discarded the parens patriae doctrine, relying on a tragic narrative that recast juvenile detention as imprisonment, a childhood lost. This characterization reversed the original declaration in *Ex parte Crouse* that juvenile detention was a school, and not a prison. The story imagined Gault's lost potential, suggested the risk for abuse, and reinforced the importance of expert judgment that transcends sentiment: "A boy is charged with misconduct. The boy is committed to an institution where he may be restrained of liberty for years. It is of no constitutional consequence—and of limited practical meaning—that the institution to which he is committed is called an Industrial School. . . . However euphemistic the title . . . [it] is an institution of confinement in which the child is incarcerated for a greater or lesser time . . . . Instead of mother and father and sisters and brothers and friends and classmates, his world is peopled by guards, custodians, state employees, and 'delinquents' confined with him for anything from waywardness to rape and homicide."[29] This procedural discipline was thoroughly stylized: the example was derived from the facts of the case, yet quite explicitly exceeded the "guilt or innocence" question of the judicial task. The opinion mourned the child's loss, laying responsibility at the feet of a byzantine world of euphemism that hid the tragedy from all but the most discerning eyes. This child was still fundamentally innocent, but this innocence supported a regime of abstract and uniform procedure, not particularized individualized character rehabilitation.

In re Gault followed *Ex parte Crouse*, *Pendergrass*, and *Lander* in describing the child as a passive object who is acted upon: "the condition of being a boy does not justify a kangaroo court."[30] Expert judgment signaled the capacity to link factual narratives to constitutional principles. The narrative moved from declarative statement of fact to commentary that evoked fears about the child's squelched aspirations. The loss of open life outcomes was an arbitrary consequence of a flawed system, not a reasonable outcome of a committed choice. Parens patriae enabled this intolerable loss of innocence, using compassion as cover for punishment.

Liberal expert judgment exposed the incongruence between stated principle and actual result. The accuracy of procedure was more important than any potential administrative burden. Parens patriae assumed that judges unburdened by cumbersome procedures would have time to make an individualized determination that may yield an ability to be "disciplined and dealt with at home."[31] But Gault's proceedings demonstrated nothing "different from [the points of concern] that would be involved in determining any charge of violation of a penal statute."[32] Because these courts were operating as criminal courts, they had to provide procedural guarantees. Recording the proceedings was the only way for a reviewing party to know whether the punishment was justified. If Gault had been over eighteen, "the maximum punishment would have been a fine of $5 to $50, or imprisonment in jail for not more than two months. Instead, he was committed to custody for a maximum of six years."[33] Only proper procedure would protect Gault from this troubling discrepancy. *In re Gault* endorsed a public sphere in which expertise, fairness, efficiency, and individual acceptance of outcome were mutually entailing so long as procedure is followed. The result is a form of expert judgment that recognizes itself as the rigorous other of the parens patriae regime that it replaced.

Finally, the opinion deployed a discourse of deference to articulate important adversarial and textual practices. It emphasized the various state legislatures' freedom to decide how to comply with its mandates. This strategy defined failures of due process while delegating to state legislatures and judges the responsibility to prescribe particular procedures. The laundry list of rights articulated here proceeded in an inevitable and mutually entailing progression that aligned procedure, efficiency, and liberty with suitable adversarial and textual practice. Adequate notice was required because "a youth's freedom and his parents' right to his custody are at stake."[34] A right to counsel marked the proceeding as adversarial, assuring that the child had "assistance . . . to cope with problems of law to make skilled inquiry into the facts, to insist upon regularity of the proceedings, and to ascertain whether he has a defense and to prepare and submit it. The child 'requires the guiding hand of counsel at every step in the proceedings against him.'"[35] Rules against forced confessions and self-incrimination advanced the adversarial symmetry of the process, founded on categorical equality between the state and the juvenile as an individual. This prevented the state "from overcoming the mind and will of the person under investigation and depriving him of the freedom to decide whether to assist the state in securing his conviction."[36] The child's transformation to liberal individual was advanced through reference to their cognitive ability. Appellate review and a record of the proceedings were valuable not to reform poor character, but to save time and prevent conflicts of interest.[37]

This approach was vulnerable to the same points of resistance that suggested themselves in *Barnette*: the child's varied capabilities meant that individual justice may prove elusive, and the opinion deflected the broader question about what happens when parents' desires (with parental rights to custody) were not aligned with their children. In displacing these issues, it is fair to consider whether and under what circumstances procedural uniformity could conceal material inequalities. The latter point served as the catalyst for the lone dissent in the case.

Rehabilitating Character Concerns: Justice Stewart's Dissent

Justice Stewart's dissent exploited the fiction that children and adults were equal in terms of their cognitive capabilities. Focusing on the aspects of individualized justice that the majority criticized, the dissent reversed the majority's appearance/reality critique of parens patriae. Faith in procedure could create the veneer of fairness—every box was checked—while legitimating systemically unjust results. Stewart's dissent argued from historical example, highlighting the injustice of flattening differences between children and adults. He worried about a dystopian public that fetishized a citizen's entitlement to procedure over care. Reviving a discourse seen in cases such as *Ex parte Crouse*, *Pendergrass*, and *Lander*, the dissent reserved a place for individualized determinations for the development of character.

Justice Stewart defined delinquency proceedings as a practice with little use for a blanket rule of criminal procedural protections. Where the majority saw a difference in name only, Stewart declared that these practices "are not criminal trials. They are not civil trials. They are simply not adversary proceedings." The argument used the language of incapacity. These proceedings addressed children who were "defective" and "dependent," in a context where the goal was "correction of a condition," not "conviction and punishment for a criminal act."[38] Inverting the argument of *Ex parte Crouse* that reformatories were not prisons, the dissent framed parens patriae as an effort to redeem the social contract's promises to children. The dissent described the purpose behind parens patriae: "dedicated men and women have devoted their professional lives to the enlightened task of bringing us out of the dark world of Charles Dickens in meeting our responsibilities to the child in our society."[39] Where the majority opinion saw categorically equal citizens injured by an overreaching and arbitrary state apparatus, Justice Powell saw a modest attempt to discharge a vital obligation to reform character. Because procedural rights were never intended as a remedy for character flaws, the dissent was skeptical that the judiciary had the proper tools to correct the social ill. Powell's dissent crafted its allure through the humility of restraint: he possessed "neither the specialized experience nor the expert knowledge to predict with any certainty where may lie the brightest hope for progress" in addressing the social problem. He understood that converting "a juvenile proceeding into a criminal prosecution" was not the answer.[40]

The dissent imagined a world in which expert judgment was ill-suited to assess and nurture character. This strategy repurposed Justice Frankfurter's discourse regarding the limitations of the judiciary. Justice Stewart warned of procedure's "inflexible restrictions," which risked retrograde treatment of juveniles because they lacked the ability to consent to decisions and be held culpable for their consequences. Stewart's anecdotal example mentions a trial from the early nineteenth century that had "all the trappings of a criminal trial": "So it was that a 12-year-old boy named James Guild was tried in New Jersey for killing Catharine Beakes. A jury found him guilty of murder, and he was sentenced to death by hanging. The sentence was executed. It was all very constitutional."[41] While this dissenting narrative retains the majority's interest in preserving youthful innocence, it exploits the majority's claims that procedure constitutes the core of citizenship because of its liberty-maximizing efficiency. The dissent's story valued individual differentiation. Citizens who lacked cognitive ability were entitled to care; individual differentiation may be less efficient in terms of maximizing liberty and administering justice, but it would make up for that deficit by reforming the child's character and life trajectory. According to the dissent, categorical equality obstructed the pursuit of liberal values: it threatened to legitimate gross injustice under the imprimatur of constitutionalism. Justice Stewart feared that the majority's floor would become a ceiling for the state's responsibility to the child. This would be no progress because it would place categorical equality above demonstrated individual need.

In re Gault was a high-water mark for the understanding of citizens as categorical equals, no matter their cognitive capabilities. Reversing over a century of policy practice, its faith in judicial procedure solidified a shift in expert judgment. Appealing to process, it synthesized the competing discourses of the proper judicial role in *Barnette*. With Justice Jackson, it emphasized a core of constitutional rights backed by tradition, and its insistence that procedure yields a more legitimate outcome consonant with policy goals appealed to Justice Jackson's ideal of persuasion among equals. It assailed mere subjective opinion and belief on similar grounds as Justice Frankfurter—what was done with good intentions would have negative unforeseen consequences on governance.

In re Gault posited a rule of categorical equality that nevertheless retained two key related discursive features of the child's place, with consequences for the relationship between cognition and the citizen that has been developed since then. First, *Gault*, like *Barnette*, continued to describe the child as a passive subject, incapable of the advanced capabilities to speak, understand, and participate. Cognitive performances, which were so important in conferring authority on judgments in prior cases, may have been made available in theory, but neither the *Barnette* nor the *In re Gault* plaintiffs did much acting on the terms of the judicial opinions. The Barnette children's thoughts were compelled by state law and repetitive oath, and the children were suspended for their silence. Gerald Gault was moved through the system impersonally, his rights violated by egregious and unfair state practices.

Second, the opinion expressed an interest in the child's development as a constitutional concern. Citing no precedent or record evidence, *In re Gault* appealed to Gerald's lost childhood. Indeed, this was the one element that bound the majority and dissent: even Justice Stewart agreed that poor defenseless children who were not fully culpable for crimes deserved protection. That investment sutured the inclusion of the child as an equal citizen with the demand that the constitutionally legitimate state justify its actions so that it may discharge its obligations under the social contract. These decisions were simply making good on promises that the Constitution made to all citizens—that they would develop free from arbitrary and damaging interference. This theme, which emerged most prominently in *Meyer* and *Pierce*, was developed further in *Barnette* and *Gault* to articulate key meanings for the rights of all citizens—the right to be free from compelled thought, and the right to procedural rigor and consistency.

Nevertheless, these expansive claims raised new concerns. If expert judgment was now recognized as the application of proper procedure, then the question of scale and administrative effect would take on more importance. Was there some limit to the burden one could place on a judge to get the decision factually correct? What kinds of pragmatic effects should be considered in predicting the outcome of a judge's decision? Concerning the citizen, both *Barnette* and *In re Gault* settled the question about whether states could act on passive citizens to deprive them of rights. But what about children who were more assertive and individualistic? And what would happen when those assertive children would challenge the norms of educational institutions tasked with cultivating habits of citizenship, beyond merely guaranteeing rights? These questions would be answered in the next landmark case that advanced the career of the child as a speaking citizen: *Tinker v. Des Moines Independent Community School District*, which addressed key questions of dissent in a time of war.

5

STRATEGIC PERFORMANCE

Tinker v. Des Moines Independent Community School District

In 1965 (one year after Gerald Gault was arrested), America was on the cusp of open cultural turmoil. The nation was living through the collective trauma of JFK's murder. Lyndon Johnson announced his vision of the Great Society in his State of the Union address. The civil rights movement was just gaining momentum and none of the other events for which the 1960s subsequently became famous—the women's movement, the assassinations of MLK and RFK, violence at the 1968 Democratic National Convention—had taken place. But shortly after Johnson's address, the escalation of the Vietnam War served as the canary in the coalmine. Although there were twenty thousand "military advisers" in Vietnam, there had been to that point no commitment of combat forces. But on March 8, 1965, thirty-five troops landed in South Vietnam. This decision met with some popular resistance, and educational institutions played a vital forum for dissent. Teach-ins at the University of Michigan and Berkeley attracted a national spectrum of activists, lecturers, and performers. Student dissatisfaction with the responsiveness of the American government and university administrations led some to introduce the topic of university takeover.

These events divided the American public. College students were joining with their professors and a host of cultural figures to protest the most important policy issue of the day. Unlike the flag salute at issue in *Gobitis* and *Barnette,* the character of their dissent was not an opt-out from a civic ritual. Nor were these students motivated by religious belief. Rather, they were arguing that a government policy was fundamentally unrepresentative of the democratic will. And they were applying pressure on institutions that went as far as threatening their dismantling if student demands continued to fall on deaf ears. By the winter of 1965, these protests had helped politicize America's involvement in the war in cities and towns across the country. John Tinker, his sister, Mary Tinker, and Christopher Eckhardt wanted to raise the issue in their schools in Des Moines, Iowa. John and Christopher were high school students, and Mary was in junior high. In December, they met (along with their parents and other adults) at Christopher's home. They were "determined to publicize their objections to the hostilities in Vietnam and their support for a truce by wearing black armbands during the holiday season."[1] The principals of the schools then enacted a policy forbidding the armbands.

Two days after the policy was adopted, Mary Tinker and Christopher Eckhardt showed up to school with their armbands on. John Tinker followed suit the next day. They were all sent home and were not allowed to return to school until after their planned time to wear the armbands had run. Their fathers filed suit on the children's behalf, seeking to enjoin the school officials from disciplining their children and asking for nominal damages.[2] The district court dismissed the complaint, arguing that the school's action was reasonable to preserve school discipline.[3] The plaintiffs appealed to the Eighth Circuit, which considered the case en banc.[4] After the Eighth Circuit split down the middle (leaving the district court decision intact), the *Tinker* plaintiffs appealed to the Supreme Court, which heard oral argument in 1968 and decided the case in 1969.

The Supreme Court ruled in favor of the students. In an opinion by Justice Fortas, it held that the students' activities were protected under the First Amendment.[5] Observing that the students' armbands were passive, the court noted that the speech the bands represented neither curtailed the rights of others nor disrupted classroom activities. The opinion remarked that neither students nor teachers "shed their constitutional rights to freedom of speech . . . at the schoolhouse gate."[6] Because there was no evidence that the school's rule was necessary to prevent substantial interference with school discipline, the speech was permitted. Justice Hugo Black dissented, disputing the source of student and teacher rights in school.[7] He distinguished the compelled speech in *Barnette* from the armbands in *Tinker*. Expressing a concern about school governance, Justice Black believed that schools could regulate the armbands because they were likely to distract students from the purpose of schooling—to learn.

Political Strategy and Civic Speech

The decision considered "the need for affirming the comprehensive authority of the States and of school officials, consistent with fundamental constitutional safeguards, to prescribe and control conduct in the schools."[8] *Tinker* holds great significance for the story of citizen and expert judgment for three reasons. First, it introduced capable performance as a requirement for the speaking child, relying on the display of strategic political thought calculation as a sign of judgment capabilities. Second, it opposed fear-driven decisions as anathema to a liberal public but observed that documentary evidence could render perceived threats more credible. Third, as a matter of expert judgment, the opinion invented from within the constraints of the genre. Deriving its authority from the subtle homology it created between the facts of the case and its doctrinal distinctions, it neither explicitly meditated on judgment nor framed its decision as the discharge of a prior (implicitly contractual) obligation. This strategy indexed the increasing complexity of the liberal project of inclusion and the demands placed on experts to confine their authority in space and time. Ideologically, this provided jurisprudential resources for the First Amendment's extension, but it also contained its own limiting principle and laid the groundwork for conservative opposition.

Reading Signs: *Tinker's* Child as Political Strategist

Tinker read signs of the child's performance capabilities in order to tame fears of speech that threatens the established order. In so doing, it created a set of evaluative markers for acceptable citizen speech. The opinion used discursive conventions to frame the speaking child as a strategic political actor, declaring relevant facts to cast the child as a purposeful, calculating agent. Its precedential distinctions supported the decision, elevating the specific speech act to a preferred constitutional status. Finally, it aligned the character of the speech act with an ideal practice of public reason for citizens, marked by a distinctive relationship between documentation, fear, and reason.

The opinion introduced a discourse about capable performance, relating that performance to a citizen's judgment to speak. It accomplished this rhetorically, crafting a narrative about the plaintiffs as savvy actors capable of calculating speech acts to achieve strategic ends. The plaintiffs "held a meeting" as a group of "adults and students."[9] "The group determined to publicize their objections" to the war and to support a truce.[10] The black armbands were coupled with a fast on December 16 and on New Year's Eve. They had "previously engaged in similar activities, and they decided to participate in the program."[11] This was a display of advanced cognition, not an unreflective emotional reaction. The characterization of the plaintiffs aligned with similar descriptions of sound judgment in *Pendergrass* and *Lander* (proportional punishment without bad intentions), as well as *Meyer* (the Nebraska legislature exaggerated the threat out of fear). The students made plans. They acted in concert with adults. They coordinated their actions for maximum effect. They imagined what their expression meant to a larger public. Even more, these displays of cognitive ability served as interpretive guideposts for the speech act, signaling its intended reception: to wear bands on their arms to protest the Vietnam War.

This factual narrative ran parallel to the opinion's doctrinal distinctions. The law, like the capable citizen, relied on fine distinctions as a condition for legitimate participation in the public sphere. Speakers were not to be held accountable for every unforeseeable effect of their speech; the ability to distinguish between speech act and its effect mattered greatly. Speech was constitutionally protected because of its public relevance as a speech act, distinct from "actually or potentially disruptive conduct by those participating in it."[12] Dissociation played a large role in establishing these capabilities. The opinion divided symbolic acts into "pure speech" and speech that tends to incite violence: "the wearing of armbands in the circumstances of this case was entirely divorced from actual or potentially disruptive conduct by those participating in it. It was closely akin to 'pure speech' . . . entitled to comprehensive protection under the First Amendment."[13] This maneuver implicitly appealed to a speaking citizen who could distinguish speech act functions based on character and audience reception. The distinction allayed fears of a public run wild: judgment included the ability to infer from the speech act a particular nonthreatening individual character.

The citizen's abilities in this area are contingent on performance, as is the status of children as constitutional rights bearers. The opinion described requirements for citizens to calibrate the likely consequences of their speech. Political speech communicates a viewpoint. But it must also be passive, and not targeted to incite or disrupt: "The problem posed . . . . does not concern aggressive, disruptive action or even group demonstrations. Our problem involves direct, primary First Amendment rights."[14] This distinction named a zone of valued expression and the conditions for its regulation. Mere personal expression and style would not suffice, as the court observed that the issue "does not relate to regulation of the length of skirts or the type of clothing, to hair style, or deportment."[15] For a speech to have a political purpose, it had to conform to prevailing understandings of topics of public concern, and it must have been designed to avoid violent reaction.

Passive expression was evidence that such speech was calibrated for political discourse. The armbands were "silent" and there was "no evidence whatever of petitioners' interference . . . with the schools' work or of collision with the rights of other students to be secure and to be let alone."[16] This passage imagined an ideal public space, and the ideal character of citizens occupying that space. Empirical reality served as the basis for this imagined public: "Only a few of the . . . students in the school system wore the black armbands. Only five students were suspended. . . . There is no indication that the work of the schools or any class was disrupted. Outside the classrooms, a few students made hostile remarks . . . but there were no threats or acts of violence on school premises."[17] The absence of any disruption demonstrated that the speech was presumptively protected. The law protected this right because of the lack of tangible violence or social disorder left in its wake.

Documenting Fear: The Textual Practices of Judgment

Where *Barnette* elevated persuasion as the ideal liberal communicative form, *Tinker* posited a public of individuals with the proper attitude in receiving discourse. The administration's "undifferentiated fear" was dismissed. Mere controversy could not make such fear reasonable. The opinion used anaphora to appeal to a public of risk, and worried about a slippery slope of state power. Because the administrators could not articulate a principle for stopping, *any* "departure from absolute regimentation" could cause a disruption, *any* "variation from the majority's opinion" could be controversial, and *any* "spoken word may start an argument."[18] The school district's reaction was an example of poor judgment because it didn't differentiate between acceptable and unacceptable risks. Attitudes tolerant of risk were necessary in a liberal democracy: a "kind of openness . . . that is the basis of our national strength and of the independence and vigor of Americans who . . . live in this relatively permissive, often disputatious, society."[19] The opinion appealed to a pragmatic concern for civic unity to justify its ruling. Just as a cluster of signs demonstrated the plaintiffs' strategic capabilities, so the school district's reaction betrayed signs of illiberality. Rejecting speech merely because it departed from regimented habit and from the views of others who share the same public space proved inapposite for the contemporary liberal public sphere.

Ironically, the opinion's focus on the evidentiary record (or lack thereof) suggested that the more effective a speech or protest was, the less permissible it would have been, since "disruption" was also a sign that speech has elicited a strong reaction. Perhaps the *Tinker* plaintiffs didn't attract enough attention. To understand *Tinker* solely as a symbol of citizenship inclusion would be to misunderstand its limitations. Children's citizenship depended on their abilities to correctly calibrate the effects of their speech. The opinion did not just declare the child to be a citizen: it also disciplined that citizen with reference to norms of the larger community grounded in a presumption for stability and order.

Finally, the opinion's inclusive gesture was grounded in a social contract model of governance. It appealed to risk regimes borne by individuals and administrators, and which could be addressed through contract. The opinion's generalized world of risk channeled state authority by identifying risk management techniques. The state must document its concerns. The objection to the administrators' response was its deviation from the assumption that liberal public life is structured like a contract. The opinion's rhetoric of inevitability retained this symmetrical structure. Inviting comparisons between the students' planning and the school district's reaction, it placed the individual and the state on equal footing.

This symmetry left the door open for the state to write the terms of that social contract. The evidentiary record justifying the school's response appeared to violate liberal neutrality principles: because the school only prohibited armbands and did not prohibit "the wearing of all symbols of political or controversial significance," the court viewed the school's actions with a skeptical eye.[20] One perspective might view *Tinker* as a blueprint for restricting speech through proper documentation practices. Future school administrators in future cases could create an evidentiary record of the kinds of speech that would be acceptable, no matter the strategic planning, supposed purity, or topical content of speech. Justice Fortas's opinion in *Tinker*, long thought to be a crucial extension of the liberal rights revolution, also provided a path for the state to reassert its power. Justice Black's dissent seized this opening, seeking to secure a liberal state under siege by protesting speakers.

Justice Black's Dissent: Institutional Order, Bureaucratic Interests, and Adversarial Relationships

Justice Black described the majority opinion as an antidemocratic break from traditional respect for local authority. The ruling "ushers in . . . an entirely new era" transferring power "to control pupils" from elected officials "to the Supreme Court."[21] This traditional argument crafted a liberal counternarrative in two significant respects. First, concerning citizen-judgment, it argued that the varied capabilities of children supported a pedagogy of hierarchy and tradition. Second, concerning expert judgment, it revived the democratic social function of judicial deference to school boards.[22] These latter stood in for liberal democracy itself, a synecdoche that Justice Black leveraged to articulate a constitutionally significant interest in protecting state bureaucracy.

First, Justice Black's dissent followed the now-long-standing discourse of differential capabilities to justify hierarchical order. Shifting the relevant legal question away from the majority's emphasis on the plaintiffs' strategic plans, Justice Black compared the speech at issue with the vast majority of students who followed the rules. Viewed this way, the plaintiffs' armbands were an antimajoritarian outlier. They were "ordered to refrain from wearing the armbands" by "elected school officials and the teachers vested with state authority," and "only seven out of the school system's 18,000 pupils deliberately refused to obey the order."[23] The students' youth suggested that they were mere mouthpieces of their parents: "One defying pupil was . . . in the second grade; another . . . was 11. . . . Their father, a Methodist minister without a church, is paid a salary by the American Friends Service Committee. Another student . . . was . . . an 11th grade pupil. . . . His mother is an official in the Women's International League for Peace and Freedom."[24] Where the majority saw cognition and calculation, Justice Black saw dependence and a lack of reflective judgment. The children were mere agents of their parents' minority beliefs, who themselves were not reflective of community norms (the "minister without a church"). The speakers were pupils, not individuals. For Justice Black, school control was justified because the child lacked the ability to act strategically. The unique nature of the child-subject and the institutional space of the school justified a "nondistraction" rule for student speech. Where the majority highlighted the school district's unqualified fear, Black noted the absurdity of unqualified rights. No person, he argued, "has a right to give speeches or engage in demonstrations where he pleases and when he pleases."[25] The dissent wished to assert institutional control to shape those children incapable of self-directed and disciplined action.[26]

"Distraction" rather than "substantial disruption" would have been far easier to satisfy with record evidence. The armbands "caused comments" and "warnings by other students," and one teacher said that a math lesson was "wrecked" because of these reactions: "The armbands did exactly what the elected school officials and principals foresaw they would, that is, took the students' minds off their classwork and diverted them to thoughts about the highly emotional subject of the Vietnam war."[27] Rather than lament the failure of administrators to document their fear, Justice Black lauded their predictive abilities.

The dissent's hierarchical model contained implicit criteria for citizenship: the state was justified to limit constitutional rights in order to develop judgment. Downplaying capacities for strategic public address, Black emphasized self-discipline for the pursuit of knowledge about a particular topic as a crucial entry barrier into the public sphere. Schools existed because the child has "not yet reached the point of experience and wisdom which enabled them to teach all of their elders. . . . Taxpayers send children to school on the premise that, at their age, they need to learn, not teach."[28] This incapacity legitimated their exclusion from public life, because of the child's diminished cognitive ability to prevent emotional material from diverting their focus: "Students . . . cannot concentrate on other issues when black armbands are being ostentatiously displayed in their presence to call attention to the wounded and dead of the war, some of the wounded and the dead being their friends and neighbors."[29] Restrictions on public participation were justified as a paternalistic principle to block trauma. Using a slippery slope to protect state institutions, Justice Black worried about a world in which children could vote and hold elected office. If children "can defy and flout orders," then "the next logical step . . . would be to hold unconstitutional laws that bar pupils under 21 or 18 from voting, or from being elected members of the boards of education."[30] This argument asserted that public order depended on the propriety of speech: that it be performed in the right place and at the right time.

Justice Black's opinion exemplified this "right place, right time" mode of judgment in his dissent, which displayed a command of topical variety integrated with technical acumen. He identified the majority's flaw as a misreading of legal precedent, arguing that the majority mistakenly relied on a long-discredited "reasonableness" test to evaluate the school board's action.[31] Black observed that recent precedent had "totally repudiated . . . the doctrine that judges have the power to hold laws unconstitutional upon the belief of judges that they 'shock the conscience,' or that they are 'unreasonable,' 'arbitrary,' 'irrational,' 'contrary to fundamental 'decency,'' or some other such flexible term without precise boundaries."[32] Following the discourse of procedural virtue in *In re Gault*, the dissent activated concerns about clarity and predictability in law.

Here, however, that discourse counseled in favor of judicial restraint. Expert deference to local governing institutions was necessary for the latter's ongoing stability. Justice Black argued that it was necessary to protect "domestic peace" from "uncontrollable liberty."[33] Empowered but incapable speakers threatened institutions: "Some of the country's greatest problems are crimes committed by the youth, too many of school age."[34] Schools imparted discipline, and this was "an integral and important part of training our children to be good citizens—to be better citizens."[35] These incapable citizens' unrestrained free speech could unravel the social fabric, because the child would not exercise the prudence necessary for the maintenance of other rights. Echoing the traditional argument that children should be subjected to authority in order to protect economic rights, Justice Black imagined child-actors who would produce social malaise, assaulting rights of locomotion ("to force students not to cross their picket lines"), property ownership ("break-ins," "property seizures," and "destruction"), and bodily integrity ("violently attack[ing] earnest but frightened students").[36] When citizens demonstrated a general inability to predict the reception of their speech, they were blind to the possible effects of their actions. These citizens arrogated to themselves which rules to follow and which to discard, placing their individual impulsive desires ahead of those with higher status and authority.

Imprudent exercise of free speech would team with civil litigation to invert the hierarchy that is the hallmark of American governance. Conjuring a slide into liberal disorder, Justice Black described a state interest in protecting bureaucracy against individuals using the state's procedures against itself to sue administrators. Black feared students would be "turned loose with lawsuits for damages and injunctions against their teachers." This sea change in constitutional principle meant that "young, immature students will . . . believe it is their right to control the schools rather than the right of the States."[37] The argument articulated both a principle of governance and sound judgment as the ability to predict system-wide effects of decisions. The majority opinion failed to understand the human psychology of the legal system, including its effects on administrators and governance. These administrators were the true representatives of the public interest, both because their authority has been democratically validated and because they possessed the capabilities of self-discipline and reflection.

Persuasive Citizens: Strategic Children and the Procedural Republic

Barnette, *Gault*, and *Tinker* are more than cases that extended individual rights. They also constituted a different model for addressing the problem of the child's status along the lines of categorical equality. *Barnette* declared that its child-plaintiffs were free-thinking individuals who could not be compelled to utter a pledge, even if the various states believed that the pledge contributed to civic unity. *In re Gault* elevated the child to equal status as an adversary against the state in criminal proceedings, dismissing the benevolent care approach of parens patriae. And *Tinker* expressly stated what *Barnette* had implied: children had constitutional rights just as adults, and state institutions could not invalidate them based on mere fears of political disorder. This model contrasts with the approach in the cases studied in the previous chapter, which advanced claims that the state had authority over the child—and, at times, the rights of their adult parents—to instill virtues in them.

In so doing, these cases reshaped the constitutional narrative of both citizenship and expert judgment. Each opinion introduced new motives and behavioral norms for the citizen. Speech, critique, and textual performance became important as performative and cognitive capabilities, replacing the earlier regime that primarily valued adherence to virtues of property and industry.

Barnette sketched a vision of a public citizen that valued persuasive communication (and, by implication, dissent and critique). Its model citizens shunned mere personal conviction as the ground for communal attachments, because it was not sufficient to demonstrate willed and thoughtful choice. *In re Gault* outlined procedure as the citizen's constitutional entitlement, and a distrust of state benevolence as a wise disposition. It required rules of transparency, tests of factual assertions, and the rigor of textual review as signs that the state's decisions to revoke liberty were legitimate. And *Tinker* used the child's assertion of the right to dissent to articulate a core of important political speech, as well as to mark the strategic capabilities that citizens required.

Novelization underwrote this transition, because the opinions altered the narrative by grounding it in familiar themes, characters, and rhetorical techniques. The temporality of good judgment justified these outcomes, a constant theme amid the differing contexts of each case. *Barnette* argued from example to demonstrate the long view of regimes whose compelled civic attachments led to their own demise. *In re Gault* noted the inability of judges to assess the effects of parens patriae on a long line of children. Both practices (parens patriae and compelled speech) were associated with ancien régimes or bygone eras. Like *Meyer*, these cases were grounded partially in the supposed differences between modern American liberalism and its outmoded, violent, barbaric predecessors.

These modes of discursive resistance and appropriation allowed new characters to embody particular traits. The fearful state actor first appeared as an abstract worry in *Pendergrass* and *Lander* in the form of the teacher who punished a child out of anger. Later, that worry structured the opposition between the calm, passive speakers and the fearful and hasty administrators of *Tinker*. *In re Gault* inflected the investment in the child as citizen with new values, converting the state's mission to instill respect for values into an obligation to maintain for the child the possibilities of a future open to individual choice. Dissents, not majority opinions, referred to economic values and respect for property, worrying about political disorder tied to student protests (*Tinker*) and overturning the authority of states and local school boards (*Barnette*).

The question of citizenship capabilities also divided these opinions. The majorities passed over alleged incapabilities, because the child was a subset of categorically equal people. Dissenting opinions exploited this omission, maintaining a discourse of differentiation for judgment and consent. Justice Frankfurter's *Barnette* dissent began the discourse with a notion of consent as committed choice, and the child's inability to freely give it. Justice Stewart noted the potential injustice of ignoring differentiation in juvenile crime settings in *In re Gault*, reviving the story of the twelve-year old sentenced to death as an example of the grave problems of declaring juveniles to be equal (and, by implication, morally responsible) adults. Finally, Justice Black advanced these concerns in his *Tinker* dissent: arguing that children lacked the requisite cognitive ability to judge, he appealed to schools to train future citizens with the capacity to do so, and raised the threat that untrained citizens would pose to democratic order. Where Justice Frankfurter worried about the pragmatic effects of invalidating state legislation, Justice Black adapted that pragmatic concern to the administrators and officials tasked with governing the school.

These cases also reshaped ideas about the role of the expert judge. The overt clash of the judge's role was most pronounced in *Barnette*, where Justice Jackson shifted the judge's task from interpreting original grants of authority to protecting core individual rights threatened by democratic process failures. This new vision directed attention to the content of that core. As it did so, it freed judges up to argue at a more general level of analysis for the relationship between the core rights of the individual and the maintenance of liberal civil society. In response, Justice Frankfurter made an appeal to the expert judge restrained by tradition, precedent, and an agreed-upon role in a far larger system of liberal democracy. On this view, not only was this the role that had shaped the vast majority of Supreme Court decisions to date, it was also the most likely way to maintain a liberal democracy that cohered around common sentiment.

Justice Frankfurter's objection was a minority view because contextual circumstances belied his very argument. It was difficult to assert that judges needed to defer to legislative decisions for the sake of civil society when confronted with legislative acts that gave impetus to social unrest. Because Justice Jackson's view seemed more responsive to the changing reality of American constitutional democracy, Justice Frankfurter's role-based vision of expertise receded into the background. It was domesticated, not vanquished: the *Gault* and *Tinker* dissents criticized the majorities' interpretive practices but focused primarily on the speculative pragmatic effects of the majorities in each case. Justice Stewart thought the *In re Gault* majority was unwise because of the possibility that it would accomplish procedural justice at the cost of grave substantive injustices. And Justice Black's *Tinker* dissent, for all of its observations about doctrinal misapplication, appealed primarily to effects that the judging, planning, and speaking child would have on institutions—the threat of lawsuits that would intimidate administrators and block them from doing what is best for civil society.

As the judicial role changed, pragmatic interest balancing in terms of the effects on individuals held sway, displacing the contractual grounding of earlier cases in favor of the expansion of categorical equality. Images of contract persisted in these discourses: ideas about consent and choice implicitly endorsed a contractual model of legitimacy. But these cases of inclusion were less concerned and self-reflective about their own potential reach. *Meyer* and *Pierce* legitimated their judicial authority with counterfactuals that limited the reach of the decisions, assuring state legislatures that their constitutional interventions would be limited. Although majority opinions repeated these gestures in miniature—*In re Gault*'s observation that states could figure out how to implement procedural rights, and *Tinker*'s self-limiting to exclude matters of student dress and comportment, for example—these nods to restraint did not prevent a counterdiscourse that the decisions were grounded in neither precedent nor tradition, and that they had abandoned the proper role of the judge by exceeding the limits of their expertise.

These three cases set parameters for the constitutional commitment to the individual citizen. But the demand that the justices themselves perform their expertise (an element endemic to the form of the judicial opinion) produced its own set of pressures—questions deferred or unanswered, choices not made, problems ignored. As the next chapter will show, the vocabulary of order, structure, rules, discipline, and bureaucracy will find its way into a new majority as the speaking child is reined in. No longer able to claim lesser-developed status as a ward, the full consequences of placing performance burdens on citizens would emerge as the progressivism of the 1960s yielded local resistance, cultural conflict, and a Nixon presidency. The Warren Court of the 1960s gave way to the Burger and Rehnquist Courts of the 1970s and 1980s, with an implicit mandate to stem the tide of constitutional progressivism with the jurisprudential tools at hand. The ensuing retrenchment would appeal to the relationship between pedagogy, experience, educational practices, and the production of liberal citizens. No inexorable march, the status of the citizen is better thought of as the movement of a pendulum. And in the 1970s it began to swing back with a revival of organic institutions and its emphatic display of incapable children needing protection from a larger public and from themselves.

Part III

THE CHILD AS REFORM OBJECT

Richard Nixon defeated Hubert Humphrey in the 1968 presidential election. That victory provided an opportunity to shape the Supreme Court. Assuming the presidency at a time of great social upheaval and change, Nixon had campaigned on the restoration of "law and order," including the need to appoint "strict constructionist" judges. These promises resisted some of the Warren Court's changes to the American constitutional order. As detailed in part 2, the court had taken on a larger role in social life and political affairs. It had arbitrated acceptable ways to produce civic bonds in a time of war, articulate constitutional procedural guarantees for deprivations of liberty, and strike a balance between protest and governing order. Along the way, the court had provoked anxious resistance to its disruptions of traditional governing practices. Local control of schools was an issue, most glaringly as a pretext for racial exclusion in *Brown v. Board of Education* but also at the level of teacher and administrator authority. Casting the role of the judge as the protection of the individual's constitutional rights triggered a heightened level of scrutiny for a host of state and local practices. Opposition to this scrutiny gained momentum throughout the 1960s. An "Impeach Warren" campaign gathered steam among conservative groups. Nevertheless, the Supreme Court carried on, having issued landmark rulings that shaped the constitutional landscape in terms of First and Fourth Amendment rights, as well as a constitutional right to privacy. This was the landscape that Richard Nixon inherited.

Over the span of his presidency, Nixon appointed four Supreme Court justices. The confirmation process for these justices was contentious. Chief Justice Earl Warren had announced his intention to retire in June 1968. The Senate rejected then-President Lyndon Johnson's nomination of Justice Fortas (the author of the *Tinker* and *In re Gault* majority opinions), formally citing corruption concerns about his personal financial dealings. Informally, the Senate also was united in its opposition to the direction of constitutional jurisprudence. Nixon nominated appellate judge Warren Burger to fill the role of chief justice; the Senate confirmed Burger in June 1969. In the meantime, Justice Fortas resigned in the wake of a second scandal surrounding another of his private financial contracts. This development opened up another seat, which was eventually filled in 1970 by appellate judge Harry Blackmun. The subsequent health-related retirements of Justice Black (who died days after his retirement) and Justice Harlan (who died a few months after his retirement) led to the elevation of Lewis Powell and William Rehnquist to the Court in 1971. In a matter of two years, Nixon had appointed four justices.

Although the Supreme Court had continued at the turn of the decade to make progressive decisions that emboldened conservative opposition—most notably *Roe v. Wade*—an emerging conservative majority had begun to put the brakes on the expansion of liberal individualism in the early 1970s. Led by Chief Justice Warren Burger, this cadre of justices was faced with a dilemma: would it undo what it likely believed to be Warren Court excesses through "strict construction" of the Constitution or would political and jurisprudential headwinds counsel in favor of maintaining the precedents of the last thirty-odd years, which had become settled law and which also likely had formed part of the baseline of many citizens' expectations?[1]

This section of the book examines three Burger Court cases about the status and judgment capabilities of the child. The cases selected—*Ingraham v. Wright, Parham v. J. R.*, and *Bethel School District v. Fraser*—typify the Burger Court's approach to the child's status.[2] Two of these cases addressed the child's right to due process and one addressed the right of the child to speak. They were socially significant because they cut to the heart of civic habits, testing the degree of independence the child had as an individual in cases where the child was clearly incapable or had transgressed social codes and mores. This chapter argues that the cases treated the child as a reform object in an attempt to revive tradition. This revival altered the landscape for citizens through the child's legal identity, but it did not explicitly overturn the precedents that had defined children as categorical equals. The strategy focused on enduring practices of local government that the categorical equality strategy had not expressly disrupted. It connected local practices to a minimal judicial role: the traditions were necessary because they were democratic, so the judiciary need not be involved. These traditions started with specific local practices that had unquestioned democratic support, but they later broadened to include appeals to traditional values (such as "family" and "civility") whose representativeness was questionable. Sound judgment was recognized as the maintenance of tradition, and judicial expertise was authorized through a combination of textual interpretation and assertion of enduring constitutional values. Perhaps as a result, the strategy left itself open to a critique that it lacked judicial rigor and was therefore more of a nonjudicial expression of preference than an exacting review by an independent judiciary. As the strategy claimed to be necessary to respect democratic community, it also produced some antidemocratic consequences.

6

TRADITION AGAINST THE INDIVIDUAL

Ingraham v. Wright

JAMES INGRAHAM AND ROOSEVELT ANDREWS WERE IN THE EIGHTH ninth grades, respectively, at Charles R. Drew Junior High School in Dade County, Florida. The county's schools employed corporal punishment as a disciplinary measure. This practice was supported by legislation that "in effect authorized limited corporal punishment by negative inference, proscribing punishment which was 'degrading or unduly severe' or which was inflicted without prior consultation with the principal or the teacher in charge of the school."[1] The Dade County School Board issued a regulation that clarified the practice in its schools. It specified punishment by instrument (a flat paddle of specific dimensions), place (buttocks), the number of blows (typically no more than five), and result (could not produce apparent physical injury).

It would appear that these regulations were not followed when Ingraham and Andrews were disciplined at Drew, which evidence suggested had a "particularly harsh" regime.[2] On one occasion, Ingraham was held over a table and struck over twenty times for the infraction of being "slow to respond to his teacher's instructions."[3] He suffered a hematoma, which required medical attention and caused him to miss school.[4] Andrews was apparently paddled many times for a series of minor infractions. One incident involved being paddled on his arm severely, which caused him to have only partial use of his arm for a week.[5]

The students filed a lawsuit as individuals challenging their specific punishments, and as a part of a class of students challenging the scheme of corporal punishment. They made two constitutional claims. First, they alleged that the corporal punishment violated the Eighth Amendment's prohibition on cruel and unusual punishment. Second, they alleged that the punishments constituted a deprivation of their liberty without due process, and they sought additional procedures guaranteeing students' adversarial rights to protect themselves against unjust punishment. The case went to trial in federal district court. The court dismissed the entire case after hearing the plaintiffs' evidence, deciding that even if all that they had introduced had been proved true, they had not stated a cause of action. The plaintiffs appealed this ruling, and the court of appeals reversed it. Specifically, it found that the individual punishments alleged were so severe that they violated the Eighth Amendment, and that the scheme violated the Due Process Clause because it did not provide adequate procedures. The case was heard again en banc (in front of the entire court of appeals), and the en banc panel rejected both the Eighth Amendment and due process claims.[6] The Supreme Court then considered the appeal.

The court ruled five to four in favor of the defendants. Justice Lewis Powell wrote the majority opinion and there were two dissents—one by Justice White and one by Justice Stevens. Justice Powell rejected the Eighth Amendment claim because its original application was in a criminal context. He argued that to apply the Eighth Amendment to corporal punishment was unnecessary because there were many safeguards in place to curb abuse, including the public nature of schooling and the presence of civil and criminal remedies for those who would perpetrate abuse. He also rejected the plaintiffs' due process claim because there were significant safeguards in place and imposing additions would be costly (perhaps even causing districts to end corporal punishment as a practice). Justice White's dissent disagreed with both of the majority's conclusions. Concerning the Eighth Amendment, he reasoned that punishments deemed too severe for crimes were certainly too severe in class, and that the Eighth Amendment should extend beyond its application to criminals because public safeguards were insufficient. Concerning the due process claim, he argued that students were owed prior procedures because the postpunishment procedures that Florida provided were too late (the pain was already inflicted) and not broad enough (they protected good faith mistakes). Justice Stevens joined Justice White's dissent, but he wrote separately to remark that postpunishment hearings may be permissible in cases where one is deprived of property instead of liberty.[7]

Disciplining Citizens through Tradition: Justice Powell's Majority Opinion

Justice Powell's opinion identified two legal issues: the first was whether "paddling of students as a means to maintaining school discipline" violated the Eighth Amendment and the second was whether the Due Process Clause entitled students who were to be paddled to "prior notice and an opportunity to be heard."[8] In posing the issues this way, the opinion marked a notable transition for constitutional controversies about the child. This conservative majority argued that procedural conceptions of citizenship disrupted traditional governing practices.[9] For Justice Powell, there was no question of the child's individual capabilities—these children were being disciplined for transgressing rules. The opinion appealed to the discourse of pragmatic tradition, much like Justice Frankfurter's opinions in the flag salute cases that worried about the effect on legislation, and like Justice Black's anxiety in *Tinker* that students would rule schools by the threat of litigation. In *Ingraham*, Justice Powell's opinion posited that due process protections would be unenforceable, unnecessary, and destabilizing for local governments. The opinion staked out a role for the judge as guardian of long-standing traditions, relating that role to a claim that there was a broad societal consensus in support of corporal punishment of the child.

First, Justice Powell's opinion employed a discourse of tradition as the proper guide to expert interpretive practice. This appeal, like Justice Frankfurter's opinions examined previously, justified ruling against the children as an act of neutrality, rather than personal motivation. Tradition served as a legitimate source of authority because it shaped previous court decisions that relied on "common law concepts," "attitudes which our society has . . . taken," the prevalent "law of the land," and "ideas of fair procedure."[10] The opinion interpreted a series of Eighth Amendment due process cases to demonstrate that prevailing traditional practices should influence constitutional interpretation. Strategically, this approach deflected attention away from the plaintiffs' injuries, the state's regulations, and the administrators' apparent inability to follow even those regulations. The opinion's mode of abstraction—to describe practices of corporal punishment as an agreed-upon policy shared across otherwise divergent local polities—recast those troubling facts of the case as outliers in a longer, continuous, civil timeline. Corporal punishment's pedigree was impressive. Its use "date[d] back to the colonial period," and it "survived" the transition from private optional education to compulsory public education.[11] Foreshadowing the opinion's argument about the Eighth Amendment, it noted that corporal punishment in schools persisted even after its "general abandonment" as punishment for convicted criminals.[12]

The discourse of tradition implied that sound judgment displayed a longer time horizon, and this time horizon justified limiting a citizen's rights. Justice Powell's explanation of punishment as tradition belittled the severity of the disagreement over its use. In spite of "sharply divided" opinions, the court could see "no trend toward its elimination."[13] Blackstone, the preeminent authority on the common law, saw the practice of a teacher's "moderate correction" permissible, and if force were excessive, most states could hold teachers civilly or criminally liable.[14] Where originally parents delegated authority to punish to teachers, contemporary wisdom held that the state had independent authority to punish the child. The authority's reasonable exercise was secured by looking at a variety of factors reminiscent of the "reasonableness" factors seen earlier in *Lander v. Seaver*—severity of punishment, infraction, and the age of the child. Of the twenty-three states that had laws related to the practice, twenty-one of them allowed its moderate use and two states had banned corporal punishment in schools.[15] This evidence advanced the discourse of tradition by crafting a single, coherent narrative. Corporal punishment expressed a commitment from trusted authorities, state legislation, and implementing regulations.

This focus on tradition deflected attention from other potentially persuasive starting points for making a judgment—both the text of the constitutional amendments and the specific plaintiffs. Conceiving the general practice abstractly aligned conservative expert judgment with the maintenance of an unbroken line of democratic government. This position legitimated practices that potentially violated citizens' rights because of their pedigree. The case of the child illustrates the ways that pedigree and tradition can sanction cruelty. The majority opinion described ruptures to the practice—the pre/post Founding shift, the shift in authority from parents to state, and the sharp public and professional disagreement—as temporary discord against a backdrop of the practice's moderate (and agreed-on) use. This frame permitted the opinion to claim authority without the court scrutinizing the practice. The strategy did double duty: not only did it permit the court to avoid addressing individual injustice but it did so by reaffirming a traditional conservative vision of expert judgment. The contrast with *In re Gault* is especially striking. In *Gault*, the court declared the child a categorical equal, and that decision was opposed because it might result in individual injustice. In *Ingraham*, the child's claims were rejected in categorical terms—no civil applications of the Eighth Amendment, because it was categorically limited to criminals—and the enabling discourse of tradition permitted the court to sidestep individual injustices.

The appeal to tradition failed to consider the issue of developing judgment in individuals as a citizenship capability. That discourse, which was prominent in *Barnette* and *Tinker*, prioritized the free speaking individual not merely as an end unto itself but also as a mode of political participation for citizens. Justice Jackson's *Barnette* opinion betrayed concerned about the psychological effects of compulsion (without explicitly referring to a psychological discourse). The opinion in *Barnette* connected the threat of punishment with effects on citizen capabilities; Justice Fortas's opinion in *Tinker* argued that "personal intercommunication among the students . . . is . . . an important part of the educational process."[16] Although neither opinion considered psychological evidence, Justice Fortas did consider social science evidence in *Gault* to argue that parens patriae did not accomplish its rehabilitative ends. The gap in these discourses—the failure to assess the psychological effects of "correction" on the development of capabilities—permitted Justice Powell's failure to address the relationship between correcting the child through corporal punishment and the goal of developing citizens with particular cognitive abilities to judge and speak.[17]

Ingraham activated an older judicial discourse that organic institutions, not the courts, were responsible for curbing abuses of a policy. This discourse, which appeared in *Pendergrass* and *Lander*, countered the argument from *Gault* that to punish a child was arbitrary and unfair. *Gault* had used an a fortiori analogy, comparing Gault's confinement against an adult's fine (for the same offense). Where *Gault* held that the child deserved more leniency than the adult, Justice Powell made a doctrinal argument that the Eighth Amendment only applied in criminal proceedings, where there is an adjudication of guilt: "The prisoner and the school child stand in wholly different circumstances, separated by the harsh facts of criminal conviction and incarceration."[18] The distinction also echoes the distinction drawn in *Ex parte Crouse*, that because the House of Refuge was a school, not a prison, the state could exercise power over the child. Activating these discourses, the opinion argued that organic institutions would curb possible abuses. The "openness of the public school and its supervision by the community" would ensure that "common law constraints [would] effectively remedy and deter excesses such as those alleged in this case."[19]

These strategies limited the scope of the judicial expert. The role of the judge, according to Justice Powell, was not to intrude in every instance of potential injustice. Enforcing the Constitution was a more limited endeavor in every way—the Eighth Amendment's restrictive application was a "longstanding limitation" to which the court conformed; each of the court's previous decisions considering the meaning of "cruel and unusual" had reviewed *criminal* punishments, not civil actions; and the local community could be safely relied upon to enforce the "legal constraints of the common law."[20] According to this approach, prudential judgment required restraint and avoidance, and that paradigm valued extrajudicial indicators of conflict resolution—governing history, legislative action, and a description of the reality of education institutions.

Finally, the opinion rejected the due process claim. Here, its strategy showed the ideological effects of expert judgment as restraint. Its description of corporal punishment and its emphasis on the extraconstitutional constraints on the practice—common law, teacher moderation, state legislation, civil and criminal penalties—prefigured the opinion's application of the relevant constitutional test (what "process" is "due" the child). The opinion implicitly assumed that the child needed authority figures to instill obedience as a virtue through physical correction. The child was not, under this construction, a citizen merely performing badly. The opinion relied on the same discourse of tradition in describing a web of practices that constituted "due process" for corporal punishment regimes. The child's liberty interest was "subject to historical limitations," and this included the teachers' privilege to administer "moderate correction."[21] It then used Florida's actions (again, not the specific teacher's punishment) as evidence that the child's liberty interest was sufficiently already protected. The state "recognize[d] . . . and strengthened by statute" the child's right to be free from excessive punishment and provided for hearings after punishment to determine whether it was excessive.[22]

In contrast to the strategy of *In re Gault*, Justice Powell's *Ingraham* analysis minimized the child's specific case to illustrate the virtues of the larger democratic process. It portrayed miscarriages of justice as "aberration[s]" and attributed their relative infrequency to the belief that teachers typically administered punishment for conduct they directly observed.[23] The strategy pivoted from the extreme example to its routine (acceptable) practice. This approach revived a dormant discourse of authority over citizens, foregoing the kind of rigorous scrutiny of specific conduct more typical of the then-prevalent due process approach. What mattered instead were the myriad counteracting causes that would prevent these extreme cases from occurring—that most of the punishments under question were permissible because the teacher personally witnessed the offending conduct; that the teacher was expected by tradition and common law to exercise prudence; that the teacher's failure to exercise restraint risked civil and criminal penalties, and so on. This case was the exception that proved the prudence of the rule.

This mode of expert judgment was conservative in several senses. Tradition provided an alternative to either interpretive practices deemed strictly textual or practices derived from inviolable rights. The former discourse derived judgments from authoritative texts and the latter constituted the prevalent progressive approach that began with the judiciary's role as guardians of individual rights. The discourse of tradition rehabilitated themes and discourses that had been previously marginalized by the legal liberalism of the post–New Deal court. It would persuade those already inclined to accept the controversial practice of corporal punishment because it argued that the persistence of the practice was a democratic fact. Cumulatively, it made a pragmatic case for expertise as restraint. The opinion is transitional in the sense that it mostly revitalized older arguments for restraint—resonance of Justice Frankfurter's hesitance to make policy (*Barnette*) and Justice Black's concern for administration (*Tinker*) could be heard in the opinion's concern over the "time, personnel, and . . . diversion of attention from normal school pursuits" required by a constitutional ruling.[24] The rationale implicitly rejected the role of the judge as the guardian of the individual and an inviolable core of rights. The primary dissent resisted these conclusions and articulated a different role for expertise.

A Text-Driven Alternative: Justice White's Dissent

Justice White dissented, joined by Justices Brennan, Marshall, and Stevens. The opinion argued that the Eighth Amendment applied in school and that corporal punishment required a hearing prior to its administration. The dissent performed expert judgment by beginning with text. Its primary appeal was its case for procedural justice as textual interpretation because that judicial discipline resulted in active scrutiny of democratic practices and protected a core of citizenship rights against the state.

First, the dissent focused on the Eighth Amendment claim. A discourse focusing on the amendment's text countered the majority's appeal to tradition. Beginning with this text signaled a belief that society's normative commitments were found in an interpretation of the Constitution's wording. The Eighth Amendment "flat[ly] prohibit[ed]" cruel and unusual punishments; the text "reflect[ed] a societal judgment that there are some punishments that are so barbaric and inhumane that we will not permit them to be imposed on anyone."[25] Justice White treated the textual absence as an inference of value. There were no "limit[s]" or "modifie[rs]," and the Framers did not use the word "criminal" in the amendment.[26] The turn to the text was important for the result: where the majority reconciled an ongoing general practice with text and court decisions, the dissent drew attention to the text of the amendment and its prohibition on specific punishments. This choice allowed the dissent to shift the focus back onto the precise examples of the case.

The textual appeal resisted tradition by shifting the operative legal question. The fact that the text of the amendment did not suggest that it didn't apply to citizens in civil contexts indicated that the important constitutional question was: what is a punishment? Justice White answered it in broad terms: punishment was "an institutionalized response to the violation of some official rule or regulation proscribing certain conduct [and which] is imposed for the purpose of rehabilitating the offender, deterring the offender . . . and inflicting some measure of social retribution for the harm that has been done."[27] The definition supported a consistent interpretation of the amendment's text while also maintaining the a fortiori analogy from *Gault*—if the state could not inflict a particular punishment on an adult for a particular crime, it also could not do so to a child. The tactic also implicitly rebutted the majority's argument that tradition was democratic: a clear definition consistent with a clear constitutional text would mean that justices enforced the Constitution in limited ways that were not unduly influenced by personal belief.

Justice White's dissent advanced a discourse of core individual citizenship rights, adding to that discourse the idea that proper judicial interpretation constituted the right procedure for discerning that core. This counter-discourse resisted the majority's argument that the open tradition of public schools and common-law remedies were sufficient to safeguard citizens' interests. It also created an autonomy for constitutional judgments by divorcing public display and acceptance from constitutional guarantee. Making a punishment public did not "render the punishment constitutional if it were otherwise impermissible," and its "openness to public scrutiny should have nothing to do with its constitutional validity."[28] Ideologically, the dissent appealed to a procedural-textual mode of discerning the substantive core of citizenship rights. The judge's role was to intervene to protect the substantive core of rights, not to tolerate the occasional injustice by letting popular local traditions rule the day. Florida's alternate ex post legal remedies bore no relevance to the issue of *whether* the punishment was cruel and unusual. Only text and precedent cases could answer that question, not tradition.

In analyzing the due process claim, the dissent activated the discourse of procedural fairness to argue that Florida's regime was insufficient. Sound judgment involved rigorous application of routinized procedures to limit the risk of errors—the same discourse from *In re Gault*. The opinion emphasized that process was there to "protect the individual from erroneous or mistaken punishment that the State would not have inflicted had it found the facts in a more reliable way."[29] Justice White performed this precision by closely reading precedent cases. This precision allowed him to spot errors in the majority's analysis. For example, the majority opinion worried that requiring additional procedures would be too burdensome, perhaps even to the point of ending corporal punishment as a practice altogether. Justice White found this to be a sloppy reading of precedent, concluding that due process could reduce errors without much burden. Citing *Goss v. Lopez,* he observed that the relevant constitutional clause "requires not an 'elaborate hearing' before a neutral party, but simply an informal give-and-take between student and disciplinarian which gives the student an opportunity to explain his version of the facts."[30] In effect, Justice White accused the majority opinion of lacking the precision that interpretive application requires for judgment. The *Ingraham* opinion arrived at an overbroad conclusion based on an improper starting point and poor reading of court precedent. Expert procedure worked best when judges were operating at their highest level to guard against excessive state authority over the individual.

The dissent characterized the majority opinion's "deference to tradition" as an abdication of judicial responsibility. It forfeited the judge's role to independently assess legal facts and the probability of harm. The *Ingraham* majority, in its haste to restore a lost tradition, detached that tradition from shared values. This mode of judicial resistance was present across both free speech and due process cases in the twentieth century. Justice McReynolds protected economic liberty in *Meyer* and *Pierce*; Justice Frankfurter sought to protect civic values and democratic processes in *Gobitis*. Justice Jackson protected the individual against village tyrants in *Barnette*. Justice Fortas protected the child against fearful administrators in *Tinker*, and against arbitrary juvenile court systems in *In re Gault*. Justice White's dissent implied that the *Ingraham* majority was protecting tradition itself. This strategy put pressure on a revanchist judicial approach by exploiting the latter's concession that whatever judicial expertise was, it had to be more than one's intention to achieve an end or personal belief in the correctness of a result. Only a commitment to judicial procedure could vindicate the need to properly assess risks.

The dissent performed that vision of judgment by dissecting one of the majority's analogies. The majority had analogized the students' punishment to an adult's arrest. Wrongful arrest was subject not to a full-blown hearing, but a later legal action to sue the police and recover money. Similarly, the majority had reasoned, these civil and criminal remedies were sufficient to protect the child's liberty. But was the child in a comparable situation? According to Justice White, the court's own previous cases said "no." The majority was misreading precedent, which applied only in criminal seizure contexts (Fourth Amendment) because the state's interest was so high. When the court had upheld warrantless arrests, it was *not* because damage suits were sufficient to protect liberty, but because the arrest itself triggered a bundle of procedural protections. In the case of the child, the social interest was lower and the liberty interest higher. The court's precedent required procedures with which a school could easily comply: "only . . . a few minutes to give the student 'notice of the charges against him, and, if he denies them, an explanation of the evidence the authorities have and an opportunity to tell his side of the story' . . . in order to avoid injustice."[31]

Ingraham signaled a transitional moment in the story of judgment appropriate for the constitutional narrative of citizenship. It elevated respect for tradition over individual development in terms of citizenship. It was an example of self-imposed limits. It tolerated individual instances of cruelty because they were aberrant, and because one couldn't—and shouldn't—"constitutionalize" every dispute. If one did, one risked upending the entire tradition. The dissent protected the individual, but made a minimalist case grounded in textual application. Justice White admitted that his own view was that although corporal punishment was acceptable, it needed to be subject to *some* constitutional limit.

Ingraham had very little to say about individual judgment. The child in this instance was presumed incapable. The opinions activated latent discourses about the social contract, including what particular institutional actors owed to the child as a citizen. The majority opinion placed faith in public scrutiny and democratic legislation—revivals of Justice Frankfurter's appeals to democracy as a system—and rehabilitated tradition as an authoritative mode of developing decision-making habits. The dissent opposed this maneuver as a matter of textual interpretation, but its argument for due process retained a kernel of faith in communicative reason—the idea that to give the child an opportunity to be heard was the way to demonstrate a system's legitimacy to an individual. In short, *Ingraham* infused the constitutional narrative with a deference principle: judges could not substitute their own judgment for a traditional one.[32] The dissent resisted on the narrow grounds that the majority misread the text, with the admonition that the judge needed to remember that deferring to other decision-makers could constitute a judicial abdication rather than a noble execution of one's proper role. The dissent's claim that the majority was "misreading precedent" failed to come to grips with the court's majority decision in *Ingraham* that would now serve as precedential support for deference.

But what about cases where the citizen seems chronically unmanageable, even for traditional organic institutions? In such cases, where there is no crime, but there is nevertheless a possibility of being institutionalized for long periods of time, should the citizen have an independent voice? In the case of the child, does the fact of apparent agreement about what is best for the child deserve the respect of tradition, even though the child does not agree? The court took up such a case with extremely high stakes—the commitment of the child to a hospital because of mental illness. From speech seemingly dangerous to the child to the seemingly dangerous child, this case provided the opportunity to recalibrate the relationship between family, child, and state, and refigure precisely what obligation the state owed individual citizens.

7

TRADITION AGAINST DEMOCRATIC MAJORITIES

Parham v. J. R.

THE CASES FROM PART 2 THAT TREATED THE CHILD AS A CATEGORICAL equal—*Barnette, Gault,* and *Tinker*—had used the narrative of a childhood lost to advance citizenship as categorical equality. The facts of *Parham v. J. R.* challenged this narrative's constitutional reach. J. R.'s childhood may already have been "lost." His early years lacked the stability thought necessary for the play, safety, adventure, and self-determination that characterize a socially healthy childhood. He was removed from his parents when he was three months old.[1] A series of foster care placements failed to create a permanent custody arrangement. When he was seven years old, his foster parents sought outpatient psychological treatment for him. According to Chief Justice Burger's majority opinion, he was "so disruptive and incorrigible that he could not conform to normal behavior patterns."[2] His foster parents asked that he be removed from their home, and the Georgia Department of Family and Children Services asked for him to be admitted to the Central State Hospital in Georgia.[3] He was admitted, based on findings that he was "borderline retarded, and suffered an 'unsocialized, aggressive reaction of childhood.'"[4] During his time at the hospital, the department tried, and failed, to place him in another foster home. In October 1975, J. R. filed suit with another plaintiff, J. L., seeking "a less drastic environment suitable to his needs."[5]

J. L.'s mother requested that he be admitted to the hospital in 1970, when he was six years old. His commitment followed two months of attempted outpatient treatment. A physician who interviewed him had "learned that J. L. had been expelled from school because he was uncontrollable. He accepted the parents' representation that the boy had been extremely aggressive, and diagnosed the child as having a 'hyperkinetic reaction of childhood.'"[6] While he was committed, J. L. lived intermittently with his parents on a furlough basis, but the arrangement was stopped at his parents' request. According to Chief Justice Burger, "several hospital employees recommended that J. L. should be placed in a special foster home," but this never occurred. Some five years after his initial commitment, J. L. filed suit seeking his release.

The plaintiffs claimed that Georgia's commitment laws violated due process.[7] In Georgia, guardians began the voluntary commitment process for a child by signing a form, which authorized the hospital superintendent to admit the child temporarily. The superintendent could then admit the child "for such period and under such conditions as may be authorized by law" if s/he found evidence of mental illness.[8] Children committed indefinitely in this way could be released in one of three ways: if a guardian requested a discharge, if a patient recovered, or if a patient improved enough that hospitalization were deemed undesirable.

The various hospitals diverged in their implementation of these procedures. The hospitals were different sizes: some of them had as few as ten children and others had committed as many as twenty-five. The hospitals were located in different communities—large cities with over one hundred thousand, and smaller cities with only ten to twenty thousand people. Some admitted voluntary patients only if it were proved that they were a danger to themselves or others, while other hospitals allowed a guardian to authorize commitment. The hospitals had different review procedures and personnel. Finally, the average stays for a child varied: some children were committed for an average of 90 days, but one hospital's average stay was over five times as long (465 days).[9]

The federal district court ruled for the plaintiffs, invalidating Georgia's procedures for commitment. Relying heavily on *In re Gault,* it ruled that the commitment process deprived a child of their liberty interest, because children were subject to physical restraints and emotional harm when they were institutionalized.[10] It concluded that the child was entitled to a hearing in front of an "impartial tribunal" and that the existing review process was inadequate. It also required that Georgia provide adequate support for less restrictive treatment facilities.[11]

The Supreme Court reversed this ruling, reasoning that Georgia provided sufficient due process to children in its fact finding prior to, and after, commitment. It balanced the child's liberty interest against the probable value of additional procedures, as well as the state's interest in maintaining reasonable fiscal and administrative burdens. It held that parents had the authority to seek care for children subject to medical expertise and that due process did not necessarily require legal training. It ruled that Georgia's procedures satisfied due process requirements because they involved an array of experts who conducted careful medical evaluations. Justice Brennan concurred in part and dissented in part in an opinion joined by Justice Marshall and Justice Blackmun. He agreed with the majority that the district court should not have required adversarial hearings in every case. But he dissented because "the right to at least one post-admission hearing can and should be affirmed."[12]

VINDICATING BUREAUCRACY: THE *PARHAM* MAJORITY

The majority opinion further developed the turn to tradition by treating the child's constitutional claim as a shared interest with the family. Concerning individual judgment, the opinion turned to tradition by reasserting the child's lack of capabilities. It used the character of the incapable individual child to advance prominent roles for the family and the elected branches of state government. In performing its expertise, the opinion revived arguments for judicial restraint through the pragmatic impact that an adverse ruling would have. This tactic amplified Justice Black's "administrative burden" discourse from his *Tinker* dissent: judicial restraint was wise not because it preserved voter preference, but because it preserved state spending allocations. In so arguing, the opinion further divorced the traditional argument of judicial restraint from its original democratic thrust. Where *Ingraham* dismissed procedural citizenship for the child because public scrutiny would correct abuses, *Parham* did so on the grounds that executive officers and bureaucrats could determine how best to apportion procedural guarantees. This approach also rendered expert judgment more opaque and narrower in scope.

First, Chief Justice Burger's opinion used the character of the incapable child to develop a theme of well-intentioned entities responding to the child's mental illness. This incapability then justified a charitable presumption toward both the child's parents (or guardians) and the state's response to the problem of childhood mental illness.[13] The opinion's legal question prefigured both an attitude toward the citizen and the case's outcome. It asked: "What process is constitutionally due a minor child whose parents or guardian seek state administered institutional mental health care for the child, and, specifically, whether an adversary proceeding is required prior to or after the commitment."[14] The question worked with the due process discourse of *In re Gault* but qualified it, suggesting as *Ingraham* had that exceptional cases could justify exceptions to general due process rules.

The opinion used the character of the mentally ill child as a limit-case for the citizen's procedural liberty. The child's inferior status bolstered the claim. *Tinker* and *In re Gault* emphasized the child's categorical equality, but Chief Justice Burger described a "minor child" in need of "health care." This frame distinguished children from adults for constitutional purposes. It related that distinction to variations in procedural justice by emphasizing the case's civil context. The exceptional minor child was passive, and the child's parents and the state were active. The opinion focused on the parents' motives and dismissed the child's desires as the poorly formed wants of an incapable person. The child was an object of parental choice and state duty rather than a free chooser. Parents "sought . . . care" from the state, and the child was a passive recipient. The opinion constructed a narrative of parental solicitude and clinical medical assessments. J. L. "was admitted in 1970 at the age of 6 years. . . . Prior to his admission, J. L. had received outpatient treatment . . . for over two months."[15] J. L.'s mother sought indefinite commitment as a last resort. The admission procedures in place were presumptively beneficial, because the clinicians thereby gained relevant information with an interview with J. L. and his parents.

This legal question fragmented the discourse of skepticism from *In re Gault*. *In re Gault* mistrusted the state's parens patriae power because it arbitrarily deprived the citizen of liberty. That idea relied on an image of childhood lost, populated by violent criminals instead of parents and play. But in *Parham*, the child's world is populated by caring parents, deflecting attention from the conditions of confinement in mental institutions. The argument strategy cultivated a theme of judicial intrusion into an otherwise benevolent and voluntary decision.

The opinion advanced this strategy in framing the case's procedural history. It ignored the district court's factual basis for its decision and the varied backgrounds of the individual plaintiffs. Instead, the *Parham* majority framed the lower court's decision as a dangerous potential disruption of local governing practices. This choice posited the primacy of those who make active choices (parental rights) and the diversity of local governing structures. The incapable minor child resisted the discourse of categorical equality and raised the inherent limitations of judicial institutions.

The opinion minimized the child's liberty by denying its proof: "The lower court relied on one of appellees' witnesses who expressed an opinion that 'some still look upon mental hospitals as a "dumping ground . . . ."' No specific evidence of such 'dumping,' however, can be found in the record."[16] The opinion did not define "dumping" and overlooked the facts that one of the hospitals had an average stay of over 450 days and that J. R.'s foster parents actively sought his placement. This line of argument used a declarative tone to make a contingent legal conclusion ("no evidence of dumping grounds") appear necessary and incontestable. Chief Justice Burger failed to mention that the named plaintiffs were both incarcerated for over five years; hospital personnel had recommended that both plaintiffs be placed in less restrictive care settings; the state's own director of mental health conducted a study that concluded that children required independent advocates (and less restrictive, home-like treatment settings) and that Georgia's system of commitment lacked both reliable data collection processes and evaluation standards. This formalistic strategy relied on the appearance of neutrality, which allowed it to deemphasize the deprivation of liberty. In the words of Amartya Sen, it was an example of a description that was accurate without being good.[17]

The opinion advanced a mode of expert judgment as a synthesis of restraint and bureaucratic protection. The former relied on a rationale similar to Justice Frankfurter's discourse of reverence for the democratic system (in *Gobitis/Barnette*); the latter repurposed an argument about the threat that litigation posed to governing institutions, similar to Justice Black's *Tinker* dissent. The end result retrofitted conservative reverence for organic institutions with the realities of a progressively complex modern liberal democracy. This model of expert judgment prioritized traditional Western values through the bureaucratic management of risk.

The special case of the mentally ill child counseled for restraint.[18] The opinion framed state caregiving efforts as benevolent trial-and-error, activating the trope of state institutions as labs for experimentation. Deference was necessary to maintain diverse government responses to the public problem of mental illness. The chief justice's opinion emphasized the personal information that a hospital superintendent had uncovered in finding facts, deepening the association between local governing institutions and individualized treatment: "He learned that J. L.'s natural parents had divorced, and his mother had remarried. He also learned that J. L. had been expelled from school because he was uncontrollable."[19] J. L.'s example stood in for the whole of similarly situated children, whose evaluators discovered parents that are caring, who shared an interest in the best living arrangements, and who sought to make the best of a difficult situation.

In discussing J. R.'s case, the opinion reinforced themes of parental and state benevolence. The opinion used the decision to commit J. R to highlight the child's lack of cognitive capabilities. The state tried less restrictive placements numerous times; he had received outpatient treatment "for several months" prior to being hospitalized; when sent to school, he was "disruptive and incorrigible," and his seventh set of foster parents requested his removal. And like J. L., the decision to admit appeared carefully thought out: the Department of Family and Children Services gave the hospital "a complete sociomedical history at the time of his admission"; the admission team conducted "three separate interviews" with J. R. before admission; and "It was determined that he was borderline retarded, and suffered an 'unsocialized, aggressive reaction of childhood.' It was recommended unanimously that he would 'benefit from the structured environment' of the hospital, and would 'enjoy living and playing with boys of the same age.'"[20] This frame supported the opinion's vision of expert judgment through deference: evidence of others' cognitive acts mitigated the need to exercise judicial authority.

The discourse of deference then suggested a discourse of state administrative burdens. It combined Justice Frankfurter's argument that "constitutionalizing issues" would invalidate too much social legislation and Justice Black's argument in *Tinker* that rights expansion deprived administrators of necessary governing authority. *Parham* conjured expansive citizenship rights as a threat to states' fiscal viability. The lower court's ruling rejected "the State's entire system . . . on both procedural and substantive grounds."[21] Instead, fiscal budgets should seemingly determine whether a state's efforts were reasonable: "Georgia . . . funds over 50 community mental health clinics and 13 specialized foster care homes. The State has built seven new regional hospitals within the past 15 years . . . . [It] ranks 22d among states in per capita expenditures for mental health and 15th in total expenditures."[22] This claim for judicial deference excised the traditional "will of the people" in favor of bureaucratic function. This strategy granted constitutional significance to a state's evidence of effort, detached from an evaluation of its normative core. Where the categorical equality model of citizenship was opposed by assertions of a slippery slope of rights, its retrenchment through tradition was slowly expanding the types of state interests deserving of judicial concern, weaving such asymmetries into the constitutional narrative of citizenship.

The *Parham* majority wished to avoid open-ended judicial intrusions into state legislative process, including the technocratic realm of budget and executive authority. The opinion deferred to executive testimony that the lower court's order would directly impact Georgia's fiscal situation: "The Governor of Georgia and the chairmen of the two Appropriations Committees of its legislature, testifying in the District Court, expressed confidence in the Georgia program and informed the court that the State could not justify enlarging its budget during fiscal year 1977 to provide the specialized treatment settings urged."[23] The state's interest in budgeting appeared as a constitutionally significant consideration, substituting technocratic and executive authority for the will of the people.

This interpretive practice equated expressions of confidence in the procedural scheme with their constitutional adequacy. This approach unwittingly exposed an irony of deferential judgment: where Justice Frankfurter had posed deference as an antidote to personal judicial conviction, here, it was deployed as an endorsement of the state's conviction of its own sufficiency. The chief justice's reliance on evidence of fiscal impact was relevant to the question of a child's right to adversarial procedures because of anxieties about courts judging beyond their capabilities. In deferring to the governor's confidence in the program, the opinion sharply contrasted with the assessments of threat in *Meyer, Pierce, Barnette, Tinker,* and *In re Gault*. Each of those opinions asked for something more than belief that a risk or threat to the public was likely. Yet here, Chief Justice Burger deferred to mere confidence in accurate results as a reason to discount possible harms to citizens.

The majority opinion criticized the lower court's emphasis on the "emotional and psychic harm" of commitment and impugned the court's assessment of evidence because it overvalued the testimony of a single expert witness.[24] Chief Justice Burger reverted back to parental motivations and beliefs as the primary evaluative lens. This strategy contrasted the practical clarity of deference to the interpretive ambiguities in the lower court's opinion. The district court's reasoning was arbitrary and susceptible to unpredictable application. The lower court ironically engaged in the type of judgment of which it complained,[25] through basing its decision on the "inexactness of psychiatry" and then later "shift[ing] its focus drastically" from a procedural to a substantive due process analysis.[26] By using the lower court as a character in the narrative, the opinion appealed to a concern about erratic and unpredictable judges wreaking havoc on democratic decisions.

To counteract this undesirable effect, the majority suggested that the state should decide its own limits, because that was the proper democratic process. The expense of litigation justified deferring to an already constitutional legislative scheme:

> In an earlier day, the problems inherent in coping with children afflicted with mental or emotional abnormalities were dealt with largely within the family. . . . Until recently, most of the states did little more than provide custodial institutions for the confinement of persons who were considered dangerous.
>
> Ironically, as most states have expanded their efforts to assist the mentally ill, their actions have been subjected to increasing litigation. . . . In this case, appellees have challenged Georgia's procedural and substantive balance of the individual, family, and social interests at stake.[27]

Activating the discourse of institutional limits, the facts of the case validated the principle. The legislature, not the judiciary, has been responsive to the emerging medical knowledge and progressive in its care for incapable children. Federal funding keyed this progress: "As medical knowledge about the mentally ill and public concern for their condition expanded, the states, aided substantially by federal grants, have sought to ameliorate the human tragedies of seriously disturbed children."[28]

The entire mode of expert judgment embedded a kernel of contempt for minority constitutional challenges. It exploited an (unstated) inference that plaintiffs who sue amid these general background conditions are either unreasonable, ungrateful, or irresponsible, because they are unconcerned about the fiscal consequences of public law litigation.[29] The opinion leveraged that attitude in order to revive earlier jurisprudential discourse that treated the child's constitutional stake as coterminous with the interest of a parent. The child wasn't the sole holder of constitutional rights but rather had an interest "inextricably linked with the parents' interest in and obligation for the welfare and health of the child," so the "private interest at stake is a combination of the child's and parents' concerns."[30]

This description downplayed the potentially divergent interests of parent and child as individuals with conflicting interests. Instead it relied on a tradition of parents as proxies for their incapable children. Moving from the general to the particular, it grounded this idea in tradition and precedent as a mirror of shared values: "Our jurisprudence historically has reflected Western civilization concepts of the family as a unit with broad parental authority over minor children. Our cases have consistently followed that course; our constitutional system long ago rejected any notion that a child is 'the mere creature of the State . . . .' Surely, this includes a 'high duty' to recognize symptoms of illness and to seek and follow medical advice."[31] Precedent supported denial of the child's constitutional claim on grounds that doing so restored traditions. Invoking language from *Pierce v. Society of Sisters*, the majority opinion in *Parham* argued that the Western reverence for the family meant that the incapable child's liberty interest involved parental obligation. Expertise involved a judgment idiom marked by presumptions, proxies, and rules of thumb, with an affinity for organic institutions.

Casting the assertion of rights within an idiom of tradition allowed Chief Justice Burger to dismiss the importance of due process for citizenship. The alternative—state power overruling parenting decisions "in all cases"—was "repugnant to American tradition."[32] Contestation and disagreement alone could not dislodge the presumption in favor of traditional substantive values. "The fact that a child may balk at hospitalization or complain about a parental refusal to provide cosmetic surgery" did not tip the scales away from parental autonomy.[33] The opinion's analogy comparing involuntary commitment to a hospital for mental disability with hospitalization for a sudden grave illness, and to child objections to a denial for an ear-piercing request, illustrated the reach of tradition's sway. Each of these objections was presumptively invalid because it threatened traditional family structure.

Parham advanced a transitional model of addressing controversies about the child by reviving tradition. Concerning individual citizen judgment, it implied that the incapable citizen's inability to perform consent required strong counterbalancing forces to make decisions in that citizen's best interests. The consequences of this description for the social contract included a declining emphasis on adversarial justice in a modern regulatory state. The opinion downplayed the potentially divergent interests of citizens (parent and child) through a narrative of care. In the place of categorical equality, it designated well-intentioned parental proxies. In the place of expert adversarial procedure, it counseled for restraint, with the troublesome twist that such restraint deferred not to democratic majorities but to the self-stated confidence and good intentions of the executive branch and its concern for fiscal limitations on constitutional rights. In the realm of citizen due process, the state could potentially define the limits of its own obligations.

The Time of Judgments and the Objectivity of Reciprocity: Justice Brennan's Dissent

Justice Brennan dissented in part because he believed that the child was entitled to "the right to at least one post-admission hearing."[34] The opinion linked the character of the vulnerable child to a discourse about the virtues of independent adjudication. Grounding the judge's role in the accuracy of procedure, Brennan contrasted that procedure to Georgia's provisions for clinical review. First, his opinion used the discourse of the temporality of judicial expertise to emphasize its objectivity and accuracy compared to immediate clinical assessments. Second, it performed that expertise through themes of contractual reciprocity. Justice Brennan argued that parental rights were limited in part by how parents exercised them. This judicial performance figured objectivity through its privileged temporal position: expertise was authorized because it could assess private sphere relationships (doctor-patient, parent-child) with detachment and critical distance.

Although Justice Brennan began from a similar place as the majority—with the incapability of the child—the dissent took the perspective of the child rather than the family unit in order to argue that the child was "entitled to more protection than are adults. The consequences of an erroneous decision are more tragic when children are involved."[35] A child suffers longer deprivations of liberty in commitment and "may bear the scars for the rest of their lives."[36]

Repurposing the discourse of lost childhood, the dissent justified rigorous judicial procedures to limit grievous errors. On this reading, judicial expertise preserved a future of open possibilities for individual citizens. The decision to commit a child to a hospital could create irreversible cognitive limitations for the child. The opinion's strategy maintained a tension between the incapable child in need of protection and care on the one hand, and the free child entitled to procedures on the other. This frame conceded the paternalistic idea that children who lacked cognitive capabilities were entitled to fewer rights. Justice Brennan's dissent envisioned a role for expertise that would protect the incapable citizen to preserve their development.

The dissent justified this judicial role with the theme of objectivity. Procedure cured errors made from "psychiatric diagnoses and therapy decisions . . . fraught with uncertainties."[37] Its longer time horizon and protocols managed the emotions involved in the decisions. Clinical settings exacerbated the risk of factual mistakes because of their timing. The clinician interviewed the child at a time of great stress. They were gathering information in situations where there was no time or process to "become acquainted" with the child in total; furthermore, "these uncertainties may be further aggravated when economic and social class separate doctor and child, thereby frustrating the accurate diagnosis of pathology."[38] This statement implied that judicial hearings could correct errors resulting from communicative misunderstandings because hearings screened emotional interference out of the process. Their differences in timing and protocol allowed an authentic voice to emerge. That authentic voice protected liberty. The risk calculus for clinicians differed: where judges were required to operate with a presumption in favor of liberty, "psychiatrists tend[ed] to err on the side of medical caution, and therefore hospitalize[d] patients for whom other dispositions would be more beneficial."[39]

Judicial expertise also checked the excesses of irrational belief, creating a role for the state opposed to the organic institution of the family. Parental error posed as much a danger to the incapable individual as the clinician. Misguided parents were free "to become martyrs" but couldn't "make martyrs of their children."[40] The martyr metaphor was particularly apt, given that martyrs' judgments looked righteous for those with similar beliefs but not to the secular world. Referring to precedent that limited custodial rights when the parent was motivated by religious belief, it made the case for judicial intervention to protect the child's right to due process.[41]

Second, Justice Brennan grounded the expert's role in a contractual logic that assessed relationships according to reason and reciprocity. Judicial review of commitment decisions was warranted because those decisions involved something different than "a routine childrearing decision."[42] The child may have been exceptional, but that also meant that the parental decision to commit them also was exceptional. The parents' decision to surrender custody ruptured family autonomy: "A child who has been ousted from his family has even greater need for an independent advocate."[43] The child's incapacities likely were caused by factors that were not a part of the child's makeup. Studies demonstrated that commitment decisions "often [were] the results of dislocation in the family unrelated to the children's mental condition," and "even well-meaning parents lack[ed] the expertise" required to decide the appropriate course of treatment.[44]

Justice Brennan's opinion was a transitional statement for the individual citizen and for the expert judge, because it reshaped the "categorical equality" model as a minority position. Its language of exception limited the role of legal expertise in guaranteeing equality for individuals both in argumentative form and in linguistic style. Redeploying the discourse of judicial abdication and misplaced faith, the dissent argued that the majority erred because it "assumed blindly that parents act in their children's best interests."[45] But conceiving of citizenship as procedural at all costs was impractical as well. A rule requiring pre-commitment hearings may "deter parents from seeking needed medical attention . . . delay treatment of children whose home life has become impossible . . . [and pit] the child and his advocate against the parents."[46]

Acknowledging these instrumental considerations demonstrated the transition away from a robust role for the judge as guarantor of a citizen's individual due process. It gave credence to the institutional limitations of the judicial process, as well as the administrative burden that the state would suffer in being required to have full hearings for every commitment decision. The result was a retreat to the insistence on post-admission review hearings. Although Brennan rehearsed the traditional benefits of due process rights, the exceptional character demonstrated that the aggressive liberal proceduralism of the Warren Court had given way to the conservatism of tradition. Justice Brennan's opposition was limited by his incrementalism and concession to flexibility.

Parham advanced the assertion of tradition against equality, tempered by the discourse of procedural justice. Chief Justice Burger's approach expanded state authority, refiguring the antimajoritarian anxieties of the court by claiming for the judicial expert the authority to define American traditions and the scope of Western morality. Complicating matters further, the bureaucratic concerns of Justice Black in *Tinker*—that litigation fears would hamstring the state's administration—were validated in *Parham*'s due process context. Transferring the trope of delegation onto the representative institutions of government, the decision appeared to give authority to the state to assess its own commitment to a legislative scheme that met constitutional muster.

This approach exacerbated the asymmetries of the democratic social contract between state and citizen. Neither Chief Justice Burger nor Justice Brennan answered the question of representation—it is difficult to legitimate majoritarian political processes when some individuals cannot participate in those processes. In deferring to the pragmatic problems of state budgets and describing individual citizenship rights as having more than one stakeholder, *Parham* further complicated the asymmetry between government officials and the people who are governed. The default presumption now would be judicial deferral concerning scrutiny of bureaucratic and professional allocations. This new approach opened the door for the state—as legislation, as tradition, as bureaucracy—to define its own obligations in the realm of due process. What did this mean for cases where the child as a nascent citizen had displayed some capacity for controversial public speech?

8

TRADITION AGAINST FREE SPEECH

Bethel School District v. Fraser

The Burger Court of the 1970s exploited the rhetorical resources of past cases to reshape the constitutional narrative of individual and expert judgment through due process controversies involving children.[1] At the level of individual judgment, it had emphasized the discourse of the individual child's incapability as a rationale for strong parental involvement and traditional state authority. At the level of expert judgment, the court was reinventing the argument for judicial restraint as an appeal to bureaucratic and administrative realities of modern government. This new role derived its mandate from constitutional tradition. It made use of the longer temporality of judgment, but as a way to divine long-standing traditions instead of potential threats to order. It deployed textual interpretations of precedent, but these were more supportive of tradition than determinative of the outcome.

In the realm of the child's First Amendment rights, the court had been relatively quiet. Its most significant pronouncement in the 1970s on the child and public speech came in *FCC v. Pacifica Foundation,* which upheld the Federal Communications Commission's authority to regulate a broadcast of comedian George Carlin's "Filthy Words" routine.[2] Carlin's performance lampooned the notion that the government could label a set of words categorically profane and unfit for public consumption. When a New York radio station broadcast the routine one afternoon, a man who was driving with his son during the broadcast wrote a letter of complaint to the FCC. The FCC issued an administrative warning, arguing that it could have chosen to sanction the station. The broadcast company then challenged the FCC's decision.

The most remarkable portion of Justice John Paul Stevens's opinion upholding the FCC's authority argued that citizens had a right to not be confronted by indecency, and that there was a special obligation to protect children from this material.[3] Like the approaches in *Ingraham* and *Parham,* the opinion appealed to the incapable, impressionable child, easily corrupted by immoral outside influences. A decade following *Tinker*, the court had yet to answer its leftover questions. If *Tinker* rested on the black armband's purity and passivity combined with the lack of a documented record of its threat to the school, what about speech that was more "active"? What type of evidence would satisfy the court that there was a risk of school disruption? Put differently, since the child was an individual citizen, when could a citizen's speech be silenced because it disrupted a broader public purpose?

In 1983 the court addressed these questions in the case of a political nomination speech delivered by graduating senior Matthew Fraser in front of approximately six hundred students at Bethel High School in Pierce County, Washington. Fraser spoke to his fellow students at a "school-sponsored educational program in self-government."[4] When he ascended to the platform, he delivered the following speech:

> I know a man who is firm—he's firm in his pants, he's firm in his shirt, his character is firm—but most . . . of all, his belief in you, the students of Bethel, is firm.
>
> Jeff Kuhlman is a man who takes his point and pounds it in. If necessary, he'll take an issue and nail it to the wall. He doesn't attack things in spurts—he drives hard, pushing and pushing until finally—he succeeds.
>
> Jeff is a man who will go to the very end—even the climax, for each and every one of you.
>
> So vote for Jeff for A. S. B. vice-president—he'll never come between you and the best our high school can be.[5]

Fraser's speech drew the ire of the assistant principal, who called Fraser into her office for discipline the next day.

Bethel High School had a disciplinary rule that prohibited "the use of obscene, profane language or gestures." The assistant principal asked Fraser to explain himself. Unimpressed with Fraser's defense, the school suspended him and removed him from a list of commencement speaker candidates. Fraser challenged the sanction through the school district's grievance procedures. A hearing officer upheld the school's decision, finding the speech "obscene" because it was "indecent, lewd, and offensive to the modesty and decency of many of the students and faculty in attendance at the assembly."[6]

Fraser then went to federal district court, which decided that the school's disciplinary action violated Fraser's First Amendment right, as well as his right to due process (because the rule it relied on had not mentioned Fraser's punishment as a possible outcome). The court awarded Fraser damages and attorney's fees. It also enjoined the school from preventing Fraser from speaking at commencement. Fraser's classmates voted for him as a write-in candidate to speak, and he addressed his class at graduation. The school district appealed the court's ruling to the Ninth Circuit Court of Appeals, which also sided with Fraser. Undeterred, it then appealed to the Supreme Court, which decided to hear the case.

Chief Justice Burger's opinion held that the school could punish Fraser's speech because it transgressed the bounds of civil discourse.[7] It reasoned that the school was constitutionally empowered to limit uncivil speech in order to educate future citizens about fundamental values (which included education about the political sensibilities of others).[8] It then ruled against Fraser on his due process claim, holding that a school did not have to specify a particular sanction, but only needed to give Fraser notice that lewd speech could be punished.[9] Justice Stevens issued the most lengthy dissent. He argued that the school had not demonstrated that Fraser's speech was actually disruptive, and that Fraser was entitled to notice about the scope of the speech prohibition and possible punishment.

Civil Traditions and Public Judgment: Leading by Example

The majority opinion in *Fraser* framed the problem as a need for citizens to follow rules of civility. Incapable speakers threatened these rules by displaying poor judgment and incapable audience members could not develop their capabilities properly if subjected to offensive material. The opinion connected individual judgment to decorum, described as the ability to respect for the rules of speech. The citizen respected decorum by displaying a respect for the varied opinions and cognitive capabilities of members of the public, and by addressing topics that are properly considered political. Concerning expert judgment, the opinion continued to connect authority to tradition. *Fraser* performed tradition through mimetic example. It identified that tradition in key civic texts, precedent cases, and analogies. Substantively, this expert judge needed respect wide administrative latitude to apply bureaucratic rules. As an interpretive practice, the opinion's juxtaposition of the discourse of tradition as civility with the discourse of deference to local governing approaches created tension, which *Fraser* resolved in an idiom of uniform institutional certitude. This certainty about civility reshaped the argument from deference, further deepening its disconnection from its popular democratic instincts.

Chief Justice Burger's opinion argued that regulating Fraser's speech was permissible because it displayed poor judgment and a lack of respect for its public. By strategically framing the legal question and positing a relationship between education and decorum, the opinion introduced a capacity for civil discourse as a necessary component of citizen judgment. Ironically, at a time when due process rights received little respect, the opinion advanced a discourse of civil respect for procedural rules, order, and discussion of intense political views as a mode of developing citizenship capabilities for political participation. By incorporating these stock concerns, the *Fraser* majority figured individual judgment as a capacity to select proper topics and calibrate their public reception at the expense of alternative expressive forms.

First, the opinion described individual judgment as the capability to discern political from nonpolitical speech. It separated speech into high and low value. This strategy developed a latent discourse from *Tinker*. Even though *Tinker* acknowledged that students do not "shed their constitutional rights . . . at the schoolhouse gate," the *Fraser* opinion emphasized the low content-status of Fraser's speech. There was a "marked distinction between the political 'message' of the armbands in *Tinker* and the sexual content of respondent's speech in this case." The citizen's free speech right changed from a natural right that traveled with the citizen in order to protect the development of the free mind to a student's "right to engage in a nondisruptive, passive expression of a political viewpoint."[10]

The opinion's legal question asked: "whether the First Amendment prevents a school district from disciplining a high school student for giving a lewd speech at a high school assembly."[11] The question prefigured the speech as lewd, rather than being politically important. It pointed to the analysis of other tribunals to justify the claim. A hearing officer found that the speech was "indecent, lewd, and offensive to the modesty and decency of many of the students and faculty in attendance."[12] Likewise, the court of appeals "proceeded on the theory that the use of lewd and obscene speech in order to make what the speaker considered to be a point . . . was essentially the same as the wearing of an armband in *Tinker* as a form of protest or the expression of a political position."[13] In recounting the procedural history, the opinion introduced differences between Fraser and the *Tinker* plaintiffs—Fraser may himself have believed that his speech had "a point," but that belief was not necessarily shared by Fraser's public.

The opinion connected individual judgment to a discourse of civility in order to bridge the gap between speaker belief and public reception. This discourse created civil performance as an important element of citizen's judgment. It declared that the "role and purpose of the American public school system" was to "prepare pupils for citizenship in the Republic. . . . It must inculcate the habits and manners of civility as values in themselves conducive to happiness and as indispensable to the practice of self-government in the community and the nation."[14]

A citizen's judgment entailed the mutual recognition of social behaviors, and a citizen's liberty required the ability to gauge to the feelings and sentiments of a public: "The undoubted freedom to advocate unpopular and controversial views in schools and classrooms must be balanced against the society's countervailing interest in teaching students the boundaries of socially appropriate behavior. Even the most heated political discourse in a democratic society requires consideration for the personal sensibilities of the other participants and audiences."[15] The opinion deployed the disfavored discourse of subjective belief as evidence that Fraser lacked the proper capability to respect others in political discourse. Adding the personal sensibilities of the larger public as a new factor that individuals must calibrate in composing speech, the court placed the responsibility for audience reception squarely on the speaking child.

The opinion declared that education was a training ground for citizenship, aligning its argument content with its form to emphasize the importance of paradigmatic examples. To reproduce polite civil citizens would require examples of traditional values in the classroom, because examples displayed in practice the abstract ideas and values of books: "The process of educating our youth for citizenship is not confined to books . . . schools must teach by example the shared values of a civilized social order." Replicating the discourse of character formation from the nineteenth-century cases, the opinion argued that "teachers—and indeed the older students—demonstrate the appropriate form of civil discourse and political expression by their conduct and deportment in and out of class. Inescapably, like parents, they are role models."[16] This strategy used the revival of tradition as a way to reconstitute the child-family-state triangle. It limited the *Barnette/Tinker* vocabularies of categorical equality for the child in the name of an imitative reproduction of citizen judgment.

The opinion used Fraser's performance to illustrate poor individual judgment. This approach constitutionalized civility as judgment about the use of particular public spaces and audiences. The record evidence authorizing the opinion's declaration of lewdness relied on the speech's reception. The "sexual innuendo . . . was plainly offensive to both teachers and students. . . . By glorifying male sexuality, and in its verbal content, the speech was acutely insulting to teenage girls. . . . The speech could well be seriously damaging to its less mature audience, many of whom were only 14. . . . Some students were reported as bewildered by the speech and the reaction of mimicry it provoked."[17] The opinion invoked past Supreme Court cases to advance its argument from tradition; these cases "acknowledged limitations on the otherwise absolute interest of the speaker in reaching an unlimited audience where the speech is sexually explicit and the audience may include children."[18] This approach made manifest what *Tinker* had left implicit: that judgment was partially a discipline of self-reflection that included the display of concern for and calibration of others hearing the speech. The discourse in *Fraser* altered *Tinker* by insisting that civility be a part of determining whether a speech was protected.

This discourse of tradition, civility, and rules inflected individual judgment with a conservative orientation toward hegemonic institutional politics. Perhaps most obviously, it punished expression about taboo topics. Its own paradigmatic example of civility was the halls of Congress. Justifying its appeal to rules-based habits, the opinion argued by analogy, observing that Congress staged "some of the most vigorous political debates in our society," and that "there are rules prohibiting the use of expressions offensive to other participants in the debate."[19] Congress prohibited impertinent speech and indecent language, while the Senate had in place rules that sanction speakers for "imputing improper motives to another Senator," or referring "offensively to any state."[20] The opinion then asked, "Can it be that what is proscribed in the halls of Congress is beyond the reach of school officials to regulate?"[21]

This embedded a stock psychological narrative about personhood in which rules disciplined emotions so that reasoned solutions to political problems would emerge (instead of violence). That narrative was consequential for individual judgment because the individual must recognize and comply with rules in order to keep conflict at bay. Procedural rules about communicative form ensured civility in political discussions. These rules disciplined communication, which was necessary because humans lack the ability to debate political issues organically without running the risk of offending others, disintegrating into violence, or reaching an unjust result.[22] The analogy first argued that Congress, as an ideal model of political discourse, required rules for sober liberal political discourse. It then extended the analogy to schools: because schools were traditionally a training ground for citizenship, these rules would be permissible in schools as a constitutional norm. This structure introduced a corrective to the development of judgment for citizenship. It now included the habit of taking others' comfort level with speech into account.

Expert Judgment: Performing Deference to Ideals

The *Fraser* majority opinion advanced the traditional argument that expert judgment deferred to the presumptively wise and democratic decision of others. The majority's language of prohibitions was bolstered by self-evidence: "Surely it is a highly appropriate function of public school education to prohibit the use of vulgar and offensive terms in public discourse. . . . Nothing in the Constitution prohibits the states from insisting that certain modes of expression are inappropriate and subject to sanctions. . . . The determination of what manner of speech in the classroom or in school assembly is inappropriate properly rests with the school board."[23] This argument framed democracy as a system to which the individual must conform. *Fraser* transformed expert judgment in two significant respects: it clothed its rationale for deference in a language of certitude, and it extended this certitude to support flexibility for administrators and bureaucrats. This frame legitimated a dangerous deference to state authorities.

First, the opinion performed a unitary interpretive practice at odds with the traditional argument for wise deference. Although the opinion's conclusion let the school's initial disciplinary decision stand, its interpretive practice exhibited tension with deference's stated virtues. Its style cultivated seemingly mandatory interpretations, with limited tolerance of viewpoint diversity for education's purpose, the meaning of Fraser's speech, the record evidence, and governing precedent. In all of these ways, even though the opinion did not contain a sustained meditation on the role of the judge, it expressed a closed vision of expertise harmful to diverse ideas and experimentation in developing civic virtue.

The opinion's performance of evidential assessment and the interpretation of precedent admit of no alternate interpretive conclusions. Burger's assessment of the record included no justification for the "lewd speech" rule itself, but only contained assertions about other students' reactions. The evidence—that fourteen-year-olds were "bewildered" by Fraser's speech; teenage girls were "acutely insulted"; teachers were "plainly offended"—accomplished a sense of dominant reception based on a questionable assessment of testimony. Most importantly, the opinion used this questionable evidence of reception as documentation of the speech's disruptive character.

The opinion extended that unitary approach to its deployment of precedent. It justified its interpretation of school action with reference to other cases that drew a distinction between the adult and the child. Even though the First Amendment's breadth was wide, the opinion posited that the "First Amendment guarantees wide freedom in matters of adult public discourse" and "the constitutional rights of students in public school are not coextensive with the rights of adults in other settings."[24]

According to this narrative, as they mature, adults develop capabilities to protect themselves against the harm they suffer as targets of lewd speech. This position admitted no opposition to the proposal that Fraser's speech was offensive, nor any alternative to censoring said speech. References to the judiciary's lack of expertise, the need for localities to experiment, and the need for citizens to develop independent thought were markedly absent.

Second, the opinion's model of expert deference emphasized administrative flexibility. This was made most clear in its due process section. Erwin Chemerinsky has argued that its most significant feature was its emphasis on "the need for judicial deference to the authority and expertise of school officials."[25] Continuing a trend first articulated in Justice Black's *Tinker* dissent and accelerated in *Parham*, *Fraser* enabled a nimble and vague administration with the authority to create its own reality by defining threatening speech. Quoting a recent case interpreting the Fourth Amendment in schools, the opinion highlighted a school's interest in "maintaining security and order," which "requires a certain degree of flexibility in school disciplinary procedures," and its "need to be able to impose . . . sanctions for a wide range of unanticipated conduct."[26]

This reasoning continued to defer to administrative experts to maintain order. Articulated in *Tinker* (Justice Black's dissent), *Ingraham*, and *Parham*, the *Fraser* opinion used the idea to analyze the fundamental fairness of the administrators' conduct. It was not used for its support of democratic choice but rather to shrink the state's responsibility to the individual. Good leaders, like administrators, plan ahead and earn deference. Distinguishing Fraser's speech from *Tinker*, Chief Justice Burger emphasized that there was a rule against the speech prior to its utterance. The regulation wasn't reactive to a fear. And Fraser was given "admonitions" by teachers "that his lewd speech could subject him to sanctions."[27]

Fraser allowed prohibitions on lewd speech. Instead of comparing the performances of strategic speakers with the fearful administration, the *Fraser* opinion highlighted the content of the speech as evidence of its character. Fraser's consultation with other teachers—typically a sign of wise judgment—was used to invalidate his constitutional claim. This conservative interpretation punished Fraser for failure to heed the advice of those with higher status. There was only unfounded fear in *Tinker*; here, the school used a disciplinary rule as the rationale for the suspension. The existence of the rule disarmed the argument that the administration was merely reacting to an exaggerated risk. The opinion granted the state great latitude to define its relationship to individuals, similar to the changed due process landscape. Since the presence of a rule justified later punishment, it was as if the administration's written declaration of risk (and its authority to punish) became evidence of such risk's probability.

Fraser shifted the emphasis of judgment's development from "preparing students for citizenship" to "prohibiting offensive terms in public discourse." The opinion's implicit pedagogy valued specific form, aversion to taboo content, and fidelity to institution over individual. It argued that even if Fraser could not predict that the "speech . . . would subject him to disciplinary sanctions," his suspension was lawful, "given the school's need to be able to impose disciplinary sanctions for a wide range of unanticipated conduct disruptive of the educational process."[28] This is expertise based on a hierarchy of preference, protecting a public sphere free of offensive content. In making that choice, *Fraser* also protected the administrators, educators, and state bureaucrats tasked with governing it. The dissent seized on this asymmetry, recasting the child-state relationship on the terms of the social contract.

Free Speech as a Committed Contract: Justice Stevens's Dissent

Justice Stevens argued that Fraser's punishment violated due process because he could not have anticipated it.[29] He argued that the rule was ambiguous, that Fraser would not have given the speech had he known of the punishment, that ambiguities should be resolved in favor of a robust First Amendment, and that the court should have deferred to the lower court's fact-finding because that court could better assess community standards. The opinion relied on a discourse of contractual fairness, blending expression with commitment. It resisted the majority's approach because it argued that *if* the state could foist an obligation on citizens to forecast the effects of one's speech on one's public, then the state was at least obligated to notify citizens of the consequences of failure. This discourse, while friendly to free speech, diverted attention from concerns of developing judgment capabilities such as independent thought and critique. It presumed the child to be a categorically equal speaker, appealing to the idea of the citizen and the state as rational parties dealing with each other at arm's length.

Justice Stevens's dissent did not focus on civility but rather analyzed the post hoc reasons given for punishing the speech at issue. This approach activated the discourse of fear used by *Meyer* (fear of an immediate threat was not sufficient to prohibit language instruction) and more prominently in *Tinker* (fear that war protest would cause violence was based in record evidence). It also evaded controversy about the speech's supposedly offensive content. Refusing the majority's discourse of civil traditions and rules, the dissent imagined how an individual would evaluate the school's justification. What distinguished sound individual judgment was that it offered intelligible justifications to individuals. Bethel High School had failed Fraser in this regard.

As an expert, Justice Stevens meticulously analyzed record evidence. Taking an approach like that of the *Tinker* majority, Stevens focused on aspects of the record that demonstrated Fraser's strategic conduct prior to the speech.

This differing starting point led Justice Stevens to assess different aspects of the case than examined in the majority opinion. He highlighted other record facts about Fraser in order to cast doubt on the majority's characterization of the speech's reception. Fraser's character showed some of the marks of a potential leader: He was "an outstanding young man with a fine academic record. . . . He was chosen by the student body to speak at the school's commencement exercises . . . he was respected by his peers."[30] According to this logic, Fraser "was probably in a better position to determine whether an audience of 600 of his contemporaries would be offended by the use of a four-letter word—or a sexual metaphor—than is a group of judges who are at least two generations and 3,000 miles away."[31]

Here Justice Stevens repurposed Justice Frankfurter's discourse of judicial restraint in order to justify protecting Fraser's citizenship rights. This expertise inverted Frankfurter's earlier rationales for judicial expertise. Where the *Fraser* majority adopted a unitary interpretive practice—the speech was lewd—to justify local governing authority, Justice Stevens's dissent deployed the discourse of restraint to cast doubt on the court's interpretation. The argument activated concerns that judges were too removed from the democratic process to review and invalidate legislation, and that the tools of the judiciary were too blunt to adequately respond to democratic problems. Justice Stevens used the court's distance from Fraser to argue that these same judges are detached not merely from the democratic process but from the social life of the public itself.

This strategy opened an avenue of attack: the *Fraser* majority inserted its own personal view about what is civil rather than an approach more in tune with the institutional capabilities of the court. Justice Stevens argued that this approach lacked precision: the more relevant question for the dissent was whether Fraser "should . . . be disciplined for speaking frankly in a school assembly if he had no reason to anticipate punitive consequences."[32] The majority was clouded by its own assessment of the speech rather than the perspective of Fraser's audience. Fraser's endorsement was frank speech offered to a receptive public.[33] Contrasting with Chief Justice Burger's pedagogy to "lead by example" with punishment, the dissent supported civil society's commitment to treat individual citizens fairly with clear consequences for actions. No matter what the judges or the school board thought of Fraser's speech after he gave it, he should not be disciplined if he had no reason to anticipate that this would be a consequence.

The dissent performed the objectivity expected of expert judges through its focus on record evidence. Fraser consulted three teachers in advance of his speech, and their warnings did not amount to an explicit notification of punishment. At Fraser's trial, one teacher did not testify; another admitted to telling Fraser that the speech would "raise eyebrows"; a third had told him that it was "inappropriate, and that he should probably not deliver it."[34] According to Justice Stevens, the review process signaled Fraser's thoughtfulness and a lack of reasonable notice that he would suffer suspension.

But . . . was Justice Stevens' analysis of Fraser's speech as "frank" off the mark? Was it speaking truth to power? Was it speaking in a manner that the audience may want to hear? Fraser's speech could be interpreted in both ways, and more. Was it a political endorsement phrased with a puerile double entendre for rhetorical effect? Was it a pretext to give a speech about sex? The speech escaped singular interpretations. There is a plausible case that the speech was political (because it endorsed a candidate), that it was "frank" (because it addressed sex in ways that were sincere to Fraser), and that it was rhetorical (because it displayed an attention to audience and frames oriented toward communicating a truth). Neither the majority opinion (which interpreted the speech as "lewd" without considering the political dimensions) nor Justice Stevens's dissent (which interpreted the speech as "frank" without considering that it was opaque and indirect) accounted for the variety of audiences, individuals, and interpretations of the speech. If citizenship rights depended on interpretations, whose interpretations and reactions should count? Surely Fraser's audience was not a monolith, and just as surely there were and are students who would view the speech as harassing.

The opinions in *Fraser* illustrated the way that the discourse of tradition both limited individual citizens' rights and compelled them to earn those rights through cognitive performances. The majority could not rely on direct precedent to deny child citizens the right to speak; it instead deployed tradition to limit the extension of those rights. At the level of civic practice, this meant a conservative mode of determining what kinds of political participation would count under the Constitution. Much like Justice Brennan's dissent in *Parham*, Justice Stevens's dissent failed to contest the basic factual premise (that civil speech is important), and instead relied on the absence of notice and the judiciary's inability to decide what is uncivil speech. The dissent also displaced the problem of differential capabilities, miscasting Fraser's speech as "telling it like it is." At the same time, it was unclear that "frank speech" was the proper political model for citizens. Given the history of the use of frank speech to marginalize minority groups, and the ways that internalizing fear of violating implicit speech codes can lead to self-censorship over important issues, the potential for *Fraser* to have a lasting impact as an example of proper political speech was dubious at best.[35]

Transitions: State Power, Tradition, and Performance Anxiety

These cases—*Ingraham, Parham,* and *Fraser*—were emblematic of a new model of addressing constitutional controversies about the child. Each opinion turned away from the constitutional emphasis on categorical equality and the presumption of the flourishing of the individual mind. In place of that model, these cases constituted a retrenchment of both organic institutions and traditional values. They emphasized particular instances of the incapable child as a reason that traditional governing practices (instead of constitutional guarantees) were required. The *Ingraham* plaintiffs were being punished for their inability to follow rules. The *Parham* plaintiffs were deemed incapable of making decisions in the first place. In *Fraser,* both the speaker and audience of Fraser's speech were incapable citizens: he was incapable of composing his speech in a sensitive manner and calibrating its reception, and his public was easily influenced and confused by the speech. This model was not a full restoration of the nineteenth-century approach to instilling virtue—such an approach was not appropriate to addressing the particular incapacities at issue in the cases examined in this chapter. Rather, these cases addressed exceptionally incapable citizens through community tradition as an acceptable response.

Nevertheless, this model limited the reach of citizens' categorical equality and reshaped the role of the judge as a steward of democratic values. *Ingraham* and *Parham* limited the reach of categorical equality when citizens defied authority or exceeded their ability to care for themselves. The limitation of citizens' interest in due process matters was extended by the Burger Court's argument for traditional civility in *Fraser*. That case oriented individual judgment toward traditional institutional participation. This statist conception implied a severe limit on the speaking subject. Parody, art, and self-expression unrelated to a political opinion were now potentially off the table as state-supported ends. Even some self-expression that *did* relate to a political opinion could be prohibited if it risked the offense of others. Individual judgment required the accurate assessment of speech reception. This assessment included each individual audience member's moral sensibilities. This vision of judgment was legitimated not in terms of empathy or ethics but in the language of power and mandate. Chief Justice Burger argued that civility was a democratic requirement, but the opinion justified state authority in the style of conservative tradition, positivism, and power. Fraser's speech was plainly "lewd" because the opinion termed it so, and the state had general authority to regulate lewd expression. Lewd speech reflected poor judgment: Congress could prohibit it;

the school had even wider latitude than Congress; therefore, the school could prohibit it.

These developments limited political participation to noncontroversial topics and unsophisticated speech styles. Crucially, *Fraser* neglected the discourse of persuasive communication from *Barnette* and *Tinker* that had grounded categorical equality. *Barnette* prohibited compelled speech in part because of a self-understanding that liberal democracy was a place where civic unity was produced through persuasion. The black armband in *Tinker* was "passive" and "pure speech," but the court used it as an example of a deliberate and sophisticated message that should not be censored by the undocumented fear of administrators. In *Fraser*, the child was no longer a youth of conscience imbricated in a family belief structure, arguing the courage of his or her convictions. He was skating the line of permissibility, drawing attention to himself, pushing boundaries, and daring the administration to act.

Concerning expert judgment, these transitional cases reverted to more implicit performances of expertise rather than explicit debates about a judge's appropriate interpretive role. This phenomenon did not deny that judges were tasked to protect individual rights. Instead, these cases suggested that longstanding and widely held values should be accorded more decision-making weight. That strategy activated a consistent discourse of judicial temporality—the perspective generated by the long view, which sees continuity and unity amid the local fractures of controversy. This approach framed the court's logic in its recurrent appeals to family, to public scrutiny of schools, to treating others civilly, and the like. These tropes placed faith in the wisdom of the people to resolve disputes. And they provoked a counterdiscourse that criticized their simplicity. If the role of the judicial expert was to produce accurate results through precise interpretations, vague references to values and presenting self-serving uses of history as legal evidence simply did not do that job. The Burger Court's traditionalism raised potential concerns (not yet expressed) that its representation of traditional values claimed to speak for more people than actually adhered to them.

In the meantime, the strategy shifted the argument for democratic deference in ways that created more distance between the constitutional judge and a democratic people. Although these majority opinions described deference to local governing entities as democratic, the relationship between deference and democratic choice was becoming more obscure. Deference in *Ingraham* and *Parham* meant deference to tradition and state bureaucracy, respectively—not to a law as the expression of the people's will. *Ingraham* expressed reverence for corporal punishment as a long and unbroken mode of discipline. In

Parham, the opinion paid tribute to the authority of family choice. But each opinion performed an interpretive practice that granted credence to state officials' self-assessment of their governing practices. *Fraser* made great legal significance out of the fact that the administration had a rule banning lewd speech. It also argued explicitly that administrators required flexibility in how they governed their institutions.

These discursive moves began to shift the social contract itself. The jurisprudence in these transitional cases maintained the child's identity as a nominal citizen. But the burden of performing one's entitlement to citizenship rights through cognitive displays of judgment allowed a bureaucratic logic to gain hold. Administrative rules signaled expectations for behavior. As citizens were entrusted with more rights, this trust signaled a renewed state authority embodied in administrative rules. The state was becoming more bureaucratic at a time when judges were limiting their roles to hold the state accountable. An increasingly conservative Supreme Court would accelerate the trend, remaking individual judgment as the assessment of risks and widening the state's authority by expanding its legitimate ends.

Part IV

The Child as Contractual Citizen

The liberal child's story began as that of a ward whose fortunes necessitated serious investment and justified state authority. Children could not consent. Since consent formed the ground of liberal constitutional democracy, it needed to be produced. This goal was akin to a mission. It seeped into popular literature and family practices, and served as a core purpose for educational institutions. It also legitimated custody and punishment. The child was stuck between parental prerogative and state authority. One side privileged liberty while the other had an interest in compelling obedience to prevent the greater harm of citizens who could not judge and whose poor decisions would menace the public sphere.

After the passage of the Fourteenth Amendment, it appeared that liberty had won out—at least for parents. The cases that sided with parents (*Meyer* and *Pierce*) did not develop consent and judgment for future citizens so much as preserve parental rights and economic property interests. The theory of liberal democracy that these cases advanced was a pluralism of individual choice. On this view, pluralism was a civic strength in the face of threats to the body politic—again, not threats to the development of consent and judgment capabilities but threats to a population bound by a common history (and racial heritage). Although these decisions stood fast against xenophobic policies, they continued to push the liberal child toward crisis—the pluralism it prized was that of individuals pursuing economic gain, and it was only a matter of time before the idea of individual liberty might be pushed to its outer bounds of inclusion.

That expansion happened during a time of extraordinary social instability marked by violence. The Supreme Court's *Barnette* decision marked a decisive turn to ground American liberal order in the free individual. Rather than producing citizens who were attached to an American creed through repetition, Justice Jackson advanced a vision of citizens bound by their individual capacities to judge and choose. As a result, the judiciary's role tilted from a self-conscious negotiation of its position relative to legislatures to that of protector of the rights-bearing individual. *Tinker* and *In re Gault* pushed this development further and emphasized aspects of the judicial method of expert judgment to justify the robust rights guarantors' new role. It seemed as if the liberal child would experience a time of continued growth.

The following decades ushered in a period of gradual decline in this trajectory. This phenomenon resulted from a combination of unfortunate facts, creative judges, and tenuous interpretations. Traditions such as civility and discipline informed these transitional decisions, which limited the child's rights of bodily freedom and speech. The decisions vindicated these traditions with reference to rules, regulations, and risks. The capability of consent was earned by a display of good judgment, but the state's responsibility was limited to rules-based justifications. In *Ingraham* and *Fraser*, these rules legitimated the decisions of individual administrators. *Parham* justified deference to a legislative process that, in the court's estimation, was the best that the state could do.

Perhaps most significantly, these decisions had reshaped the public character of citizenship and the social contract. Their mid-century articulation was premised on persuasion, meaningful political speech, and the virtues of judicial procedure. Cases from the ensuing transitional period reasserted countervailing concerns to temper these earlier premises. According to Chief Justice Burger's *Fraser* opinion, political persuasion required civility, and civility required rules. Justice Powell's opinion in *Ingraham* and Chief Justice Burger's opinion in *Parham* both observed the need to temper judicial procedure with the need to make governing decisions that respond to the contingencies of the time. Even though *In re Gault* emphasized the strengths of judicial procedure, these safeguards could prove burdensome. As *Ingraham* and *Parham* demonstrated, the court was unwilling to sacrifice traditional governance for those safeguards.

Still, it was not yet apparent whether these cases constituted a limit on the expansion of the child's citizenship or a reversal of the gains that had been achieved. Part 4 examines three cases that answered this question. It begins with *Hazelwood v. Kuhlmeier*, a case that evaluated a principal's decision to censor student-written articles from the school newspaper because of their controversial content. It then studies the tragic case of *DeShaney v. Winnebago County*, in which the court took up a severely abused child's claim that Winnebago County social workers bore responsibility for his injuries because they had failed to exercise judgment to remove him from the home. Finally, the chapter analyzes *Morse v. Frederick*, a case that passed judgment on a principal's decision to punish a student for displaying a banner at an off-campus school event celebrating the Olympic Torch Relay.

The main argument of part 4 is that these contemporary cases used the child to advance a comprehensive strategy of contractual citizenship. Its contours borrowed from prior models. It posited the categorical equality of the child, emphasized the importance of judicial process, and related the performance of judicial process to respect for democracy. But the Supreme Court reinvented these argumentative elements to formulate its strategy. The categorical equality of the child was used to justify risks—since the child was a citizen just like everyone else, the child had to act as responsibly as others. The state and the individuals involved in these cases were parties to a contract, and the terms of that contract were found in the documents that governed the relationship—including student handbooks and disciplinary rules. The judicial role still mattered. Where past strategies had relied on traditions to develop a vision of a rounded individual citizen, the contractual citizenship model rooted judicial expertise in hierarchical interpretive practices. Practically, this meant beginning with the Constitution and then distilling and synthesizing precedents with a judicial philosophy wedded to clarity. Where ambiguities arose, judges construed them in favor of the state; the strategy disavowed any state obligation to develop the child's citizenship capabilities. Finally, the strategy authorized itself as the only option for a constitutional democracy. The contractual citizenship advanced in the cases that this chapter studies grounded democracy in the predictability of texts and appeals to abstract democratic interests detached from citizens' practical concerns for self-government.

These features shaped the legal identities of children as citizens, and those identities in turn influenced contemporary understandings of the social contract between state and citizen. The implications are as follows. The Supreme Court's new strategy shifted responsibilities onto the liberal individual under the guise of long-standing democratic tradition and rigorous judicial practice. At the same time, the decisions' justifications authorized an expansion of state authority. For individual judgment, these cases used the categorical equality of the child to justify the responsibility to protect oneself from risk, to downplay the state's obligation to protect the child, and to ignore the state's duty to develop judgment capabilities in citizens. For expert judgment, these opinions fragmented the court's prior cases into a multiplicity of doctrinal lines and fact patterns, expanding the description of the state's interests in its authority. The court's interpretive practices have highlighted the challenges to a shared liberal tradition more than revived a common civic mission, leaving the liberal project with an uncertain future.

9

LIMITED STATE OBLIGATIONS

Hazelwood et al. v. Kuhlmeier

Hazelwood East High School in Hazelwood, Missouri, had a school newspaper called *Spectrum*. Hazelwood East staffed the paper with students enrolled in a journalism class, whose teacher supervised the paper's content and production. In spring of 1983, *Spectrum* ran into a problem that pitted its journalism students against the school administration. That year, the journalism teacher left his job just a few weeks before the scheduled release date of a *Spectrum* issue. His replacement stepped in mid-cycle and submitted page proofs to Principal Robert Reynolds for review prior to publication.[1]

Principal Reynolds didn't care for two of the articles. One of them "described three Hazelwood East students' experiences with pregnancy" and another "discussed the impact of divorce on students at the school."[2] According to the court's opinion, Principal Reynolds objected to these stories' journalistic integrity. He worried that readers would be able to identify the pregnant girls, even though false names were used in the story. He didn't agree that students should be exposed to that story's references to birth control and sex. The divorce story concerned him because its student-author did not offer her parents the opportunity to either respond or to consent to its publication.[3]

Because only three days remained before the scheduled press run, Reynolds decided there was no time to make changes to the stories. He believed that his choices were to either eliminate the two pages of the newspaper dedicated to them or to eliminate the entire edition of *Spectrum*. He chose the former. The students who worked on the stories filed a lawsuit, claiming that Reynolds's act violated their First Amendment rights. After a bench trial, the district court found that no First Amendment violation had occurred. The students appealed to the Eighth Circuit. The Eighth Circuit panel reversed the district court's decision. Relying on *Tinker*, it noted the importance of *Spectrum* as a public forum, a "part of the school adopted curriculum" that was "intended to be and operated as a conduit for student viewpoint."[4] The Eighth Circuit was skeptical that the articles "would have materially disrupted classwork or given rise to substantial disorder in the school."[5] The Eighth Circuit panel reasoned that because the articles did not expose the school to liability—meaning that the subjects could not recover for any damage done by the stories—Principal Reynolds's "journalistic integrity" justification violated the students' First Amendment rights.

The Supreme Court reversed the court of appeals decision in an opinion by Justice White.[6] Justice Brennan filed a dissent, joined by Justices Blackmun and Marshall. Justice White's majority reasoned that the child's First Amendment rights were subject to the special characteristics of the school setting. Because the school provided the platform for speech, it could regulate that speech in a way consistent with its mission as the school determined it. So even if a school had little latitude to restrict expression on the general grounds of the school, it had greater authority to do so where these restrictions were "reasonably related to legitimate pedagogical concerns."[7]

Hazelwood continued the dialectical development of a recent tension between individual speech and audience incapacity to comprehend it. *Fraser* had introduced rules of civility as a theme through which taboo topics could be controlled under the guise of noncompliance with rules. Like *Fraser*, the articles in *Hazelwood* included discussion of taboo topics such as sex, pregnancy, divorce, and family matters. Unlike *Fraser*, the form of the speech and its place in the school were markedly different. These students were participating in professional training in journalism, and the product was a part of the curriculum. They were learning how to investigate and compose stories of public interest.

Justice White's majority opinion shaped the meaning of citizen judgment as the capability to parse bureaucratic rules. First, it highlighted a discourse of state control of dangerous speech by synthesizing past precedent. This choice emphasized tradition in discussing *Tinker* and *Fraser*. This reframing permitted state control of citizen speech when the state has designed a special purpose for a public space.[8] Second, the opinion introduced a discourse of reciprocity, further deepening the connection between contract principles and citizenship rights. The opinion argued from the doctrine that the paper was not a "public forum," resisting the discourse of the state's obligation to develop citizenship. This approach prefigured speech by contract principles: that is, whether the school honored its own promises when it removed the articles from the newspaper. Such a discourse reshaped the relationship between state and citizen, introducing a distinction between the *obligation to tolerate personal viewpoints* and a *refusal to promote viewpoints* on a state-run platform. It also altered the kinds of citizenship capabilities that the Constitution implicitly valued. *Hazel-*

wood accelerated *Fraser's* discourse of state control by stripping down the obligations the state owed to its citizens. The citizen now needed the capacity to decipher increasingly complex and poorly circulated promises, and those (potentially self-serving) declarations set the terms for whether citizen speech was calibrated accordingly. Sound citizen judgment now conformed to the status quo on the state's terms.[9] The result devalued individual thought and the introduction of different perspectives. It also entrenched a state that prioritized self-protection, abrogating its obligations to develop forward-thinking citizens.

State Control of Dangerous Speech: Tradition Over Precedent

The *Hazelwood* opinion synthesized *Tinker* and *Fraser* into a new rule that limited the child's First Amendment right, focusing on the school's authority to control the curriculum. It relied on a discourse of novelty to creatively apply past precedent to the distinct facts of the case. It emphasized a tension between *Tinker* and *Fraser*, downplaying *Tinker's* commitment to citizens' right to free expression—and that opinion's dismissal of administrative fear as a reason to limit citizen speech. Instead, the opinion construed *Tinker's* facts narrowly, characterizing the students' antiwar protest as "merely . . . expressing their personal views on the school premises."[10] Against that seemingly limited right, the opinion noted *Fraser's* emphasis on the school's power to determine the speech appropriate to its educational mission. This synthesis shifted the practice of judicial expertise from a precedent to tradition. Excising any trace of *Tinker's* radical political significance in the progression of speech rights that travel with students across physical spaces and institutions ("in the cafeteria, on the playing field, or on the campus"), Justice White's description of that case recoded past precedent, endorsing a mode of judgment that understands governing structures as systems with distinct functions to limit to individual expression.

The enduring theme of childhood exceptionalism supported the reversion to respect for authority. The opinion exploited language from *Tinker* that acknowledged the "special characteristics" of the school, arguing that *Fraser* had interpreted that language to include the interest of the school in rejecting "student speech that is 'inconsistent with its basic educational mission' . . . even though the government could not censor similar speech outside the school." This description included the discourse of deference to administrator motive and belief, sacrificing concerns about citizens' free expression and its differing contexts because "the determination of what manner of speech in the classroom or in school assembly is inappropriate properly rests with the school board . . . rather than with the federal courts."[11] The synthesis activated a theory of government that respects local decision-making bodies, evoking Frankfurter's dissent in *Barnette* and Black's in *Tinker*.

This discourse deflected *Tinker*'s rejection of undifferentiated fear as a basis for restricting citizens' rights to speak. The opinion appealed to a public with the cognitive ability to consider local administrative reaction before participating in political speech. It also prioritized institutional fidelity to its own public commitments over an independent evaluation of their representative quality. Framed as a mere extension of *Tinker*'s logic, the opinion's interpretive gloss endorsed a citizen who could cognitively obey a chain of command: administrators had power to decide the institution's mission and to determine which speech damages or threatens that mission. This approach excluded from sound judgment speech that critiques the institutional mission. The school communicated its mission partially through punishing such speech. *Hazelwood* reintroduced fear as a legitimate motive for regulating citizens' political participation.

Citizenship: The Social Contract Atrophies

The opinion introduced a discourse of thin reciprocity between citizen and state through a doctrinal argument about whether the paper was a "public forum." This move allowed the opinion to strip the state's obligation to the individual down to mere conformity with its own promises. White employed the doctrine as an analytical gatekeeper determining whether the school's decision would trigger strict judicial scrutiny or deference. The doctrine's roots stretch back to *Hague v. CIO*; it holds that the state can restrict speech based on content to public space and political participation: "Streets and parks . . . have immemorially been held in trust for the use of the public and, time out of mind, have been used for purposes of assembly, communicating thoughts between citizens, and discussing public questions. Such use of the streets and public places has, from ancient times, been a part of the privileges, immunities, rights, and liberties of citizens."[12]

This public forum analysis placed administrators on one side of an implied contract that granted them control over public space. It shifted the analytical focus from speaker-speech-character to the state's concern about the character of the institution. Because schools were not like streets and parks, they were subject to different scrutiny. This strategy shifted the analysis from an independent judicial examination of the speech's consistency with curriculum to a deference to the local administrator's decision that censorship was consistent with public statements it had already made about *Spectrum*'s purpose. Correspondingly, the capability for citizenship moves from individual expression and development of the free mind to the ability to read the terms of the social contract governing the relationship between citizen and state relationship.

The strategy subverted speech rights to contract rights by recasting the issue in terms of what the state has promised to provide in a zone of public space. The opinion found that *Spectrum* was not a public forum because the school didn't call it one: a forum is only public if school authorities have "opened those facilities 'for indiscriminate use by the general public,' . . . or by some segment of the public, such as student organizations. . . . If the facilities have instead been reserved for other intended purposes, 'communicative or otherwise,' then no public forum has been created."[13] This approach used the discourse of child exceptionalism to confer legitimacy on institutional protocols. Because the child's rights were not coextensive with the rights of adult citizens, school administrators could decide their scope. This argument implied a cognitive capability of citizenship to decipher content from form, and grasp state articulations of a platform's purposes. The less capable citizen could share personal views, but a full citizen-subject must differentiate individual views from the platform.

The argument authorized bureaucratic deference as an essential aspect of the social contract. The opinion diverted the narrative focus from the free speech value of the *Spectrum* articles to the conditions that Hazelwood East's school officials placed on the speech. As the focus of speech and speaker changed, so did the cognitive criteria for evaluation. Consistency with prior statement became more important because it served as a proxy for fair warning to speakers. The relationship between citizen and state had shifted from a vocabulary of individual character and rights to a vocabulary of agents and authority. The school newspaper was a place for professional skills, not personal expression. The Hazelwood East Curriculum Guide described the Journalism II course as a vehicle for developing "journalistic skills": "a laboratory situation in which the students publish the school newspaper applying skills they have learned in Journalism I. . . . School officials did not deviate in practice from their policy that production of *Spectrum* was to be part of the educational curriculum."[14] Hazelwood administrators controlled the forum, selecting editors and publication dates, the number and types of stories, and reserving the principal's right to review the final product prior to publication.[15] The school's control over student speech was the performance of a promise, not a disturbing fact. This description imbued the administrators' management techniques with a sense of fairness, constitutionalizing their power to define the expectations of participating individuals.

The opinion downplayed citizens' aspiration for change and praised realistic expectations. The *Spectrum*'s Statement of Policy must be "understood in the context of the paper's role in the school curriculum";[16] moreover, it merely stood for the proposition that "the administration will not interfere with the students' exercise of those First Amendment rights that attend the publication of a school-sponsored newspaper."[17] Expectation conferred legitimacy on the school's action. As long as the school did not violate the precepts of its own statements of purpose, it could censor student speech. This approach devalued any independent interest in developing the individual judgment to evaluate difficult public topics, and limited individuals' ability to engage in deliberative practices when they run contrary to the state's own declared interests.

The State Personified: Tolerating Others, Promoting Oneself

Cumulatively, the opinion's strategy created a constitutionally significant state interest in what contemporary culture might understand as brand management. This interest distinguished between state toleration and promotion of speech. It appeared neutral, preserving the appearance of public fairness, yet remained detached from a public good. It applied to "educators' authority over school-sponsored publications . . . that students, parents, and members of the public might reasonably perceive to bear the imprimatur of the school."[18] Resisting the discourse in *Barnette* and *Tinker* of toleration as a way to build civic unity through risky speech, the *Hazelwood* opinion emphasized the "special role" of educational institutions in community life as a marriage of local democracy with bureaucratic regulation. This new standard "is consistent with our oft-expressed view that the education of the Nation's youth is primarily the responsibility of parents, teachers, and state and local officials, and not of federal judges."[19] It argued that school boards and principals were more attuned to the local community and were better situated to make decisions about its formation.

Appealing to tropes of the now-familiar childhood lost, the opinion emphasized the importance of innocent children. Administrators could now invoke less capable citizens as a reason to be concerned with how the school broadcast its own values. The school could remove an article about teen pregnancy, because the article was "presumably taken home to be read by students' even younger brothers and sisters."[20] A divorce article could be purged, because "an individual publicly identified as an inattentive parent . . . was entitled to an opportunity to defend himself as a matter of journalistic fairness."[21] What began as a material distinction between toleration and promotion of particular messages became a constitutional sanction for state brand management. It elevated the state's interest in preserving a particular image in the eyes of unnamed third parties to justify limits on active citizen participation. It prioritized the state's consistency with its own statements over its substantive obligations. Where *Barnette* emphasized the development of free thought, Justice White's future citizen must prepare for an adversarial world in which the state defined its own commitments and the individual citizen must grasp those detailed rules and commitments in order to claim the right to speak. *Hazelwood* implicitly endorsed a relationship between citizen and state in which community values were declared and speech that countered those values was cleansed from the public sphere.[22]

The opinion created its authority through a central irony. It subverted the value of individual judgment to local community values, yet presumed a citizen savvy enough to weed through a maze of regulations to calibrate acceptable speech. Much like the school administration could create its purposes and obligations in establishing a newspaper, the court clarified to litigants the purposes and obligations of its prior statements of constitutional law. The opinion remade *Tinker* into a reservoir of judicial discretion to make other decisions for cases that did not fall within the scope of its narrowly construed promise. This strategy reconstituted a conflict between the categorically equal citizen and the smooth function of the state. Dangerous speech could have a substantial impact on the school's mission. The decision expanded the state's authority to regulate such speech and granted the state the authority to define its purposes in self-serving ways. The case also redefined citizenship as conformity to the state's image of itself.

A Relational Social Contract: Justice Brennan's Dissent

Justice Brennan's dissent argued that Principal Reynolds's act was unconstitutional censorship. The student articles did not "disrupt the classroom [or invade] the rights of others,"[23] and so were protected under the First Amendment. The dissent criticized the majority for seeming to limit *Tinker* rather than applying it. It characterized the majority opinion's rationales as a "tangle of excuses," arguing that the majority "denude[d] high school students of much of the First Amendment protection that *Tinker* itself provide[d]."[24] The metaphor performed the critique of the school district's decision through its critique of the majority opinion—a post hoc justification that engineered a result instead of a thought-out defense of community values.

This strategy exploited the majority's neglect of civic practices. Where the majority opinion emphasized administrative authority, the dissent counterposed the need to form a strong community. The dissent advanced this argument in two ways. First, it relied on a vision of individual judgment as the critical capability to take on a different perspective. This vision repaired the type of contractual relationship advanced by the majority opinion, emphasizing citizens' expectations instead of administrative control. Second, the dissent occupied a space in between the doctrinal formalism of Justice White's opinion and the principles of the categorical equality model advanced by earlier cases. This prudence appealed to traditional values and historical precedent, reintroducing the discourse about longer time horizons to generate a fuller sense of civic values.

First, the dissent began with the imagined viewpoint of the students in order to portray them as having exercised sound judgment based on their expectations: "When the young men and women of Hazelwood East High School registered for Journalism II, they expected a civics lesson."[25] This maneuver suggested an alternate standard of judgment for the case, focusing on the decision's effects on students' preparation for citizenship. The dissent imagined that the state took on explicit commitments to the greater public good. Guarantees, broken promises, and expectations described the case, evidence of the school board's flawed commitment to a free press: "The Hazelwood East administration breached its own promise, dashing its students' expectations."[26] Moving from broken promise to illegitimate motive, Justice Brennan wrote that Reynolds did not remove the articles from the *Spectrum* "because any of the articles would 'materially and substantially interfere with the requirements of appropriate discipline,' but simply because he considered two of the six 'inappropriate, personal, sensitive, and unsuitable' for student consumption."[27] The majority misunderstood the function of the First Amendment in the educational public sphere—personal sensitivity to a viewpoint was not grounds for curbing viewpoint diversity.

Second, Justice Brennan performed judicial expertise in maintaining this contractual vision through his interpretive style. The dissent framed the majority opinion as a radical departure from tradition, because of its departure from relevant precedent. Reading precedent—including *Brown v. Board of Ed.* and *Ambach v. Norwick* (which upheld a New York law that required noncitizen teachers to manifest an intention to apply for citizenship as a condition for permanent licensure)—to unite around public education's role in developing civic values, this style of judgment contrasted sharply with Justice White's structure of doctrinal application.[28] Where the majority proceeded doctrinally in order to justify a host of inexorable conclusions (and preferred values), the dissent invoked a set of like cases that coalesced around the theme of relating education to the training of citizens. The performance established the dissent's authority through the unifying principle of a traditional theme (citizenship) rather than a deferential principle.

The reference to *Brown* resisted the majority's discourse of local community values that were not worth preserving (and may bear a mark of shame). Having established the moral case for change, the dissent then cited the court's long history of acknowledging the role of educational institutions to prepare individuals for participation in a complex democratic society. This society prized open information, citizen contribution, and leadership. The ideal citizen would judge with one eye on the dynamism of history, maintaining the ever-present possibility of change. This citizen's continued renewal depended on a vigorous First Amendment in school.

The dissent used this discourse of citizenship to resist the idea that educators deserved deference. The importance of the public educator's role required exacting scrutiny. This argument created a homology between the sophisticated pedagogy of a school administrator and the good judge's ability to decide a case. The public educator's job "demands particularized and supremely subjective choices among diverse curricula, moral values, and political stances to teach or inculcate in students, and among various methodologies for doing so."[29] The majority's theme of deference to administrators imagined a monolithic state eliminating speech for "mere incompatibility with the school's pedagogical message."[30] This kind of social contract ran counter to the concerns of citizenship, which argued that the state must commit to modes of instruction that teach future citizens to discriminate between their own views and views that diverge from their own perspective.

The dissent appealed to the cognitive capability of critique, itself performing this capability by critically questioning the majority's parsing of *Tinker*. The majority perverted *Tinker* to create "a taxonomy of school censorship, concluding that [it] applie[d] to one category and not another."[31] In its place, the dissent served a social contract that prohibited active resistance to a core curriculum but supported dialogical questioning. A "young polemic" who "deliver[s] an eloquent political diatribe" in calculus class would be prohibited, but a "student who responds to a political science teacher's question with the retort, 'socialism is good'" may be acceptable. The latter contradicts the school's message "without directly interfering with the school's expression" of that message.[32]

The dissent's critical questioning was democratic because it held authority publicly accountable. The opinion enacted this strategy by dissecting the majority's "tangle of excuses." None of the excuses held up under questioning. The first was a pedagogical justification. But Justice Brennan skeptically observed that "the principal never consulted the students before censoring their work. . . . Further, he explained the deletions only in the broadest of generalities."[33] This tactic appealed to advanced modes of procedural judgment—it insisted on consistency, precision, and a validating process. It held the principal's justification to the record evidence and a standard of citizenship that expected administrators to be specific and collaborative. The school's responsibility was to reproduce common values not only as administrators see them but as they were developed with engaged students.

The majority's second excuse was to shield "an impressionable high school audience from material whose substance is 'unsuitable for immature audiences.'"[34] But this justification could easily become cover for schools policing students' thoughts. The dissent here criticized a relationship between citizen and state that made itself unaccountable for anything outside of itself. Rather, the state should bear an obligation to perpetuate a liberal community grounded in students' critical participation in their own leadership preparation. The last excuse was one of viewpoint confusion: that someone may confuse a student article with the administration's opinion. In dismissing this excuse, the dissent took issue with the state's means of redress. It could have issued a disclaimer, a clarifying statement, or rebuttal. Instead, the "Court approve[d] of brutal censorship," instead of "acknowledging the less oppressive alternatives."[35]

Hazelwood demonstrated an important contrast in views about judgment appropriate to the liberal social contract. Justice White's contract model demoted the educational institution from its perch as preparer of citizens to just another state-created institution. What this choice gained in objectivity and neutrality it lost in value. The state owned this public space, and its public commitments framed the terms of its power in schools. So long as the state discharged the obligations it had agreed to undertake, it owed the individual nothing more. Justice Brennan's dissent reminded us that any liberal public entails an element of imagination about its citizens as end products. He offered an alternative vision for this larger purpose—the free-thinking citizen, asking critical questions, exercising judgment linked to functions, and seeking diversity of opinion at the level of individual experience.

Hazelwood, like *Tinker* and *Fraser*, began with the structuring question of appropriate public sphere topics in order to produce meaning for a citizen's right to speak. *Hazelwood* coded this constitutive problem of disagreement regarding topical inclusion, endorsing a relationship between citizen and state that punished the offending speaker in order to restore civil communication (like *Fraser*). Second, *Hazelwood* continued to diminish the state's civic responsibility to include only the protection of those deemed less capable. Because *Fraser* raised due process concerns, the question of the child's free speech became linked to the state's obligations to the speaker to notify them of the rules. *Hazelwood* clarified that the state doesn't owe the speaker much beyond what it has stated that it will take on.[36] Finally, a new interest in message management assumed constitutional significance. *Hazelwood* extended *Fraser*'s interest in rules-driven civility to include a state interest in a monolithic message free of audience confusion. This interest emphasized strategy over ethics, elevating a school's reputation over its curricular mission. Now severed from any common mission but empowered to define the mission and silence different perspectives, these decisions shifted what it meant to be a citizen by granting to the state the ability to limit political participation, and by supporting a narrow view of traditional values as the goal of citizenship development.

This refigured relationship provoked the court into drawing additional distinctions depending on the physical place of the speech—out of class but on campus, as a part of the curriculum, in an auditorium. At the same time, the social contract logic expanded state authority. In a sense, these developments can be seen as part of a dialectical relationship instead of a conservative retrenchment: after all, if the child was a categorically equal citizen, on what grounds could these citizens argue that the state needed to treat them in a manner more solicitous of their needs than the arms-length treatment every citizen expects? How far would the court be willing to go to entertain that description, and with what consequences? Just how free and equal was the child, and how responsible would the state be for its well-being? In order to fill the composite out, we must shift gears, to a tragic case of abuse.

10

THE IMPOVERISHED SOCIAL CONTRACT

DeShaney v. Winnebago County DSS

Joshua DeShaney was born in 1979. His parents divorced (in Wyoming) and his father, Randy DeShaney, was granted custody in 1980. Randy and Joshua moved to Winnebago County, Wisconsin. Randy abused Joshua severely. In 1983 there was a police report of child abuse and Joshua was taken to the hospital. The Department of Social Services of Winnebago County obtained a court order for custody of Joshua and formed a child protection team. After three days in the hospital, Joshua was released back into his father's custody under the condition that he permit periodic DSS visits. DSS workers recorded their suspicions of child abuse frequently on these visits. A few times the DSS worker was told that Joshua was sick and could not be seen. "I just knew the phone would ring some day and Joshua would be dead," is a quote attributed to Ann Kemmeter, a social worker assigned to Joshua's case.

In 1984 Randy DeShaney took Joshua to the hospital, claiming that he had fallen down the stairs. In fact he had been severely beaten, as a result of which he fell into a coma. The surgeons who operated on Joshua found evidence of brain hemorrhages indicative of continued severe head trauma. It was expected that Joshua would be incapable of living an independent life. His father served two years in prison for child abuse. Joshua's mother brought a lawsuit on Joshua's behalf, alleging that the state had deprived Joshua of his constitutional rights without due process of law. She claimed that the state violated Joshua's due process rights when it failed to intervene to stop the abuse, because Joshua had a liberty interest in his bodily integrity. The district court dismissed her claims at the summary judgment stage, and the court of appeals affirmed that decision. The Supreme Court took the case because of inconsistent applications of legal doctrine and because of the "importance of the issue of the administration of state and local governments."[1]

The Supreme Court ruled against Joshua. Chief Justice William Rehnquist wrote the majority opinion, which held that the Fourteenth Amendment provided Joshua no avenue for recovery because it did not obligate the state to protect him from the actions of private parties.[2] Justice Brennan dissented, arguing that the majority focused on what the state did not do instead of focusing on the state's attempts to protect Joshua. For Justice Brennan, that latter perspective meant that Joshua should have been allowed the opportunity to demonstrate that the state's failure to help him "arose, not out of the sound exercise of professional judgment . . . but from the kind of arbitrariness that we have in the past condemned."[3] Finally, Justice Blackmun issued a separate dissent lamenting the majority's embodiment of the "dispassionate oracle of the law."[4] Justice Blackmun exhorted the court to take up an alternate reading of the Fourteenth Amendment, "which comports with dictates of fundamental justice and recognizes that compassion need not be exiled from the province of judging."[5]

DeShaney reconfigured the role of the judge through the characterization of the incapable child.[6] Justice Rehnquist's majority opinion authorized judicial expertise through interpretations that favored clear and unequivocal rules. The opinion viewed Joshua as a categorically equal and free individual, and it used that discourse to advance a limited state obligation through a limited practice of textual interpretation. In contrast, Justice Blackmun's dissent argued that the good expert judge pursued justice, and that pursuit of necessity required an acknowledgment of human emotional connection to those before the judge. Justice Blackmun's dissent emphasized Joshua's lack of capabilities and autonomy. His arguments, like Justice Brennan's reasoning in *Hazelwood*, activated prudential concerns of history as a way to capture values that were relevant to the contextual relationship between citizen and state, but which had evaded the strictures of the majority's textual interpretation.[7]

Free Individuals and Minimal State Responsibilities

The majority opinion subtly prioritized an ideology to insure the state against risk for harm deemed private. It accomplished this through three primary strategies. First, it framed the legal question and relevant facts from the perspective of the state DSS. This strategy activated a discourse of pragmatic governance, which amplified a concern for interpretive clarity and certainty about the bounds of the law. Clarity became the most important function for judicial expertise. Second, it illustrated this expert practice through performance, using an interpretive method wedded to a primary text, construed narrowly. Finally, it deployed a discourse of democracy as a broad system, arguing that the particular incapable child in front of the court was a form of constitutional sacrifice, the political price to pay for the general good of certain, confident administration of government.

First, the opinion framed the legal question and the case's facts in order to amplify the concerns of the state. This general strategy—a declarative tone deployed to focus on a particular perspective as if that perspective were neutral—is not specific to this line of cases but has been deployed in them to great ideological effect for constructing meaning in the citizen-state relationship. Justice Jackson's decision to take the perspective of an individual student speaker in *Barnette,* Justice Fortas's decision to do the same in *Tinker,* Justice Black's concern for teacher liability in his *Tinker* dissent, and Justice Burger's affirmation of the good faith of parents in *Parham* each prefigured specific legal conclusions that advanced particular ideas about capabilities for judgment and speech.

Here, the opinion advanced the state's perspective. Similar to Justice Burger's *Parham* strategy, it emphasized nonstate actors as the cause of Joshua's permanent lack of capabilities. Joshua's father was the bad actor. After receiving notice from Joshua's stepmother that his father was abusing him, the county's department of social services "interviewed the father, but he denied the accusations, and DDS did not pursue them further."[8] When, a year later, Joshua was admitted to the hospital with bruising, a doctor suspected abuse and again notified DDS. DDS "immediately obtained an order . . . placing Joshua in the temporary custody of the hospital. Three days later, the county convened a 'Child Protection Team'—consisting of a pediatrician, a psychologist, a police detective, the county's lawyer, several DDS caseworkers, and various hospital personnel—to consider Joshua's situation."[9] The team recommended that Joshua enroll in preschool, that his father receive counseling, and that his girlfriend (by this time he was divorced from Joshua's stepmother) move out.[10]

These facts prefigured the constitutional question. Justice Rehnquist emphasized a locus-of-injury perspective, which obscured Joshua's position in the social arrangement. Joshua was a citizen without a choice: it didn't matter whether his father or the state was the immediate locus of his injuries, because he could not free himself from either party and had neither the standing nor cognitive ability to challenge his condition and improve it. For the majority, focusing on DSS's conduct helped advance a different narrative that emphasized Joshua's father as his abuser and the state as responsive to Joshua's plight. This discourse of responsibility, present in *Parham* as a mode of framing the state as doing the best that it can with limited resources, helped to shift the focus away from Joshua's injuries, and onto the injuries that the state may suffer if saddled with constitutional liability.

Administration and state power were the court's institutional motives for deciding the case, and the starting point for its legal analysis. The court's task was to determine "when, if ever, the failure of a state or local governmental entity or its agents to provide an individual with adequate protective services constitutes a violation of the individual's due process rights."[11] Cuing the theme from the pledge cases and *Ingraham* that democracy is a system that functions according to rules, the opinion emphasized interpretations that produced clear meaning. Judicial expertise required clear interpretations to fulfill the judiciary's democratic function, because ambiguous terms yielded uncertainty around legal risks and impeded governmental action (for fear of liability). The opinion used the discourse of categorical equality to create the fiction that Joshua was as free and capable as every other citizen. Certainty mattered. Administrators needed to know the bounds of the law so that they could follow it. This theme—that textual clarity aided practical governance—incorporated a longer tradition of judicial restraint echoed in past cases concerning the child. It motivated Justice Frankfurter's *Barnette* dissent, which advocated for restrictive standards for legislative review. It animated Justice Black's fear in his *Tinker* dissent that children would use the threat of frivolous lawsuits to seize control of schools from frightened administrators. It also justified Chief Justice Burger's majority opinion in *Parham*, which deferred to the state of Georgia's budgetary provisions. *DeShaney* shifted the constitutional narrative by juxtaposing the categorical equality discourse with concerns about deferential pragmatism.

The opinion illustrated how its method of textual interpretation could resolve constitutional controversies through a clear rule. Chief Justice Rehnquist quoted the text of the Due Process Clause and then argued that "nothing in the language of the . . . clause itself requires the State to protect the life, liberty, and property of its citizens against invasion by private actors."[12] The textual argument was inflected with a parsimonious style that informed the interpretive practice.[13] It invested in intention, assuming that clause drafters would have mentioned such an obligation if they intended one.[14] Absence of evidence was evidence of absence.

The opinion then generalized the claim with a discourse of history and tradition. This connection posed the interpretive practice as an antidote to anxiety about state risk exposure for private harms. Chief Justice Rehnquist cited three recent cases to support his argument that the clause's "purpose was to protect the people from the State, not to ensure that the State protected them from each other. The Framers were content to leave the extent of governmental obligation in the latter area to the democratic political processes."[15] This style claimed to be practical for reasons opposed to the particular circumstances of the case. Relying on discourse similar to that found in *Ingraham*—leave it to the political process if the people wish to prevent these harms—the opinion's chief concern was that states would be able to predict their own liability exposure for constitutional injuries.

The opinion extended this style in interpreting Joshua's claim as exceptional. After dismissing the claim that the Due Process Clause obligated the state to "provide the general public with protective services," the opinion considered the argument that the state and Joshua had a special relationship because the state "specifically proclaimed, by word and deed, its intention to protect [Joshua] against th[e] danger [of abuse]."[16]

The opinion expressed a restrictive attitude toward exceptions to restrictive rules. Reviewing the precedent cases that had established the "special relationship" exception, it seized on the particulars of those cases to bar recovery because those particulars were not present in *DeShaney*. State force of restraint was the marker of a constitutional relationship. *Estelle v. Gamble* recognized a duty to provide medical care, "because the prisoner is unable, 'by reason of the deprivation of liberty [to] care for himself.'"[17] *Youngberg v. Romeo* extended this duty to the care of "involuntarily committed mental patients" under a "lesser includes the greater" logic. If the state couldn't hold convicted criminals in an unsafe condition then it couldn't do so for those involuntarily committed to hospitals "who may not be punished at all."[18]

This construction of precedent narrowed the doctrine's applicability. It aligned expertise with an exacting attitude of clarity and precision. The opinions implied that DeShaney's argument rested on a mistaken and careless understanding of those cases: "Taken together, they stand only for the proposition that, when the State takes a person into its custody and holds him there against his will, the Constitution imposes upon it a corresponding duty to assume some responsibility for his safety and general wellbeing."[19] Ideologically, the practice resolved the recurrent crisis of the child by managing state risks, articulating "state custody" as a metonym for past cases and a limiting principle for future ones.

The opinion's perspective cared not about justice but about predictable rules. Categorical pronouncements worked best for this goal, because they portrayed DeShaney's claim as exceptional, and hence, unpredictable. The state's "affirmative duty to protect arises not from . . . knowledge of the individual's predicament or from its expressions of intent to help . . . but from the limitation it has imposed on his freedom to act on his own behalf."[20] This maneuver animated the social contract with an emphasis not on what the people agree to do but on what the state may be held accountable for, derived entirely from categories of state action and administrative choice.[21] Joshua's case was the exception that proved the rule. Although "the State may have been aware of the dangers that Joshua faced in the free world," it "does not become the permanent guarantor of an individual's safety by having once offered him shelter."[22] Pairing the case with the rule captured the apex of this mode of constitutional decision-making. Chief Justice Rehnquist characterized Joshua, a three-year old child suffering serial abuse from his father, as an "individual" living in the "free world" and the state as a Good Samaritan whose intervention exposed Joshua to no more harm than if it had not acted.

This claim described a social relationship between the citizen and the state by seizing on the fiction that Joshua DeShaney was a categorical equal in fact. Joshua could not vote, drive, or work, and he lacked meaningful choice in his living arrangement. He no more fit the category of "individual" navigating the dangers of the free world than would a prisoner. The opinion's formal reason constructed a strict separation between individual and state that effaced the position of the judge as individual. Its formal and empty qualities sanctioned cruelty. Judith Shklar wrote that "liberalism's deepest grounding" was in the belief that "cruelty is an absolute evil, an offense against God and humanity."[23] For Chief Justice Rehnquist's opinion, cruelty was the price of government by the rule of law. The emotionless bureaucrat was the true master of this domain: "Judges and lawyers, like other humans, are moved by natural sympathy in a case like this to find a way for Joshua . . . to receive adequate compensation. . . . But before yielding to that impulse, it is well to remember . . . that the harm was inflicted . . . by Joshua's father. . . . In defense of [state workers] . . . had they moved too soon to take custody . . . they would likely have been met with charges of improperly intruding into the parent-child relationship . . . based on the same Due Process Clause."[24]

This expertise claimed authority as the inevitable application of pragmatic principle. It concealed the choice to embrace one virtue (clarity) at the expense of another (sympathy) under the guise of neutral compulsion—the text made the court do it. This approach activated the discursive opposition between benevolent care and rational process cultivated by Justice Fortas's *In re Gault* opinion: emotion was something to be worked through, checked, or held back so that the genuine work of rational decision-making could proceed. Proceeding from linguistic abstraction, enacting the fiction of Joshua as an individual, and elevating concerns for the bureaucratic risk management of state workers, it removed a constitutional vision of care and state responsibility from the horizon of possibility.

Judgment through the Eyes of a Victim: Justice Blackmun's Dissent

Justice Blackmun's dissent was brief, fiery, and pointed.[25] Quite unlike the vast majority of Supreme Court dissents that embrace a similar frame and assess similar precedents to the ones found in the majority opinion, it revived the deep disagreement about how to judge. The dissent argued that the majority's approach was rotten to perfection, referring pejoratively to the court as "the dispassionate oracle of the law, unmoved by 'natural sympathy,'" and lambasted the majority's retreat "into a sterile formalism."[26] The dissent used the incapable child to articulate a contrasting vision of expertise. That vision had the following features: (1) it acknowledged an emotional connection with the parties before the judge and (2) it looked beyond the text to historical analogues and dissociative maneuvers in a search to do justice. The dissent constitutes a road not yet taken, an alternative to contractual understandings of obligation rooted solely in rational inference.

First, Justice Blackmun created a place for emotion in expert judgment by coding his own interpretations in emotional language.[27] Taking aim at Justice Rehnquist's rigid approach, he wrote that it ran counter to the "broad and stirring Clauses of the Fourteenth Amendment . . . . [which] were designed . . . to undo the formalistic legal reasoning that infected antebellum jurisprudence."[28] In its place, he opted for an open, sympathetic reading of constitutional law, because that reading "comports with dictates of fundamental justice and recognizes that compassion need not be exiled from the province of judging."[29]

The dissent legitimated this mode of expertise with an extended analogy between Joshua's claim and the injustice of slavery. It implied that expert judgment in the face of uncertainty required an imagination to connect cases based on their common qualities, in stark contrast to the majority's approach to exceptions. Chief Justice Rehnquist, like antebellum judges, perfunctorily acknowledged the brutal result of his decision, but assuaged moral concerns by appealing to a conviction that the law compelled it. Justice Blackmun resisted this approach, claiming that justice (and emotion) matter. Proper expert judgment should have acknowledged that a just result for Joshua turned on how one chose to interpret relevant precedents to create a textual opening for action. Plausible interpretations that did justice were preferable to clear interpretations that did injustice. The dissent's emotive conclusion—Poor Joshua!—lamented the loss of both judicial conscience and principle.[30] It charted a different path, admitting precedential indeterminacy informed by emotional reactions to an event.

For the dissent, compassion was not a primitive feeling to be overcome, but served as a ground for judgment. The opinion derided inaction in the face of uncertainty,[31] encouraging "moral ambition" to cope with an incomplete sketch of humanity and referring to compassion as "our only guide and comfort."[32] This appeal began with a common ground in feeling and moved to constitutional principle. It presumed that all judges had compassion. Where Chief Justice Rehnquist wrote and judged against that feeling, Blackmun translated it in words for readers as an interpretive guide. The dissent articulated a role for the judicial expert through critical distance rather than deference. The judge's detachment was a virtue that could avoid the bias of a singular perspective. Justice Blackmun's distance permitted him to take on Joshua's perspective. Extending the slavery analogy, Justice Blackmun described Joshua's father as one would term a slave to his emotions, utterly lacking sound judgment and making impulsive abusive decisions—"an irresponsible, bullying, cowardly, and intemperate father." The state workers did "essentially nothing except . . . dutifully [record] these incidents in [their] files."[33] Describing the state workers this way drew a fine parallel between the sterile, rote, textual process of judgment and what was in fact the abdication of role. Chief Justice Rehnquist thought he was performing fidelity to his constitutional obligation, but Justice Blackmun thought this a "sad commentary on American life," a fundamental hypocrisy that condemned Joshua "to live out the remainder of his life profoundly retarded" while the nation uttered "proud proclamations about 'liberty and justice for all.'"[34] Here, the dissent echoed the consistent objections to judicial inaction through righteous unmasking seen in the previous cases studied in this book—just as Justice Jackson debunked deference to village hamlets that could harbor village tyrants and Justice Fortas chided the fatherly judge who claimed to act in the best interests of the child but was in many instances destroying childhood.

The weakness of the dissent was its vagueness. It appealed to procedure as protection, but the contours were fuzzy. The strength of Justice Blackmun's alternative was its analysis of liberal shortcomings. Because the ongoing struggle for an inclusive polity required practices of imagining oneself in the place of another, judges needed to see the world through different eyes. The weakness emerged in how to translate the sentiment into a disciplined practice of judgment. Justice Blackmun's reference to psychiatry represented an analogy that may not hold. Psychiatrists owe professional allegiance to patients. One's compassion may be an important foundation for open doctor-patient communication and for doing the best for one's patient. But it is easier to provide support to a solitary patient than it is to show compassion to litigants and the citizens and governmental agencies that must support a constitutional decision. Compassion can produce blindness.

The disagreement between Chief Justice Rehnquist and Justice Blackmun in *DeShaney* marked the tension between justice as an entitlement premised on a particular situation and justice defined in general terms according to a social contract.[35] This tension is expressed in the two different children the opinions saw. Chief Justice Rehnquist's child was a categorically equal citizen who navigated a free world. Joshua was simply a victim of bad luck, which the state had no obligation to repair.[36] Justice Blackmun's child lacked any meaningful sense of control or choice. He was "assigned" to live out his life in a severely diminished capacity, and he "and his mother . . . deserve[d] . . . the opportunity to have the facts of their case considered."[37] His emotional lament for childhood lost revived the discourse of investment in future citizens as a reason to intervene. Justice Fortas's opinion in *In re Gault* referred to Arizona's arbitrary procedures that condemning Gerald Gault to a childhood populated by guards and criminals. Chief Justice Burger's opinion in *Parham* implied a family at the end of its rope, parenting a child with psychological problems as best as they can, and committing their child as a last resort. In *DeShaney*, Justice Blackmun's child was more like a slave, and the majority was reinventing antebellum jurisprudence. Considering child abuse as slavery represented a broader interpretation of the Thirteenth Amendment of the Constitution, and may point to interpretive practices for an alternate social arrangement that demands robust state action and broader public obligations.[38] Resistance to these alternatives was grounded not merely in competing expert interpretations but in covering over the contingent choices about the expert's role that produced them.

11

THE NATIONAL INTEREST

Morse v. Frederick

ON JANUARY 24, 2002, JUNEAU, ALASKA, HOSTED THE OLYMPIC TORCH Relay as it made its way to the winter games in Salt Lake City, Utah. Juneau-Douglas High School Principal Deborah Morse saw the relay as an opportunity for community building and allowed staff and students to attend it as an approved school event. As the torchbearers passed by (accompanied by a camera crew), student Joseph Frederick and his friends unfurled a fourteen-foot banner that read: "BONG HiTS 4 JESUS," easily readable from the other side of the street. Principal Morse told the students to take it down. Everyone but Frederick complied. Morse took the banner and suspended Frederick for ten days. Morse "thought [the banner] encouraged illegal drug use, in violation of school policy."[1] The Juneau School Board prohibited "any assembly or public expression that . . . advocates the use of substances that are illegal to minors," and a separate board rule applied the same standard of conduct to "pupils who participate in approved social events and class trips."[2]

Frederick fought his suspension and the school superintendent reduced it to eight days. The superintendent judged that Frederick's speech was not political because he wasn't, "advocating the legalization of marijuana or promoting a religious belief." It was a "silly message promoting illegal drug usage in the midst of school activity, for the benefit of television cameras," and it was "clearly disruptive of and inconsistent with the school's educational mission to educate students about the dangers of illegal drugs and to discourage their use."[3]

Frederick sued the school board and Principal Morse for violating his constitutional right to free speech. The federal courts considered two broad issues. The first concerned the legitimacy of Morse's decision to suspend Frederick, and the second was an interpretive question about Morse's "qualified immunity" defense.[4] The Ninth Circuit Court of Appeals sided with Frederick, holding that the suspension violated his First Amendment rights. The case provided an opportunity for the Supreme Court to clarify its decisions in *Tinker, Fraser,* and *Hazelwood.* The "*Tinker* Trilogy" had confused lower courts and schools, as both institutions still wrestled with the problems of classifying speech, the intention and purpose of the speaker, and the mission of public education.

The Supreme Court reversed the Ninth Circuit's decision, holding that Morse's belief that Frederick was encouraging drug use was reasonable and that this belief justified his suspension. Chief Justice Roberts's opinion reasoned that *Fraser* had clarified that *Tinker* was not the sole mode of analysis for acceptable speech, because it didn't conduct a "substantial disruption" analysis. Suggesting an "appropriateness" test for limiting the child's rights at school, Chief Justice Roberts emphasized the national problem of drug abuse by the young to support his argument that school officials could prohibit speech like Frederick's due in part to its potential impact on the school's anti-drug use message. Justice Alito concurred with the opinion, writing separately to emphasize his opinion that the *Morse* result should not be used to limit political speech. Justice Thomas wrote a concurrence emphasizing his belief that *Tinker* was wrongly decided because the First Amendment did not apply in schools.

Justice Stevens dissented, joined by Justices Souter and Ginsburg. Justice Stevens's dissent challenged the majority's interpretation of the banner, arguing that it was more akin to a nonsense message than anything persuasive. The dissent agreed that the principal should not have been held liable for punishing Frederick, but that the school's interest in prohibiting drug use could not extend to Frederick's banner, which was motivated by a desire to get on television. Even though it referred to drugs, Justice Stevens desired a rule that permitted speech so long as it did not "violate a permissible rule" and did not "expressly [advocate] conduct that is illegal and harmful to students."[5]

Interpretive Judgment and Transcendent Principles: Chief Justice Roberts's Opinion

The court rejected Frederick's claim. Chief Justice Roberts's opinion justified this decision in part by marking the signs of cognition necessary to infer sound judgment. Three important aspects stood out: (1) leaders exercised judgment with swift and certain action; (2) judgments that involve interpretive labor (decisions about meaning) should be consistent with hierarchical consensus; and (3) citizens who failed to communicate intention in speech could pose a threat to state interests. The majority opinion performed these cognitive signs by taking the doctrinal confusion of *Tinker, Fraser,* and *Hazelwood* and distilling these cases' collective meaning by identifying their core common principles. It deepened the association between citizen and state as contractual and further winnowed the state's obligations to citizens by introducing a discourse that justified expanding authority to enact its own policies.

The opinion highlighted the display of swift decision-making as a hallmark of sound judgment in comparing Morse's and Frederick's performances. This rhetorical tactic partook in a discourse introduced in *Tinker*: using a declarative tone to present legal facts that align a legal conclusion with a desired public value. The result was to introduce the character of the confident leader who exhibits certainty of direction. Where the *Tinker* majority detailed the strategic planning of the student speakers to wear their armbands (aligning strategy with a constitutional notion of political speech), *Morse* emphasized Principal Morse's motives in her actions and the school board's written policies. The opinion depicted a savvy strategist who acted swiftly, certainly, and clearly: "Morse . . . decided to permit staff and students to participate in the Torch Relay as an approved . . . class trip. . . . Students were allowed to leave class to observe the relay from either side of the street. Teachers and administrative officials monitored the students' actions."[6] This declarative tone crafted Principal Morse as the model of a successful manager. She seized the opportunity of the torch relay to add to her students' education. She exuded control over the school with unambiguous orders to the students and her staff. You can leave the school and observe the relay from either side of the street; the staff will monitor your behavior at all times. When Frederick and his friends unfurled their banner, Morse again quickly reacted, "immediately cross[ing] the street and demand[ing] that the banner be taken down."[7]

Morse's actions embodied sound judgment by conforming to the formalistic hallmarks of contract—speed of action in conformity with prior written commitments. Her conduct met expectations based on what had been previously written down. The opinion quoted the relevant school board policies at length in a litany; this tactic supported an inference that her swift action was supported by forethought. One rule prohibited public expression that advocated the use of substances illegal to minors; another applied in-school conduct rules to students on school-sanctioned social events and class trips. These facts posited a relationship between the character of her decision and a sense that the decision was predictable.

Morse's interpretive judgment also was validated by hierarchical review. The school superintendent supported her after Frederick appealed. Frederick, by contrast, embodied the character of a disorderly slacker. He was late to school and was grouped at the rally with other students, "not all [of whom] waited patiently. Some became rambunctious, throwing plastic cola bottles and snowballs and scuffling with their classmates."[8] Chief Justice Roberts described the banner only in terms of its length, words, and a judgment that students on the other side of the street could easily have read it. Strategically, the opinion shifted the legal focus to the reasonableness of the administrator. The opinion left Morse and Frederick in equipoise, and there could only be one winner. Morse was a good individual judge. She was an efficient and purposeful leader. Acting for the benefit of most, she swiftly removed the banner to enforce the school's mission, to protect other students from the message, and to demonstrate the certainty and confidence of a principal. These actions reassured the student body and the community. Frederick, by contrast, showed up late for school. When he finally arrived, he joined a rabble of students milling around without purpose. His classmates were "observing" the events unfolding, as if Frederick was influencing them with his poor behavior.

The opinion doubled this model of judgment in interpreting Frederick's message, performing objectivity in evaluating competing interpretations of the banner: "The message on Frederick's banner is cryptic. It is no doubt offensive to some, perhaps amusing to others. To still others, it probably means nothing at all. Frederick himself claimed 'that the words were just nonsense meant to attract television cameras . . . .' But Principal Morse thought the banner would be interpreted by those viewing it as promoting illegal drug use, and that interpretation is plainly a reasonable one."[9] This analysis recasts the operative legal issue from *Tinker*'s focus on the individual citizen to a state-centric approach—"Was the administrator's interpretation reasonable?" This new question shifted the burden from the administrator onto the citizen. The comparative technique of the parties' behavior placed more weight on interpretive skill in determining a message's political efficacy.

The chief justice resolved the conflict with an interpretive practice that yielded unitary and consistent results. In comparing Morse's and Frederick's performances, Roberts favored Morse's "plainly reasonable" interpretation of Frederick's speech. This maneuver activated the discourse of obvious meanings that Chief Justice Burger had used when he characterized Fraser's speech as "plainly lewd." Grafting this discourse onto Morse's interpretive act, the opinion elevated the cognitive display of consistency as a part of the core of sound judgment. Morse's declaration provided Roberts with a permissible motive for action: "When she saw the sign, she thought that 'the reference to a "bong hit" would be widely understood by high school students and others as referring to smoking marijuana.' . . . She further believed that 'display of the banner would be construed by students, District personnel, parents and others witnessing the display of the banner, as advocating or promoting illegal drug use'—in violation of school policy. . . . ('[Morse] told Frederick and the other members of his group to put the banner down because [she] felt that it violated the [school] policy against displaying . . . material that advertises or promotes use of illegal drugs.')."[10] This character sketch implied a gulf between the incapable citizen (Frederick) and the ideal type to which he should aspire (Morse). Looking beyond the post hoc character of Morse's account (she had incentives to fabricate it to protect herself from legal liability), the opinion relied on the phrasing of her testimony. Nothing outside of Morse's own statements about her intentions validated the interpretation—she "thought" it was advocating drug use, she "believed" that is how students would receive it, and "felt" that it violated policy. The opinion's declarative style performed its legitimacy by positing its own objectivity.

In contrast, Frederick's account of his speech appeared wildly polysemous. The opinion noted that "the best Frederick can come up with is that the banner is 'meaningless and funny,'" and that the dissent described "the sign's message" with a series of adjectives that connote a fundamental unintelligibility: curious, ambiguous, nonsense, quixotic.[11] The opinion thought that each interpretation overlooked the message's content: "dismissing the banner as meaningless ignores its undeniable reference to illegal drugs."[12] The opinion imposed an interpretation by celebrating the objective elements of legibility. Clarity also mattered. Recasting the question in the case—"whether a principal may, consistent with the First Amendment, restrict student speech at a school event, when that speech is reasonably viewed as promoting illegal drug use"—passively buried the subject of interpretation, concealing the fact that Roberts determined reasonableness by virtue of his own preferred interpretive criteria.[13]

That interpretation interposed meaning on Frederick's unclear speech through judicial performance. Just as Morse interpreted Frederick's speech by distilling the core principle from confusion, the majority opinion identified grounding constitutional principles by clarifying muddled precedents. This performance reimagined the nature of "political" speech. Like Frederick's strange banner, the court's past student speech cases were a thicket of confusion. They responded in an ad hoc fashion to crises without concern for future effects. These cases were not necessarily wrongly decided, but they called out for a decisive and clearly organized synthesis linked to a democratically shared purpose. This synthetic act of reading precedent was simultaneously authoritative, pedagogical, and aspirational.

Roberts read *Tinker* in a parsimonious style, emphasizing the capabilities a citizen must possess to claim that their speech is protected by the First Amendment. The character of a speech's content was an interpretive question. Political speech had to manifest both a topic of public importance and intention to persuade. "The students sought to engage in political speech, using the armbands to express their 'disapproval of the Vietnam hostilities and their advocacy of a truce, to make their views known, and, by their example, to influence others to adopt them.'"[14] This interpretive gloss deflected the progressive character of *Tinker*. It downplayed the lack of evidence that the speech was disruptive and took cognitive strategy as a metonym for political speech. The opinion's interpretation of *Tinker* as only pertaining to "political speech" allowed it to avoid its "substantial disruption" test (there was no evidence that Frederick's banner caused a substantial disruption). The opinion observed that "the only interest the [*Tinker*] Court discerned underlying the school's actions was the 'mere desire to avoid the discomfort and unpleasantness that always accompany an unpleasant viewpoint. . . .' That interest was not enough to justify banning 'a silent, passive expression of opinion, unaccompanied by any disorder or disturbance.'"[15] This description recast *Tinker* as a limited case that protected a specific type of speech (political) when the state advanced a particular type of interest (fear of disruption).

This artful description legitimated the court's new rule: if Morse could prove an interest beyond a mere desire to avoid conflict, then Frederick's speech could be prohibited. *Tinker* simply didn't apply, because it was one of a multitude of tests. Reducing *Tinker* to its new formal category, Roberts implied that it no longer dictated the analysis. The entire maneuver illustrated the way the opinion's performance of objectivity invented within the rhetorical form. Roberts's interpretive practice opened the way for judicial creation.[16]

The opinion then marked *Fraser* as a confusing case: like Frederick's banner, Fraser's speech required an act of authoritative interpretation to distill governing principles: "The mode of analysis employed in *Fraser* is not entirely clear. The Court was plainly attuned to the content of Fraser's speech. . . . But the Court also reasoned that school boards have the authority to determine 'what manner of speech in the classroom or in school assembly is inappropriate.'"[17] The opinion used this mode to justify its conclusions: (1) that children's rights to free speech in school are not coextensive with adults' rights in nonschool settings and (2) "that the mode of analysis set forth in *Tinker* is not absolute."[18]

This contested precedential history appeared as uncontroversial objective fact.[19] The chief justice's interpretive practice performed judgment against transparency, a stylized resolution whose appeal to objectivity denied its existence as style.[20] The opinion creatively misread the *Fraser* majority and Brennan's concurrence. Roberts's supposed objectivity thus shifted: each self-stated application of basic concepts of liberal community included the strategic and selective exploitation of ambiguity in the name of a new principle. The opinion built on *Kuhlmeier*'s principle of the state's interest in controlling its message as national policy. Even though the opinion conceded that "*Kuhlmeier* does not control this case because no one would reasonably believe that Frederick's banner bore the school's imprimatur,"[21] Chief Justice Roberts, a self-proclaimed minimalist, used it as further proof that *Tinker* does not govern all student speech cases.[22] But the interest was even more ambitious. The principles he found cut across other cases, supporting an argument that emphasized schools as an exception: schools may be bound by the Constitution, but that limit could be transcended in the name of the school's special institutional place. He reminded the reader that Fourth Amendment jurisprudence has argued that "the school setting requires some easing of the restrictions to which searches by public authorities are ordinarily subject" and that in deciding whether a school could require drug testing as a condition for participating in an extracurricular activity, the court had opined that "the reasonableness inquiry cannot disregard the school's custodial and tutelary responsibility for children."[23] The opinion's use of the monologic voice articulated what "the Court" has decided in previous cases, rewriting the history and context of those cases. It also changed the relationship between state and citizen: under the banner of "special circumstances" of the school, the opinion created a new state interest in protecting its desired policies.

The State's Expanding Authority over the Citizen: *Morse*'s Implications

This discourse of "national interest" broadened the state's control over citizen speech. It used the discourse in *Hazelwood* that was concerned with local traditional community values to develop an interest in limiting speech inconsistent with the school's mission. The *Morse* opinion expanded the state's authority over citizens by adding "national policy" to the state's constitutional interests. This interest is only legible if one makes an assumption about the child's cognitive capabilities—themes developed in *Fraser* and *Hazelwood*. Both of those majority opinions were concerned about the risk of speech reaching an audience that lacked the ability to process the message as intended. Although neither opinion developed evidence about this claim, each instance was concerned about the relative ability of the audience to cognitively process emotions of confusion, disgust, hurt, shame, and impulse control that the speech was perhaps designed to produce. The impressionable young girls in *Fraser* and the students in *Hazelwood* may simply have been incapable of "getting it," which meant in the former case that they were not cognitively capable of processing the connotative meanings of Fraser's tawdry endorsement. Frederick's banner may have referred to drug use (and it may have been literally illegal), but it may also have simply been a message that everyone wrapped up in Olympic nationalism should "chill" and "get religion."

In this way, the contract model of citizenship expressed a strategy of emotional management through censorship. The strategy's hallmarks for producing capable citizens appear to update an earlier discourse of virtue and tradition for modern times—the need to be aware of shared values as those values are expressed in handbooks and national legislation. It downplayed the value of Frederick's speech because it was nonpolitical, but paradoxically justified censorship to prevent illegal drug use—undoubtedly political goals. As with Chief Justice Burger's opinions in *Parham* and *Fraser*, this opinion made use of record evidence and general references to reform an argument for judicial restraint. Chief Justice Roberts's opinion exploited the tactics of preceding cases to justify his conclusion. This included the portion of *Tinker* that noted that the school hadn't demonstrated its interest "on this record" (implying that a different record would yield a different result), Justice Black's anxiety in *Tinker*—repeated in *Hazelwood*—that the students not be allowed to control an institution through speech, and Justice Frankfurter's caution that the judiciary not frustrate legislative action.

Roberts detailed the effort that Congress has put into anti-drug use policy, having "provided billions of dollars to support state and local drug-prevention programs."[24] He referred to a congressional statute, the Safe and Drug-Free Schools and Communities Act of 1994, which asked that fund recipients "convey a clear and consistent message that . . . the illegal use of drugs [is] wrong and harmful."[25] After that, he notes that Frederick's high school is one of "thousands of school boards throughout the country . . . [that has] adopted policies aimed at effectuating this message."[26] These declarations structured a seemingly simple argument: Frederick's banner supports illegal drug use; deterring drug use is an important interest of the state; and the school can censor messages that run counter to that interest.

This position evoked the discourse of judicial restraint in the name of democratic decision-making, deploying arguments about the substantial investment made in this national policy through a host of examples. The legislature's dedication of public funds to support a clear antidrug message stood in as an expression of popular will through national action. "Thousands" of school boards, those paragons of local democracy that Justice Frankfurter had praised in *Barnette*, followed suit. And this policy received the court's constitutional imprimatur, ratified by its past decisions in the area of drug testing. Taken together, Roberts built a cumulative democratic case through declaration of authority and fact.

This move scaled up the state's authority significantly, expanding *Hazelwood*'s interest in maintaining the school's public image to now hold significance in a school's support for national policy.[27] The majority's decision inverted the original rationale for restrained judicial expertise from reverence for diverse and pluralistic local democratic choice to a unitary statement of national consensus. The opinion displaced liberal democracy's need to cultivate capable citizens when it described Frederick as incapable. It reserved the court's own interpretive authority regarding political expression when it figured Frederick's speech as a chiasmus that was both nonpolitical nonsense and advocacy of drug use that threatened national policy.

The opinion's use of precedent made the argument for judicial deference more antidemocratic. It appealed to liberal democracy as the consensus of majority over the diversity of democratically chosen preferences. Justice Frankfurter's original case for deference to local school boards turned on their diversity of approaches to social and cultural policy (combined with the institutional incompetence of the courts). Chief Justice Roberts built an argument premised on national policy executed by local school boards as a condition for receiving federal funds. Its democratic power derived from its expression of a national majoritarian will backed by substantial funding. Perhaps not coincidentally, this emerged alongside a bureaucratic desire to "stay on message" as a means to protect the public investment, which privileged the school's interest in keeping consistency and avoiding confusion on behalf of audience members.

The *Morse* majority completely neglected the discourse of categorical equality that connected speech to citizenship capabilities. The anticensorship themes introduced in *Barnette* and *Tinker* linked those outcomes to the development of the citizen—future leaders who must exercise their abilities to think and speak. Even *Fraser* justified its censorship in the name of creating a civil public discourse. The *Morse* majority was silent about the obligation to produce citizens with these qualities. A capable citizen does not speak like Frederick, because his banner opposed national policy in a subversive but curiously unintelligible way. Rather than interpreting that message independently, considering various possibilities—its connotations, and its timing to gain attention, for example—the opinion chose the simplest one in order to broaden state power over citizens.

This characterization raised the final important consequence of *Morse* for judicial authority—it pushed judicial expertise from Justice Jackson's core of rights to the performance of authoritative interpretations. Interpretive practice has always been a part of a judge's role. But *Morse* highlighted the extent to which its complexity has overtaken the role of identifying and balancing constitutional rights. Chief Justice Roberts used interpretive acumen to define away the conflict—*Tinker* simply didn't apply. The critical faculty exhibited through speech is both a necessary capability for citizenship, and one that the state must manage antidemocratically. This legal interpretation embedded a political contradiction: how could Frederick's speech threaten a consensus-driven national policy and simultaneously be nonpolitical, even gibberish? The majority opinion stated that the banner was not deliberative, observing that "not even Frederick argues that the banner conveys any sort of political or religious message. . . . This is plainly not a case about political debate over the criminalization of drug use."[28] Yet it was hard to grasp the reason to regulate this speech if it was not political. If "advocacy of drug use" is the banner's most reasonable interpretation, and anti-drug use campaigns are an important national policy, then Frederick's banner would appear to be advocating against that policy. Indeed, the more effective the speech would be in persuading others, the more threatening it would be to the state's stated goal.

Relying on the trope of the child as easily influenced, the opinion worried that Frederick's banner may influence a public through circulation. It disciplined the citizen by insisting on a particular form of deliberative communication. Where *Tinker* contributed to a tradition of open expression through persuasive public appeals that neither overvalued unanimity nor exaggerated fears, here Chief Justice Roberts maintained administrative barriers to alternate modes of expressive participation. This result was justified on the ground that administrators could set the terms of public deliberation, as well as their interpretation of potential threats to that imagined public space. This was a public sphere that sacrificed diversity of opinion and expression to order performed through consistency and consensus, enforced with swift certainty.

Disagreement and Political History: Justice Stevens's Dissent

Justice John Paul Stevens wrote the primary dissent, joined by Justice Ruth Bader Ginsburg.[29] The dissent's position was simple—a school should only be able to punish speech that "violates a permissible rule" or expressly advocates conduct that is "illegal and harmful to students."[30] Because Justice Stevens viewed Frederick's speech as "a nonsense banner," he believed that the majority damaged the First Amendment in allowing the punishment of speech with which the school disagreed.[31] The dissent implicitly assessed Principal Morse's individual judgment, expecting her to assess the probability that Frederick's banner would have harmed the students. It also preserved a place for judgment to distinguish expressive speech from persuasive advocacy. Concerning judicial expertise, Justice Stevens's dissent used the argument from historical example to activate the discourse of temporality and sound judgment. Working with examples of the Vietnam War and the Prohibition Era, the dissent implied that Chief Justice Roberts's interpretation justified only his own subjective belief about the speech's propriety. In its place, the dissent offered a different interpretation better suited to the long historical memory in which momentary passions and attitudes about policy can change . . . but the court's rigid interpretations may not.

Justice Stevens's dissent figures the child as a capable speaker whose expression should be encouraged in the name of progress. At first blush, this seems counterintuitive, since he conceded Morse's authority to remove the banner because of the negative attention it would have brought on the school. But he refused to accept Frederick's suspension. The dissent sought a space between Roberts's autocratic interpretive practice and an unfettered profusion of citizens' public expression. The dissent attempted to maintain a more pluralistic vision of the public amid concerns over an outsized state and the now attenuated social contract.

First, the dissent introduced the discourse of judicial risk assessment in demanding that administrators assess the probability of harm when they judge speech worthy of punishment. Hearkening back to the cultural context of speech in *Tinker*, Justice Stevens argued by a fortiori analogy: if a school had to permit a war protest in the heat of a political conflict, then it surely could have tolerated Frederick's banner. Although the stakes in *Tinker* were extremely high, the court permitted the armbands because punishing a speaker for advocating illegal conduct is only justified if the advocacy is "likely to provoke the harm that the government seeks to avoid."[32] The authority to censor political speech should be premised on an assessment of probability and harm. The majority disposed of this inquiry altogether, substituting a belief in harm rather than documenting it. Grounding decisions in mere belief and opinion was not a judge's role; the dissent preferred a rule of inclusion for speech in the educational public sphere, even where speech might appear threatening to an administrator. After all, the public speech in *Tinker* subjected dissenters to accusations questioning their patriotism.

Concerning judicial expertise, the dissent doubled this critique of mere belief as the ground for altering citizen's rights, suggesting that Chief Justice Roberts's legally formalistic approach served as cover for his own subjective belief. Rather than appeal to context, the majority generated an abstract taxonomy of speech categories that prefigured legal results—passive speech, lewd speech, speech as part of curriculum . . . and now speech at a school event. This arid interpretive practice produced antidemocratic results. Justice Stevens argued that it remade the court's approach to public speech into one that "trivializes the two cardinal principles on which *Tinker* rests" and "invites stark viewpoint discrimination."[33] Linking these principles to the educational public sphere, he argued that the Constitution required exposure to a wide range of expressive viewpoints.

The dissent spoke to a future time when alternate contexts—different justices and different controversies—may call for the return of these liberal principles. The dissent refuted the majority's discourse of authority as being grounded in mere fear of diverse viewpoints. Justice Stevens described Frederick's banner as nonthreatening advocacy. His argument was that the state should maintain a public sphere that tolerated speech that did not expressly advocate law breaking. Even if Frederick's banner crossed that line, there is a "vanishingly small category of speech that can be prohibited for its feared consequences."[34] The majority rule would allow the state to curb too much citizen speech that was in the public interest.

The dissent distinguished the banner from express advocacy of drug use, and in so doing, it performed the kinds of capabilities for judgment and speech reception that it expected citizens to develop. It used record evidence to argue that the likelihood that the banner would have disrupted school activities was insignificant. Justice Stevens was concerned that the majority was merely expressing its subjective disagreement with the message, rather than a method for distilling constitutional principles. Frederick testified that he just wanted to get on television, and there was no evidence that the banner "'willfully' infringed on anyone's rights or interfered with any of the school's educational programs."[35] The banner may not be vital speech, but the majority's interpretation vested the subjective listener with de facto constitutional authority, because the listener's beliefs now dictated whether the speech should be allowed: "To the extent the Court defers to the principal's ostensibly reasonable judgment, it abdicates its constitutional responsibility. The beliefs of third parties, reasonable or otherwise, have never dictated which messages amount to proscribable advocacy. Indeed, it would be a strange constitutional doctrine that would . . . permit a listener's perceptions to determine which speech deserved constitutional protection."[36] Justice Stevens feared an illiberal public that reinforced its own beliefs and silenced opposition through the shortcut of censorship—the same structure that Justice Jackson had condemned in *Barnette* over sixty years ago. The folly in this governmental structure was its lack of wisdom and perspective. What type of judgment was required to prevent it? Justice Stevens closed his opinion by suggesting a wisdom informed by the longer context of the sweep of history.

Justice Stevens drew on the discourse of temporality to cultivate an expertise required to make judgments amid uncertainty. His examples—Prohibition and the Vietnam War—highlighted historical moments in which consensus opinion at the time did not win out over the long course of citizens' democratic discussion. The dominant opinion of the Vietnam War at the time of *Tinker* was that it was a reasonable conflict. It also was popular with the public. Those who opposed it faced censure, vilification, and even prosecution (here Stevens referred to the demonstrators in Grant Park at the 1968 Democratic National Convention). But *Tinker* struck a blow for an open democratic society and marked that openness with vigorous dissent. Indeed, permissiveness in speech was inextricably linked to that democratic vision.

Stevens's second example was Prohibition. Alcoholic beverages, once "condemned with the same moral fervor that now supports the war on drugs," now are seen as "ordinary articles of commerce."[37] The justice saw a similar long-term attitude change possible with the war on drugs, but worried that "the fear of disapproval by those in the majority is silencing opponents of the war on drugs. Surely our national experience with alcohol should make us wary of dampening speech suggesting—however inarticulately—that it would be better to tax and regulate marijuana than to persevere in a futile effort to ban its use entirely."[38] These examples filled out the sketch of a tolerant citizenry because they encouraged frank talk about public issues that contributed to evolving public opinions. These issues were cultural and did not lend themselves easily to right/wrong answers. For this society to progress and evolve required citizen contribution to the discourse, however little it conformed to traditional modes of expression. The artfulness and eloquence of that speech mattered less than the fact that it preserved future pathways for different, changed times.

The Asymmetrical Social Contract: Citizens Bound and (In)capable

The court's approach to citizenship in the cases discussed in part 4 shifted from a revival of tradition to a mode of contractual management and expectations. Tending to the ways in which the court novelized the public sphere has revealed the role that novelization played in reshaping the constitutional narrative: this includes the opinions' construction of relationships between students and administrators, the themes of citizenship, and the performances of judgment by characters in the cases and the justices themselves. This contractual model produced a state with increasing authority over citizen speech without the traditional commitment to develop citizenship capabilities, and the Supreme Court justices recast their commitment to provide independent, careful judicial evaluation of the particular facts of the situation. Instead, authority in these cases was produced with the certainty of published rules. These rules claimed democratic legitimacy because their publication reflected the popular will. The latter was depoliticized, detached from the values of communication and critique that had characterized earlier cases.

Hazelwood and *Morse* altered the citizen's right to speak through reliance on rules. This reliance responded to *Tinker*'s discourse of a fearful public. Where *Tinker* had discounted this fear because it was not properly documented, *Hazelwood* and *Morse* pointed to handbook regulations and disciplinary rules. This dialogical response to *Tinker* adopted the latter's approach to categorically equal citizens in their descriptions of the speaker (writer, displayer): these cases compared the performances of the students with the decision-making processes of the administrators. In the process, the explicit themes of democratic value from prior cases—the value of persuasion in *Barnette*, of political strategy, risk, and democratic criticism in *Tinker*, of civility in *Fraser*—dropped out. In their place stood the value of judicial expertise—the doctrinal dismissal of the claim in *Hazelwood* and *Morse*'s interpretive synthesis of the entire line of cases. These performances vindicated the values of responsibility for speakers, and the certainty of clear rules. In this way, they implicitly evoked the discourse of judicial restraint in *Gobitis*, *Barnette* (dissent), *Tinker* (dissent), and *Parham*. The constitutional narrative privileged textual rules, and where there was ambiguity, these opinions would reduce such ambiguity to clarity through their interpretive practice. Whether this development represented an evolution of a pragmatic state or a devolution into injustice depends on one's perspective.

If clarity of rule represented a principle of judgment, *DeShaney* highlighted the resistance that such discourse could provoke. In *DeShaney*, the majority relied on the clarity of the constitutional text. Clear rules determined the state's obligation to intervene to protect free individuals. As with the free speech cases, a pragmatic discourse justified this judgment. Social workers could not fairly be expected to have acted—such obligations might cause them to incur other liability risks, including the intrusion onto parental rights. Like *Hazelwood* and *Morse*, *DeShaney* developed the categorical equality of the child as a citizen. The state had no duty to protect Joshua from the dangers of the free world. And like those cases, *DeShaney* emphasized written rules of governance. Justice Rehnquist supported his restrictive reading of the Due Process Clause with *In re Gault*'s skepticism of state care. Because the benevolent state had demonstrated itself to be both untrustworthy and inefficient, it was not to be trusted. *DeShaney* took these ideas to their extreme practical conclusions in treating the child citizen at arm's length.

The kinds of cognitive capabilities this model valued were not found in the children and adolescents involved, because the opinions presumed their categorical equality rather than drawing on their performances to highlight their capacities. Instead, the connection between cognition and citizenship emerged in the actions of bureaucrats and administrators. *DeShaney* prized the inaction of the social worker, because of an implied knowledge of their role in the state's governing hierarchy. They did their job according to textual mandates, and that was sufficient to display sound judgment. This role-based knowledge was to the letter, matching the stingy interpretation that Justice Rehnquist gave the Constitution. It is not surprising that this strategy relied on the deferential discourse of the judicial role made famous in Justice Frankfurter's opinions (Justice Rehnquist was Justice Frankfurter's clerk). It also cultivated a detached attitude toward injustice. Echoing the physical punishment jurisprudence from previous cases, *DeShaney* also appealed to a discourse of public harms left to alternate public checks. *Ingraham* had appealed to public scrutiny of school uses of corporal punishment; *DeShaney* appealed to publics who would need to alter the legislative or constitutional landscape to address Joshua's assertion of citizenship rights to protection.

In the realm of the citizen's right to speak, *Hazelwood* and *Morse* elevated the cognitive displays of administrators; this strategy emphasized a reading-and-notice relationship between the individual citizen and the state. The curriculum guide (*Hazelwood*) defined the operation and end goals of the course, and school administrators needed only to act in accordance with those written statements to be justified in their censorship. *Morse* broadened this beyond the curriculum to the national policy against drug use, citing the protection of students as a rationale. This shift placed a contractual model on top of the law of free expression, which substantially increased the capabilities that the child is expected to have. Where originally rights were bestowed on the child so that the child could develop capabilities for citizenship, now there were requirements whose display was integral to the child earning protection for speech rights.

The contractual model of *Hazelwood, DeShaney,* and *Morse* altered the constitutional meaning of citizenship in favor of a state with the commitment solely to be consistent with its own statements and commitments. The requirement to develop citizens dropped out in favor of a host of policies, rules, and regulations. *Hazelwood* began this process with reference to curriculum and the school's message—the state must control its curriculum, both in terms of the unintended circulation of speech and the potential that members of the public might confuse the school's tolerance of speech as endorsement. *DeShaney* used a parsimonious construction of state responsibilities. *Morse* furthered the impoverishment of the social contract by allowing schools to prohibit speech that they reasonably believed to disavow important school policy. Although Justice Roberts's opinion used recent court precedent and national legislation to show the popular and expert endorsement of these policies, he employed that as evidence not for their wisdom but for silencing dissent about them.

The resistance to the contract model of citizenship in these cases emerged in dissents that brought questions of citizenship to the fore in two ways: by rehabilitating care of individual circumstances, and by activating the discourse of time horizons as signs of wise judgment. Concerning the former, the opinions opposing the advance of state rules and regulations to govern citizens highlighted the state's obligations. Each dissent prioritized the perspective of the child. Justice Brennan's *Hazelwood* dissent worried about the relationship between the state and citizen when characterizing the unmet expectations of the students who received a tangle of excuses instead of a civics lesson—first from their teachers and principal, then later from the court. Justice Blackmun's dissent—Poor Joshua!—lamented the litany of failures to prevent a fate over which Joshua never had control: the intemperate father, the dutiful social worker, and, ultimately, the arid and passive court. Each actor had an opportunity to intervene, but each ultimately abdicated on the basis of texts that offered them plausible deniability of obligation: they were not compelled to intervene, therefore they did not. Finally, Justice Stevens's dissent in *Morse* noted that even though Frederick's banner may have seemed nonsensical, the majority opinion had given the swift acting and certain administrator a pass—citizens deserved an individualized determination of risk that their speech would harm the school's mission.

Each of the dissents also offered an alternative vision of sound judgment by appealing to temporality as a path to connecting judgment to commonly shared values. This discourse made use of a familiar theme and exploited the vulnerability of a contract discourse shorn of such values. Justice Brennan argued in *Hazelwood* for citizens of a democracy where civics matters and criticism holds administrators accountable for inconsistencies in their decision-making. Justice Blackmun's *DeShaney* dissent utilized an argument from analogy to compare the situation of childhood to slavery. Like slavery, child abuse was being justified by legal formalism; and the court was disconnected from both moral compass and the centuries of legal precedent that came later. Finally, Justice Stevens argued that the *Morse* majority was too invested in protecting legislation from dissent. A long view of history—embodied by the examples of Prohibition and the Vietnam War—demonstrated the danger that a judgment linked to protecting consensus can have.

This contractual model had not yet resolved the paradox of the (in)capable citizen: how can a constitutional democracy simultaneously ground itself in a core of inviolable citizenship rights, and yet suspend those rights in the name of producing citizens in a democratic political order? If each of the models of the previous chapters demonstrated alternate strategic responses to this enduring situation, the contractual model likewise failed to provide a definitive resolution. The majorities in each of these cases addresses the categorical equality of the child as citizen, yet invokes citizens' incapacities as justifications for denying citizenship rights. The free speech cases treat the child as a citizen with the right to speak. But in denying that right as exercised, each opinion relied on the fear that the speaker's public was incapable of using the speaker's message in the project of democratic self-rule. *Hazelwood*, like *Fraser*, invoked the discourse of confused and distracted students whose incapacities would stir emotional reactions to taboo subjects. Morse, too, was preoccupied with the impact that a "nonsense banner" might have on a supposed national consensus against drug use. This conclusion only makes sense if the opinion gave interpretive weight to a general idea about the speech's audience that could capably decipher the message and uncritically follow its dictates to violate the law. In the area of a citizen's due process, *DeShaney* held that the child was categorically free (like all citizens), yet it also assumed the citizens' incapacities in its zeal to protect the state from incapable actors—overzealous litigation that might bankrupt the state, overzealous judges who could misinterpret ambiguous rules, and the like. In short, if the strength of the contractual model of citizenship lies in its statements of categorical equality, its discursive weakness lies in the web of fictions about individual social relationships. This leads to the possibility that Supreme Court judgments are partially abdications of judgment: the state can frame the terms of its own authority, as it becomes increasingly detached from substantive obligations and responsibilities.

CONCLUSION

Citizenship and Judgment in Uncertain Times

What makes a good decision, and how do we know? This question matters to individuals faced with choices about how to live their lives, to social groups carving out distinct identities, and to governments addressing public controversies over distributions of resources and a sense of national character. Judgment is simply unavoidable in a culture that prizes individual thought and democratic action. It is a faculty for making life decisions, a social currency for those who do it better, and a lightning rod for controversy when people employ different judging practices to make collective decisions. In a liberal society, a life without judgment would be degraded: a life without individual choice, without public criticism, without evaluations of the better and worse elements of existence. It sounds good to those of us who would escape the pressure of constant decision but its connection to freedom and self-determination makes the prospect unimaginable.

The preceding chapters demonstrated how judicial opinions negotiated precedent, judicial philosophies, and the pressure of contingent legal facts to shape our understanding of children as citizens. The analysis focused on the ways that both the products of these opinions (what they said about the contours of the child's rights) and their process (how these opinions authorized these outcomes) shaped the legal identity of citizens. The analysis revealed that children as citizens were limited (and sometimes enabled) by their capabilities. The cases studied in this book dealt with marginal subjects; their marginality may have proved to be a virtue, because the pressure of deciding the contours of citizenship on the margins served as an impetus for articulating the contours of citizenship for all. The chapters grouped clusters of cases together because each cluster formed a distinctive model or strategy for addressing the recurring problem of the child's citizenship. Together they constituted a repertoire whose moves, appeals, tensions, and shortcomings can be activated in any given controversy. In concluding, I would like to recapitulate the distinctive strategies and clarify their status as a narrative trajectory. I will also make more explicit the connection between the narrative trajectory and its implications for citizenship and the judiciary. Finally, I want to make an argument about the resemblances between the courts and our broader public culture. In drawing on some of the examples that opened the book (and a few others), I would like to show that the narrative arc across the court cases I analyzed reveals a range of possible policies, rationales, arguments, and appeals that can be taken up at any time in diverse settings. These possibilities also come with the pressure that precedent and other conventions effect over time. That pressure shapes a society's capacity for making good policies and good judgment.

This study does not make an explicit argument about *the* proper definition of the child-citizen. In fact, quite the opposite: the book has argued that the understanding of the child's status as a citizen has changed across time, a product of context-sensitive judicial opinions. At the same time, the study did not merely argue that every individual decision was solely a product of judicial rhetoric. To attribute so much power to the strategic choices of individual judges would be both unsatisfying and unrealistic. Judicial opinions are more than mere personal whim, or belief. The preceding chapters made a different argument with broader implications for the study of legal rhetoric and the study of citizenship in public culture: they argued that the judicial opinions constructed the legal identity of the citizen through discourse. To that end, the book identified four specific models for addressing the problem of the child as citizen. Before reviewing those models, a brief review of the specific affordances of the book's approach is appropriate to clarify the status of the models of judgment that it put forth.

The Status of the Judicial Models: The Child as Representative Anecdote and the Novelization of Citizenship

The book has argued that the problem of the child is a representative anecdote for a larger set of social and political relationships. As highlighted in the introduction, it references a model that is typical of a certain kind of discourse (Kenneth Burke referred to "motives"). What this approach sacrifices in causality claims, it gains in its ability to tease out and understand a repertoire of discursive practices. To approach the problem of the child as a representative anecdote thus provides a vocabulary for further analysis and understanding the problem of judgment in a variety of situations to the extent that it structures the motives within the discourse. The child's development is a problem to be managed because the child is a future citizen (necessary to reproduce political order); at the same time, the child lacks the capabilities to make social and political decisions responsibly. For these reasons, the family, the church, the school (and where necessary, the government) act in the child's interests so that the child is prepared to live independently and participate in political life. As a representative anecdote, the child's (un)readiness for full citizenship has implications for the structure of political controversies. Children's exemplary performance of judgment makes them especially compelling for political leadership, in part because of the display of character traits that adults (who are supposed to possess them) lack. At the same time, the (typical) child who lacks these traits of judgment is an object of cultivation and protection.

This representative anecdote structured the motives in the judicial opinions that the book has studied. In the course of answering how to manage the problem of the child in accordance with American constitutional principles, the opinions produced a repertoire of discursive maneuvers that can be seen operating in broader public discourse. These judicial opinions novelized the public sphere, deploying characters and themes in a dialogic relationship to authorize their decisions. The models do not predict outcomes in particular cases, which are dependent on a variety of additional factors. Nor do these models focus on a causal relationship between a specific legal case and a behavioral outcome for a specific group at a specific time. To focus on novelization is to argue that discursive elements place pressure on judicial opinions, which limits what they can do in a given case. The outcome of this study is a repertoire of argumentative appeals and figures that are used in these important cases of citizenship (and, as I suggest, in the broader public culture). By focusing on this repertoire, the book does not merely list a series; it also locates a structure of topics and tensions that scholars of citizenship could take up at various discursive sites.

To see the child as a representative anecdote for the problem of citizenship in US public culture reveals the importance of sound judgment as an informal qualification for citizenship, displayed through cognitive skill. As the study demonstrated, judicial discourse has historically qualified sound judgment by the assessment of one's capabilities. The narrative arc showed that the child's "unreadiness" for citizenship produced meditations on just what it was the child lacked. In the beginning, the lack was a lack of virtue and respect for property; this shifted to a lack of critical capacities to think, plan, and execute political speech and how that lack should shape the state's response.

The "child" began as a broad category exempted from the requirements (and rights) of citizenship because they lacked the virtues of citizenship—primarily respect for property. This exclusion shifted to inclusion as a citizen, but the lack of cognitive capabilities remained as the engine for that shift—the state could not strangle the child's free mind. The kinds of cognitive abilities shifted as speech took on more importance. The book identified four distinct models for addressing the problem of judgment, corresponding to the four parts of the volume and their cases.

The first model was the "Child as Ward." These cases understood citizenship as the possession of particular virtues, which the incapable child lacked. The state was limited because citizens were "naturally free"; the state could limit this natural freedom (of the parents) to discipline the child. This discipline was intended to instill citizen virtues, which emphasized economic production and respect for property. The children in these cases were incapable because of either moral failings or of their threatening critical behavior or speech. The state's goal was to reform character by forcibly separating the child from immoral and corrupt influences. Sound judgment was performed by teachers and judges through the display of cognitive capacities. This model derived its authority with mixed appeals to hierarchy and foundational documents; most crucially, it relied on performances of temporality in order to distinguish sound judgment from decisions that were irrational or overly emotional. The "role of the judge" in these cases was one in which judges adapted prior hierarchical models of expertise to the particularities of a liberal political order. Two pivotal cases at the beginning of the nineteenth century, *Meyer* and *Pierce,* set limits on this model: the state could not treat the child as ward when the former mischaracterized the threat to civic unity, because parents and teachers had liberty interests. That limit raised questions about the extent to which the child could claim such interests, and whether liberty interests could block state efforts to develop virtues. These cases also foreshadowed questions concerning the "role of the judge" by beginning two significant trends: they started to develop complex factual narratives of the parties, and they introduced rhetorical tools that were designed to limit the potential reach of their interpretive expertise. Both of these tactics conformed to an idea that democracy was best done through deference to private economic activity and representative institutions.

These lingering questions precipitated a series of controversies that shaped the second model: the "Child as Categorical Equal." That model advanced a legal identity of the child as a citizen with equal claims to free speech and due process rights. Avenues of competent citizen performance opened up to the child. This model posed persuasive communication as the driver of civic unity and individual thought and criticism as primary citizen capabilities. Because civic unity was political, citizens embodied the cognitive markers of sound citizen judgment by displaying their strategic planning, marked by intentional goals, the reflective suggestion of proper speech form, and consistency between stated intentions and prior texts. This shift also introduced a more explicit controversy concerning the role of the judge. Judges were protecting individual rights and downplaying anxiety about limiting the judiciary's reach. As a result, discourse about the role of the judge began to focus on its distinctive rigorous factfinding method and evaluation of evidence. Its relationship to temporality shifted: where before the judge displayed "critical distance" from the real-world facts of particular cases, the categorical equality model emphasized the judge's ability to mark American cultural values as a break from prior premodern traditions. It also removed hierarchical vestiges like parens patriae as an empirical failure. The primary alternative to this model argued that to assume this judicial role rendered democratic government impossible because it would impede representative institutions and produce unjust results. According to this critique, categorical equality was too arid and abstract to do justice to the recurring situations of differently classed citizens.

The third model was the "Child as Reform Object." This model exploited the vulnerabilities of the categorical equality approach, emphasizing respect for the authority of tradition in constituting a culture of citizenship. The children of these cases were individually incapable—they disobeyed authority, lacked the cognitive capacity to function in a family, and crossed civil bounds with their controversial speech. These circumstances rendered them unworthy of meaningful citizenship rights. The prior model contained a theory of how citizenship capacities were transmitted to new citizens. The reform object strategy posited shared values and insisted that children respect them. Nor was it important in these opinions that sound judgment be displayed by the state actors. All they needed to demonstrate was their well-meaning intention and their knowledge of tradition. Temporality in expert judgment was figured differentially. The majority opinions did not have recent precedent on their side. Instead, they claimed expertise by locating long-standing values—they deferred to democratic practices and habits of government, organic institutions such as the family, and norms of civility. These traditions were posed against constitutional guarantees as a mode of social order. Although the justices claimed to vindicate long-standing democratic practices, they were deferring to increasingly unrepresentative processes. In addition to the fiction that children were meaningfully represented, these opinions deferred to medical experts, administrative state bureaucrats, and the like. Because the approach rested on questionable legal interpretive practice (because it had difficulty reconciling recent precedents), it left itself open to the criticism that its outcomes were the reflection of mere personal belief.

The final model was the "Child as Contractual Citizen." In a sense, it perfected the preceding models by providing the synthetic interpretive grounding that justified broad state authority. Its children were presumed equal. This presumption extinguished the need for a special investment in the child—gone was the concern that the state not "strangle the free mind at its source" or squelch the possibilities of childhood. Instead, the child was presumed to be on equal footing to other citizens, and, it would seem, the state. As a result, the strategy implicitly indulged in the fiction that the child was as capable as any other adult citizen—to avoid private violence and to read handbooks that claimed to define the relationship between the state and the citizen in school. Citizens were expected to internalize the state's written mandates rather than acquire virtues, learn critical skills, or practice traditions. Bureaucrats performed sound judgment by adhering to previously authored scripts: the social worker who recorded threats, and the administrators who hewed to student handbooks and disciplinary guides. Judicial expertise made itself in this image. Construing state authority in a manner that limited the state's obligations to its citizens, the judicial opinions narrowly interpreted constitutional text and precedent while broadly interpreting the administrators' grants of authority. Judicial expertise performed asymmetrical interpretations that supported an asymmetrical social contract—the state now had broad authority to act in terms of vague "national interest" or "community mores" but without the responsibility to develop the capacities of citizens under its control. This model was vulnerable to a variety of criticisms. It lacked the perspective and wisdom of longer time horizons; the dissents in these cases pointed out that the majority opinions disrespected long-standing legal traditions as well as the specific relationship between individual and the state actors. Dissents also argued that the model neglected the child's need for benevolent development.

These models figured judgment in two senses. The first was the sense of judgment to be developed in children as future citizens. The other sense of judgment involves the judges themselves. The figure of the "child" has implications not only for citizenship and how we define personal agency but also for the very role and identity of the judicial system itself. The judiciary was not comfortable assuming this role and turned to novelization as a technique of managing its claim to status in our constitutional democracy. The problem of cognitive capabilities was not merely a barrier to the child's access to citizenship. It also was a mandate for judges in authorizing their opinions. Judges wield a large amount of power in a constitutional democracy to interpret the reach of the law and the meaning of the Constitution. Their decisions must authorize this power to not only bind the litigants but to change local, state, and national governing practices. So just as these judicial opinions were articulating the meaning of citizenship as the cognitive display of judgment, they were rhetorically claiming their own authority with a series of parallel displays. These judicial displays built an argument on abstract interpretive principles to assuage others that the opinions were not asserting more control over citizens than was necessary.

A vocabulary of deference emerged: judges would not second-guess teachers; benevolence compelled judicial action in order to avoid cruelty, and so on. And, as mentioned, temporality was a factor: judges showed the ability to take the long view, which was a display that they took a reasoned (rather than impulsive and emotional) perspective on controversy. As the child's status became more complex, this complexity put added pressure on judges to perform. When the child's status moved from that of ward to categorical equal, the judicial role was subject to the criticisms of deference: its role as protector of individual rights stepped outside what judges were institutionally equipped to do, and what they should be doing. This concern demanded a performative response: judges' distinctive method of inquiry made them more dispassionate decision-makers, and this rigorous method embodied the long view by taking critical distance from a controversy. Contemporary jurisprudence advanced the complexity of the judge's role in parallel to altering the child's status. By the time the child came to be considered a contractual citizen, the judicial role supporting this shift claimed authority through the rigor of synthetic interpretations.

These shifts were necessitated by the general demand that judges perform their expertise and the specific demand that they ground their opinions in the precedents and themes that preceded them. The opinions considered in the categorical equality model still framed their decisions in terms of the wardship concerns—the child's citizenship capabilities and the need to maintain an open future for children. Their opponents accused them of poor judgment because they were acting on mere personal belief. Both the reform object and contractual citizen models deployed the tenets of the categorical equality model, if for no other reason than that they had to account for those prior cases as influential precedent.

To understand these models as part of a judicial repertoire means to grasp the role of discourse in the construction of legal identities. These argument forms can be reactivated in different circumstances at different times to take on somewhat different meanings. Their political valence cannot be determined in advance. In the following section, I would like to push the argument further by suggesting a resemblance between the judiciary and the broader public culture.

The Judicial Repertoire and Public Culture

The judicial repertoire detailed in the book would appear to resemble aspects of the public discourse on display in the controversies that opened the book: the Trump administration's policy of separating immigrant families at the US border, the public discourse around gun violence in schools, and the climate activism of Greta Thunberg. Their presence in these controversies indicates that elements of the repertoire persist as public arguments about the character of democracy as well as competing attitudes about the time, place, and style of judgment appropriate to citizens. They support an inference that the way that we construct the capabilities of others also shapes the judgments that we make in the public sphere. This analysis won't offer a policy proposal to resolve specific controversies or wade into the veracity of the various claims made, though each of those areas of inquiry is important. But perhaps it can help to inform policy and the role of truth in public life by showing that our attitudes about what we owe to one another are influenced by how capable we see each other to be.

One recurring element of the judicial repertoire examined in this book has been the use of the narrative of childhood lost to justify judgment. That narrative motivated the Quaker child-savers who established the House of Refuge in the early nineteenth century. It also was invoked in *Pendergrass* to distinguish between reasonable and unreasonable punishment (based on its permanent traces). Justice Fortas relied on this narrative in *In re Gault* as a justification to end parens patriae. And Justice Blackmun's "Poor Joshua!" dissent in *DeShaney* lamented his fate to live his life out with permanent brain damage. Joshua's lost childhood was a sign of judicial abdication, a desire to follow a strict construction of the letter of the law, when a more compassionate approach was required.

Media stories detailing the effects of the Trump administration's family separation policy on children illustrated the argument that a liberal democracy should prevent irreversible cognitive damage. One report from the *Atlantic* recounts the experience of Anita and her six-year-old child, Jenri, who were separated while crossing the border to seek asylum. After release from detention, Jenri is reprimanded by a shelter employee for touching a flat screen tv:

> "No, no, honey," Sister Margaret said. "Don't touch that." The reprimand seemed to bring Jenri's month in government custody rushing back. "No touching!" Jenri said. "No touch! . . . ."
>
> Jenri began to perseverate on the phrase. He screamed "No touch!" again and again. Then, he threw himself face down on the bed and yelled

> at Anita through tears. "Just take me back to jail," he cried. "You're not my mom anymore."
>
> When he finally fell asleep, Anita stood in the darkness outside. "The separation was so long," she said. "My son has changed so much."[1]

This excerpt demonstrates how the family separation policy is criticized via an appeal to avoid the loss of normal childhood development. Jenri's experience has destroyed his cognitive and self-reflective capabilities. He utters words and phrases automatically because of the hold that a horrible past event has on his thought processes. He cannot moderate his emotions, but instead has disproportionate and uncontrollable reactions to words. He "perserverated on the phrase," until an emotional explosion compelled him to declare his familial bond severed.

Defenders of the policy deflected attention from these outcomes. President Trump argued that it prevented violence, singling out MS-13. One statement from his Twitter feed noted, "Democrats are the problem. They don't care about crime and want illegal immigrants, no matter how bad they may be, to pour into and infest our Country, like MS-13."[2] A host on *FOX & Friends* (one of President Trump's preferred news programs) circulated the claim about MS-13, adding narrative to connect immigration to MS-13: "We are $20 trillion in debt. We have classrooms that are overrun. . . . But these kids get fanned out to working class neighborhoods into our society. And then they have to be paid for by English as a second language. And then they got to be schooled and a lot of them, sadly, in my neighborhood, turn into MS-13."[3] These strategies respond to the claim of irreversible damage by pivoting to another element of the repertoire: the public threat these children posed. Just as the legislatures in *Meyer* and *Pierce* stoked fears of immigration to justify restrictive education policies, and just as the administrators in *Tinker* banned speech because of a fear that it would disrupt school activities, so does this strategy exploit the fear of insecurity in one's person and property to justify the child separation policy.

These arguments typically emphasize either the state's lack of responsibility to the child or the unknown consequences of state actions. Justice Stewart's dissent in *In re Gault* worried about miscarriages of substantive justice legitimated by procedure visiting adult judgments on undeserving children. This argument was reshaped in the majority opinions in *Parham* and *DeShaney*. Judicial deference in these cases was justified in a variety of ways: as a general incompetence to properly assess risks of particular policies in developing civic unity (in *Gobitis*), and as the need to tolerate periodic injustice because the dictates of judicial practice require that it place its faith in alternate actors to prevent gross abuse (*Ingraham* and *DeShaney*).

In the case of public discourse surrounding family separation, the argument appeared in terms of the lack of discretion and, at times, the child's just deserts. The Trump administration's Attorney General Jeff Sessions and White House Press Secretary Sarah Huckabee Sanders most notably advanced the "lack of discretion" case. Sessions, who announced the policy in April 2018, made a religious argument, justifying the policy with reference to a Bible passage that he interpreted as a mandate to "obey the laws of the government because God has ordained the government for his purposes."[4] Sanders extended this approach in the following exchange with CNN reporter Jim Acosta:

> ACOSTA: They're with their parents, and then suddenly they're pulled away from their parents. Why is the government doing this?
>
> SANDERS: Because it's the law. And that's what the law states.
>
> ACOSTA: It's not. It doesn't have to be the law. You guys don't have to do that. It's your policy.
>
> SANDERS: You're right, it doesn't have to be the law. And the President has actually called on Democrats in Congress to fix those loopholes. The Democrats have failed to come to the table, failed to help this President close these loopholes and fix this problem. We don't want this to be a problem. The President has tried to address it on a number of occasions. We've laid out a proposal. And Democrats simply refuse to do their job and fix the problem.[5]

The trope served as the ground for conservative/populist judgments about the policy, claiming its authority with a definitive textual interpretation. Sessions invoked the Bible as a defense of the policy's morality while Sanders argued that the administration was compelled by a statute. In any case, the "open-and-shut" character of these justifications is propelled by the case of the child, who forced a crisis on the administration that seeks to deflect responsibility for its policy's direct effects. Most concerning, the appeal that alternate public practices would correct abuse—common in the examined judicial opinions that turned away from injustices—has been abandoned.

In the case of #NeverAgainMSD, the "innocence lost" trope was deployed to highlight the depths to which liberal democracy had sunk due to policy paralysis. The Never Again MSD movement argued for political action so that other innocent lives could be saved. Policy makers must address gun violence not only because of its morality but because the lived experience of the liberal child is cognitively disrupted. They have seen something that interferes with the normal development of their capabilities, and this is beyond the pale of what a child should have to experience to move through life.

As mentioned in the introduction, the high school students' exceptional communication capabilities have attracted nationwide public attention. This theme hearkens back to Justice Jackson's statement in *Barnette* about communication, persuasion, and the individual mind, and *Tinker*'s focus on planning, intention, and effect. The Parkland students' communication capabilities also structured the opposition to their public intervention. Because they had performed their status as sound decision-makers, their opponents assailed their authenticity and capable character. One approach called them crisis actors, implying that they were paid to pretend to have gone through the tragedy as part of a wide conspiracy.[6] Even though pundits attribute the reaction to the proliferation of falsehoods and troubles with the digital media ecosystem, the general mode of attack is not new. Justice Black questioned the plaintiffs' independence in *Tinker* and both Fraser and Frederick were made to seem buffoons. A child is presumptively not politically competent, and if they appear so, it must be because of some sleight of hand. The general appeal delegitimized the speakers' authenticity and claim to witness (they are being paid for their testimony). It also offered an alternate explanation for the students' exemplary performance.

Another tactic framed Emma Gonzalez, one prominent public voice and face of the movement, as a threat to traditional values (á la *Fraser*). One popular assertion was that her bullying of the alleged shooter was an indirect cause of the murders. This argument implied a shift in the frame of causation from the availability of weapons to the individual's mental health. The strategy implied Gonzalez's incivility. A blog post typifying this approach argued that "Emma and her peers who ostracized the Parkland shooter since middle school should have a march against bullying" instead of "200,000 or so dumbasses [who] marched against the right to own guns."[7] Asserting the child's lack of capabilities has become a protocol of abuse, implying that the #NeverAgainMSD students were a cause of the very tragedy they are working to prevent.

Another character attack referred to Gonzalez as "Sinead O'Connor," the head-shaven singer who controversially ripped a picture of Pope John Paul II on Saturday Night Live in 1992 to protest the Catholic Church's mishandling of child sex abuse cases. Gonzalez also appears in public with a shaved head. Opponents circulated numerous references on social media to Gonzalez being a lesbian, with an altered image of Gonzalez ripping up the Constitution (the original image depicted her ripping up a target).[8] Worry about the image's authenticity misses the way that arguments from the judicial repertoire resemble the structure of the conflict. Like Justice Burger's concern in *Fraser,* the assertion hinted at Gonzalez's willingness to go to any lengths to achieve her goal. Like Justice Black's objection in *Tinker,* it activated a long-running worry (dating back at least to the House of Refuge) about the threat that youth posed to the right to be secure in one's person and property. Ideologically, the incapable child here constructed Gonzalez—and, by extension, the entire movement—as a threat to American liberty.

Finally, the case of Greta Thunberg's climate activism demonstrates the ways that public discourse resembles the repertoire from the judicial opinions. Thunberg's opponents focused on her cognitive incapacities and unregulated emotions, inverting the claim that she was acting more adult than the adults. President Trump combined "lack of emotional control" with gendered arguments about Thunberg's disposition, suggesting that she "work on her Anger Management problem, then go to a good old fashioned movie with a friend."[9] Other media sources developed the point in a more explicit way, asserting that Thunberg was letting the "so-called climate emergency" become a "personal torment" because "her parents and the climate industry have exploited her youthful idealism and rigid obsessions" (this latter reference is to Thunberg's Asperger's Syndrome).[10] A less ideological version of this line of attack argued that Thunberg was the latest example of a "media [that] now gives too much weight to the opinions of teen activists . . . Young people—even ones who can credibly claim to have been especially harmed by some crisis—do not generally have special insights or strong knowledge of public policy."[11] Here, the opposition to Thunberg has centered on her unregulated emotions, her susceptibility to misinformation from her parents (and a broader public campaign of fearmongers), and her inability to focus on relevant matters (getting stuck in "rigid obsessions"). These argument forms bear a strong similarity to judicial arguments in favor of restricting the child's political participation. Justice Frankfurter and Justice Black doubted the independent thought of child plaintiffs in *Barnette* and *Tinker* respectively, positing that the child was being manipulated by parents or religious influence. They also point to a claim that Thunberg, like the adults and scientists feeding her misinformation, are poor assessors of risk.

Throughout the study, I have argued that these controversies were important for American citizenship in part because the child's cognitive ability signaled a capacity to exercise sound judgment, and hence an ability to consent to democratic government. In this final section, I want to point to the second sense of cognition and judgment, which was the judicial performance of expertise, in order to suggest how the rhetorically grounded notions of judgment that I have highlighted can help us approach a broader crisis of democratic legitimacy in a way that can preserve strong democratic practices as a way forward.

Liberalism at a Crossroads

The 2016 presidential campaign in the United States framed a political crisis in terms of citizen apathy, polarization, and limited ability to make reasoned decisions. The resulting Trump administration posed a direct challenge to American institutions and democratic norms. The attacks emanated from a leadership style and political environment that circulated misinformation selectively and rewarded appeals to a narrow base of intense and unwavering supporters.

During the Trump presidency, we appeared caught between what Yascha Mounk has called the tension of illiberal democracy on the one hand, and undemocratic liberalism on the other hand. Mounk argues that decades of "undemocratic liberalism"—expanding individual rights that frustrate the will of the people—have given rise to populist regimes that promise democracy but deliver few rights.[12] He identifies the prominence of technocratic elites making unaccountable decisions for the people, the rapid rise of immigration, and the proliferation of social media. This study has argued that there is a tension at the core of a public culture that relies on the people to hold government accountable by insisting on justifications to curtail liberty. This culture requires a form of reasoned consent that is fictive. People don't explicitly consent to each and every action the government undertakes, they have varied relative abilities to reason, we dispense with consent processes in a crisis, we negotiate over what consent looks like when the matter requires technical expertise, and so on. The preceding chapters have made the case that the status of the child is an important site not only for justifying curbs on liberty but for articulating norms and standards of good judgment so we know it when we see it. The children in these cases succeeded or failed to the extent that they performed their capabilities. Judges writing opinions authorized their expertise in doing the same.

For communication studies, the concept of "cognitive capabilities" can serve as a hermeneutic for these times. It complements Martha C. Nussbaum's and Amartya K. Sen's influential use of the term to measure a society's commitment to human equality.[13] Defined as "the opportunity to achieve valuable combinations of human functionings—what a person is able to do or be," this approach amends traditional social contract theory, which insists on rough equality and freedom among its subjects.[14] The child's status is particularly important, because these controversies involve the kind of asymmetries of power where such freedom and equality do not exist.[15]

Rhetorical practices demonstrate the ways that communication capabilities are culture variant. Nussbaum derives a list of capabilities inferring the well-being of a society from their relative presence. That list includes practical reason, defined as "being able to form a conception of the good and to engage in critical reflection about the planning of one's life."[16] This study suggests a challenge to this approach and a method appropriate to continuing these inquiries for the study of public culture. It identified a constitutive tension between the individual subject of rights and dignity on the one hand, and the pressure to "perform these rights" through the display of capabilities for judgment on the other. This public culture produces future citizens equipped to judge and participate in the public sphere through discourses of management that appraise performances. This constitutive tension, and the genres of performance through which it plays out, can be used to investigate other exceptional cases in the public sphere that sit at the edge of inclusion for individual rights.

We should also reflect on the use of capabilities as a discourse that justifies authority, sometimes to unjust ends. The Nussbaum-Sen inspired capabilities approach identifies an abstract metric to identify the traits that are necessary for human flourishing, then measures the presence of those traits to assess the justness of a government's policies. I have tried to show how the idiom of judgment capabilities can be deployed to instantiate norms and manage subjects with antidemocratic consequences. It is not merely a measuring stick to see how healthy a people are; it is also a discourse used to mark those with lower status and exclude certain kinds of participation.

It is in this sense that the book has argued that the problem of the child is a representative anecdote for a larger set of social and political relationships. This anecdote serves as a distributing principle of authority and power. Consider criticisms of a "feminine style," or the pervasive noxious notion throughout American history that Black slaves were not "ready for citizenship" (including the terrible on-going legacy of Jim Crow and a regime of mass incarceration that historically has deemed convicted felons incapable of voting or unemployable). The list can be expanded to include questions of economic market regulation and areas where social capital intersect with constitutional rights. Is the consumer "capable" of making a meaningful choice when taking out a subprime mortgage? When is someone demonstrating capabilities to make decisions to end one's life? To consent to sexual relations? Reading generic performances in these and other areas would demonstrate a potentially fruitful line of inquiry in the study of public culture.

This discourse reminds us that some of our most important judgments are the ones we make to cede authority to others. The widening income gap has been attributed in large part to the abdication of political responsibility by elites and the corporate domination of politics. From the right, scientists reporting on the causes and effects of climate change are treated with skepticism. From the left, people have attacked centrism as a liberal consensus for its supposed fidelity to technocratic rule at the expense of tangible gains for the people in terms of healthcare, education, labor rights, and environmental protections. Social media may also play a role: in a world in which any of us can participate, few of us have the time and attention to vet information quality, and extremes are rewarded with attention. Expertise is under duress.

This seems appropriate in our time of struggle between forces of nationalism, populism, and constitutional authority. The public controversies from the introduction typify the struggle. Each controversy has roots in the failure to secure rights to life, liberty, and property due to contemporary crises that seem utterly out of our personal control to address. It is difficult to think about regulation of guns without acknowledging the culture of fear that has grown (especially since 9/11) to oppose it, it is difficult to think about immigration without considering the role of scapegoating, and it is difficult to think about climate change without the expanding stratification of wealth and opposition to regulations. It is difficult to think about all of these problems without also admitting that many people doubt liberal democracy's ability to secure the rights of the individual. Liberal democratic norms, it would appear, are on the ropes and there is an appetite for alternatives.

Analyzing the ways that judges perform their expertise can reveal much about the choices we make for the kind of democracy we want to have. The tensions, ironies, and possible judicial missteps of the judicial repertoire may serve as the building blocks for a new public culture. At the very least, they can provide a possible guide to avoid traps and expose weaknesses. The narrative trajectory of the models suggested that judgment principles intended to preserve democratic decision-making slipped into deference to the administration of things. In a complex rule-driven world that has become more detached from the people subject to these rules, whatever the fate of liberal democracy—retrenchment, reform, revolution, or something in between—the connection between expert judgment and democratic government likely will still matter. I have suggested a catalogue of attitudes clustered around the role of the expert, and the way that role is performed in relation to particular ideologies of democracy.

The story told is ironic, which is to be expected given the countermajoritarian nature of judicial opinions. One irony involves the fate of the liberal individual. Liberty expanded with a twist that refigured the state's authority over the individual, and deemphasized civic responsibilities. By the late twentieth and early twenty-first centuries, the state's interests have shifted drastically—bureaucracy carries the weight of constitutional interest. This interest has been paired with an interpretive disposition that prizes clear command, limits the state's obligations, and broadens its own interests. This disconnection from democratic decisions and this shift toward national interests strengthens the state's hand against the individual, even as it claims to prize the individual's rights.

A second irony lies in the regressive movement of judgment, because conservative approaches have taken on antidemocratic features and progressive approaches to judgment have become entangled with restrictive principles. Traditionally, judges were experts because they were able to derive an abstract quality from factual assertions and divide it into greater and lesser concerns; the abstractions were linked directly to an argument about the resolution of the case. These interpretive acts performed the limits of their authority. They referred to counterfactuals (the things their decisions did not cover) and the mutual entailing of seemingly competing values to cultivate democratic acceptance.

Post–World War II cases produced a fundamental split in the terms set by their predecessors. Here were extended meditations on the role of the expert judge itself. Should an expert bring a personal sense of desirable ends to the table? The concerns of the mission-driven state were being sloughed aside for the expansion of the liberal individual, and the frame shifted to the question of whether this new kind of judicial expert properly fit into a larger democratic system. The conventions of earlier cases remained: there was a preferred hierarchy of texts, decisions needed to justify themselves with reference to commonly held values, and judges who advocated for an expansion of rights needed to rhetorically justify their decision to assure a broader public that the judgment would not set an antidemocratic precedent. In the process, progressive judges began to make reference to both the exceptional character of the expansion and the procedural-contractual character of expert judgment.

When more conservative judgment reasserted itself in the reform object and contractual citizen models, it was saddled with the language, justifications, and strategies of the expansion period. State authority was framed in terms of a rehabilitation of a venerated tradition of civility, and a return to deference. But these cases did not overrule the liberal precedents so much as limit their growth. They grounded their strategies in specific incapable children, because that figure permitted a return to conservative tradition through state and parental authority. It was also mappable, because it had been an enduring theme across the four models discussed. This maneuver has exacted a democratic price at odds with traditional conservatism. In the name of protecting a limited government to maximize freedom, decisions have insisted on deferring to rules in school manuals and arcane budgetary allocations to define state obligations. And decisions are justifying these outcomes on strident interpretations that leave less and less room for disagreement and diversity.

Rhetorical studies can evaluate the character of deliberation and decision in public discourse as well, informed by ideas about what composition choices imply about subjectivity and the communicative relationships among the familiar social organizations of liberal society. More than this, scholars could extend the analysis of rhetorical form to study public culture as a profusion of diverse and plural positions within a system of public address: how different genres novelize public culture. The judicial opinions studied here offered one path, creating a wide variety of figures, interests, and motives: the individual thinker/leader, the incapable child, the frustrated bureaucrat, the earnest protestor, the puerile adolescent, the cool manager, the technocrat, the prophet. This process of novelization is itself an account of how public culture articulates its ideas about judgment, citizenship, pluralism, and social obligation.

The problem of the child and the issue of inclusive citizenship it represents are unlikely to shrink in importance. The former is a sign of the practical problem of justice. The latter indicates a broader crisis that requires reconnection with democratic rule. As new forms of government and social relationships challenge the social contract model, the problem of the judgment will continue to be important. I have contributed to its study by showing how a promising beginning can become impoverished. It offers a glimmer of hope that we can see our constraints as opportunities for invention. And it provides counsel for us to stay ever vigilant to maintain a worthwhile public culture.

NOTES

Introduction

1. Elizabeth Chuck, Alex Johnson, and Corky Siemaszko, "17 Killed in Mass Shooting in High School," *NBC News*, February 15, 2018, https://www.nbcnews.com/news/us-news/police-respond-shooting-parkland-florida-high-school-n848101.

2. Quinn Scanlan, "Florida Teen Shooting Survivors Announce 'March for Our Lives' Demonstration in Washington," *ABC News*, February 18, 2018, https://abcnews.go.com/Politics/florida-teen-shooting-survivors-announce-march-washington-demand/story?id=53178265.

3. Susan McFarland, "Fla. Governor Signs School Security, Gun Control Bill; NRA Sues to Challenge," *United Press International*, March 9, 2018, https://www.upi.com/Top_News/US/2018/03/09/Fla-governor-signs-school-security-gun-control-bill-NRA-sues-to-challenge/5961520617500/; Gabriella Borter, "Parkland Massacre Survivors Post Sweeping U.S. Gun-Control Plan ahead of 2020 Election," Reuters, August 21, 2019, https://www.reuters.com/article/us-usa-guns/parkland-massacre-survivors-post-sweeping-u-s-gun-control-plan-ahead-of-2020-election-idUSKCN1VB1KE.

4. Ginger Thompson, "Listen to Children Who've Just Been Separated from Their Parents at the Border," ProPublica, June 18, 2018, https://www.propublica.org/article/children-separated-from-parents-border-patrol-cbp-trump-immigration-policy. For the conditions of the facilities, see Zolan Kanno-Youngs, "Poor Conditions Persist for Migrant Children Detained at the Border, Democrats Say," *New York Times*, August 29, 2019, https://www.nytimes.com/2019/08/29/us/politics/homeland-security-migrant-children.html.

5. Maria Sacchetti, "'Kids in Cages': House Hearing Examines Immigration Detention as Democrats Push for More Information," *Washington Post*, July 10, 2019, https://www.washingtonpost.com/immigration/kids-in-cages-house-hearing-to-examine-immigration-detention-as-democrats-push-for-more-information/2019/07/10/3cc53006-a28f-11e9-b732-41a79c2551bf_story.html. See also David A. Graham, "Are Children Being Kept In 'Cages' at the Border?": A Semantic Debate Is Raging over What to Call the Pens Where Migrant Kids Are Being Held after Separation from Their Parents," *Atlantic*, June 18, 2018, https://www.theatlantic.com/politics/archive/2018/06/ceci-nest-pas-une-cage/563072/.

6. Greta Thunberg, "Transcript: Speech at the U.N. Climate Action Summit," *NPR*, September 23, 2019, https://www.npr.org/2019/09/23/763452863/transcript-greta-thunbergs-speech-at-the-u-n-climate-action-summit.

7. Robinson Meyer, "Why Greta Makes Adults Uncomfortable," *Atlantic*, September 23, 2019, https://www.theatlantic.com/science/archive/2019/09/why-greta-wins/598612/.

8. Elizabeth F. Cohen, *Semi-Citizenship in Democratic Politics* (Cambridge: Cambridge University Press, 2009). Semi-citizenship is a framework to describe categories of people such as immigrants, children, and the disabled, who are neither noncitizens nor full citizens. Cohen understands the category to be an inevitable feature of democratic government. See also Elizabeth F. Cohen, "Neither Seen nor Heard: Children's Citizenship in Contemporary Democracies," *Citizenship Studies* 9, no. 2 (2005): 221–40.

9. "Child" can be defined simply as a person "below the legal age of majority," and "adolescent" can be defined as a person "in the process of developing from a child into an adult." I use the terms interchangeably, because the child's citizenship is marked partially by their status (below the age of majority) and partially by the process of maturing into a fuller citizen.

10. Cohen, "Neither Seen nor Heard," 238.

11. The phrase "categorical equality" here describes a common rhetorical strategy, not an empirical fact. One of the goals of this book is to trace the consequences that follow from judges' decisions to justify opinions with reference to the child's supposed equality to adults. The book does not argue that children are equal to adults without qualification or should be treated that way in every instance. Rather, it suggests that judges sometimes have used this appeal to resolve constitutional crises, and this approach maintains a tension with other opposing rhetorical strategies. Indeed, these opposing rhetorical strategies often exploit the fact that treating children as "categorical equals" does not often square with our experience of how the social world is organized.

12. On the benefit of rhetorical study for understanding this aspect of citizenship, see Robert Asen, "A Discourse Theory of Citizenship," *Quarterly Journal of Speech* 90, no. 2 (2004): 189–211; Robert Hariman and John Louis Lucaites, *No Caption Needed: Iconic Photographs, Public Culture, and Liberal Democracy* (Chicago: University of Chicago Press, 2007), especially pp. 16–19, and Christian Kock and Lisa S. Villadsen, "Rhetorical Citizenship: Studying the Discursive Crafting and Enactment of Citizenship," *Citizenship Studies* 21, no. 5 (2017): 570–86.

13. Citizenship status here means that the child's rights are limited by their incompetent display. The judicial opinions express conditions, stipulations, and qualifications that relegate the child's political voice and choice to lower status.

14. Kenneth Burke, *Philosophy of Literary Form* (Berkeley: California Press, 1967), 293–304. Burke elaborated on the social function of dramatistic vocabularies—which include terms whose interactions provide societies with certain affordances (while denying others) in *A Grammar of Motives* (Berkeley: California Press, 1962), *Permanence and Change* (Berkeley: California Press, 1965), *Language as Symbolic Action* (Berkeley: California Press, 1966), among other works. This study does not explicitly assume the methodological approach of the Burkean pentad, which, while useful for developing discursive motives at a general and abstract level, is not the most productive way to illuminate the

role of judicial opinions addressing the problem of the child as citizen. Instead, the book attends to the ways that the conventions of judicial discourse refigure the social problem by explaining how the opinions generate a repertoire of argumentative moves that resolve the conflict that the child-as-citizen presents.

15. Barry Brummett, "Burke's Representative Anecdote as a Method in Media Criticism," *Critical Studies in Mass Communication* 1, no. 2 (1984): 161. I am not "looking for the anecdotes" in the following judicial opinions in order to then fit the opinions' arguments into a Burkean analysis. Rather, I am arguing that the story of the child's journey to full citizenship serves as a "basic narrative structure shared by the texts" that I am studying. Bryan Crable, "Burke's Perspective on Perspectives: Grounding Dramatism in the Representative Anecdote," *Quarterly Journal of Speech* 86, no. 3 (2000): 319. This analysis is related to, but different from, some more recent uses of the approach, which argue that the texts under consideration *are* representative anecdotes. See, for example, Calvin Coker, "Romney, Obama, and the 47%: Gaffes and Representative Anecdotes in the 2012 Presidential Campaign," *Argumentation and Advocacy* 53, no. 4 (2017): 327–43; and Martha S. Cheng and Julian C. Chambliss, "The 1909 *Plan of Chicago* as Representative Anecdote: Constituting New Citizens for the Commercial American City," *Rhetoric Review* 35, no. 2 (2016): 91–107. For the purposes of this study, the representative anecdote serves as a departure point for analyzing the selected texts for the way that they inflect the characters in the narrative with attitudes, actions, dispositions, capabilities, values, and so on. Some readers familiar with scholarship on public culture may see affinities between this approach and scholarship on "social imaginaries" propelled by the work of Charles Taylor and others. Charles Taylor, *Modern Social Imaginaries* (Durham: Duke University Press, 2004).

16. Cohen, *Semi-Citizenship*, 180.

17. The scholarly agreement about the in-between character of childhood citizenship echoes earlier works investigating the status of the child in modern life. These include Philippe Aries, *Centuries of Childhood: A Social History of Family Life* (New York: Vintage, 1965), which argued that ideas about the child as a private object of family affection are a modern evolution. Viviana Zelizer's *Pricing the Priceless Child: The Changing Social Value of Children* (Princeton: Princeton University Press, 1994) noted the emotional investments in children that emerged in America in the early 1900s, which drove up their "price." Neil Postman's *The Disappearance of Childhood* (New York: Vintage, 1994) lamented the evaporation of these humane attachments through pervasive multimedia influences.

18. Jessica Kulynych, "No Playing in the Public Sphere: Democratic Theory and the Exclusion of Children," *Social Theory and Practice* 27, no. 2 (2001): 231–64. See also Ruth Lister, "Why Citizenship: Where, When, and How Children?" *Theoretical Inquiries in Law* 8, no. 2 (2007): 693–718, and Elizabeth F. Cohen, "Neither Seen nor Heard."

19. David Tyack and his collaborators have documented the relationship between the institution of public compulsory education and the development of the early American republic, including the production of diversity, tolerance, and civic virtue. David Tyack, "Ways of Seeing: An Essay on the History of Compulsory Schooling," *Harvard Educational Review* 46, no. 3 (1976): 355–89; David Tyack and Elisabeth Hansot, "Conflict and Consensus in American Public Education," *Daedalus* 110, no. 3 (1981): 1–25;

David B. Tyack and Elisabeth Hansot, *Managers of Virtue: Public School Leadership in America, 1820–1980* (New York: Basic Books, 1982); and David Tyack, *Seeking Common Ground: Public Schools in a Diverse Society* (Cambridge: Harvard University Press, 2003). For a contemporary update to this position, see David Archard, "Children, Multiculturalism, and Education," in *The Moral and Political Status of Children*, eds. David Archard and Colin M. Macleod (New York: Oxford University Press, 2002), 153. On the potential conflicts between rights claims and liberal toleration, see Eamonn Callan, *Creating Citizens: Political Education and Liberal Democracy* (Oxford: Clarendon, 1997).

20. Brian S. Amsden has analyzed the rhetorical consequences of this tension in a series of articles. See Brian Amsden, "Negotiating Liberalism and Bio-Politics: Stylizing Power in Defense of the Mall Curfew," *Quarterly Journal of Speech* 94, no. 4 (2008): 407–29; "Democratic Prudence and the Youth Suffrage Debate," *Argumentation and Advocacy* 48, no. 1 (2011): 22–38; and "Performing Maturity in the Parental Consent and Notification Judicial Bypass Procedure," *Communication and Critical/Cultural Studies* 12, no. 1 (2015): 1–18. Amsden's work returns time and again to the ways that the law is a force to discipline and limit the freedom of the child. My analysis argues that the conventions of legal discourse constrain and enable the various responses to the problem of the child and produce a repertoire of positions for a broader public culture. The fields of political theory and childhood studies also have taken notice of the problem, for example in Jeremy Roche, "Children: Rights, Participation, and Citizenship," *Childhood* 6, no. 4 (1999): 475–93. See also Cohen, "Neither Seen nor Heard"; Allison James, "To Be (Come) or Not to Be (Come): Understanding Children's Citizenship," *ANNALS of the American Academy of Political and Social Science* 633, no. 1 (2010): 167–79; and John Wall, "Can Democracy Represent Children? Towards a Politics of Difference," *Childhood* 19, no. 1 (2011): 86–100.

21. Lister, "Why Citizenship," 698. See also Mehmoona Moosa-Mitha, "A Difference Centered Alternative to Theorization of Children's Citizenship Rights," *Citizenship Studies* 9, no. 4 (2005): 369–88; and John Wall, "Can Democracy Represent Children?" Any theory of differentiation must tend to the ways that children have been racially marked. See Robin Bernstein, *Racial Innocence: Performing American Childhood from Slavery to Civil Rights* (New York: NYU Press, 2011). For an argument that "childhood" as a category is not available to communities of color, see Erica R. Meiners, *For the Children? Protecting Innocence in the Carceral State* (Minneapolis: University of Minnesota Press, 2016).

22. Lauren Berlant explores this theme in "The Theory of Infantile Citizenship," *Public Culture* 5, no. 3 (1993): 395–410. For Berlant, the trope of the innocent infant serves as the obverse of a cynical adult citizen whose hard experiences have forced them to give up on achieving a political culture vastly different from the status quo.

23. Early American governing practices acknowledged the confounding relationship between the child-citizen and the American republic. The child provided both an aspirational metaphor and a practical problem: "The potentiality and insufficiency embodied in childhood pervade the primers, political treatises, and novels through which the colonists in eighteenth-century America were conceiving a new national identity." Gillian Brown, *The Consent of the Governed: The Lockean Legacy in Early American Culture* (Cambridge: Harvard University Press, 2001), 10. For Locke, the child's natural position vis-á-vis its parents was consensual. This theoretical move didn't merely denaturalize sovereign

authority: it rendered parental authority private and temporary, and it connected citizenship to the maturing child: "The child's consent . . . ratifies his dependence on the parent as well as his future independence from the parent. Father and magistrate rule by the child's and citizen's consent." Brown, *Consent of the Governed*, 22.

24. Nineteenth-century American women constitute a strong example of family as stewards of civic virtue. See Linda K. Kerber, "The Republican Mother: Women and the Enlightenment–An American Perspective," *American Quarterly* 28, no. 2 (1976): 187–205; and *Women of the Republic: Intellect and Ideology in Revolutionary America* (Chapel Hill: University of North Carolina Press, 2000). The dissolution of the family unit is one site at which children's agency in determining their interests can be studied. Bren Neale, "Dialogue with Children: Children, Divorce, and Citizenship," *Childhood* 9, no. 4 (2002): 455–75. Anne C. Dailey advocates for a federal interest to shape the early caregiving relationship so that it can foster "a citizenry with the skills of critical self-reflection and emotional mastery usable in times of political crisis." "Developing Citizens," *Iowa Law Review* 91, no. 2 (2006): 481.

25. Engin F. Isin and Greg M. Nielsen, eds., *Acts of Citizenship* (Chicago: Zed Books, 2008).

26. Thunberg, "U.N. Speech."

27. Bill Weir, "Greta Thunberg: The Teenage Old Soul of the Climate Crisis," CNN, September 20, 2019, https://www.cnn.com/2019/09/20/us/greta-thunberg-profile-weir/index.html.

28. Meyer, "Why Greta Makes Adults Uncomfortable."

29. Alyssa Newcomb, "How Parkland's Social Media-Savvy Teens Took Back the Internet—and the Gun Control Debate," *NBC News*, February 22, 2018, https://www.nbcnews.com/tech/tech-news/how-parkland-students-are-using-social-media-keep-gun-control-n850251.

30. Van Jones, "'This Week' Transcript," *ABC News*, March 4, 2018, https://abcnews.go.com/Politics/week-transcript-11-18-white-house-chief-staff/story?id=53487441.

31. Ginger Thompson, "A Border Patrol Agent Reveals What It's Really Like to Guard Migrant Children," ProPublica, July 16, 2019, https://www.propublica.org/article/a-border-patrol-agent-reveals-what-its-really-like-to-guard-migrant-children.

32. Christopher Sherman, Martha Mendoza, and Garance Burke, "U.S. Held a Record Number of Migrant Kids in Custody This Year," *Frontline* and the Associated Press, November 12, 2019, https://www.pbs.org/wgbh/frontline/article/u-s-held-record-69-thousand-migrant-children-in-custody-in-2019/.

33. Thunberg, "U.N. Speech."

34. *CNN News*, "Transcript: Stoneman Students' Questions to Lawmakers and the NRA at the CNN Town Hall," CNN.com, February 22, 2018, https://www.cnn.com/2018/02/22/politics/cnn-town-hall-full-video-transcript/index.html.

35. Child's World America, "Petition from Mental Health Professionals: Stop Border Separation of Children from Parents!" accessed November 4, 2020, https://childsworldamerica.org/stop-border-separation/stop-border-separation-text-preview/.

36. Zyhana Bryant, the student who started a petition to remove the Robert E. Lee statue in Charlottesville (the same location of the Unite the Right rally that resulted in the murder of Heather Heyer and acts of racially motivated violence), said, "Thanks to a

school assignment on 'how to make change,' I took an even closer look at public places like parks and thought about how we could change them to be more inclusive." Amdé Mengistu, "This Teenager Made History and Pissed Off Racists Everywhere," *Vice*, February 27, 2018, https://www.vice.com/en_us/article/8xdkj5/this-teenager-made-history-and-pissed-off-racists-everywhere.

37. In re Cassandra C., 112 A.3d 158 (Conn. 2015).

38. Brown v. Board of Education, 347 U.S. 483, 493 (1954).

39. Barbara Woodhouse marked the role of the child as property of the parents and has advocated for a more child-centric view of children's rights. Barbara Woodhouse, "Who Owns the Child? *Meyer* and *Pierce* and the Child as Property," *William and Mary Law Review* 33, no. 4 (1992): 995–1122. See also *Hidden in Plain Sight: The Tragedy of Children's Rights from Ben Franklin to Lionel Tate* (Princeton: Princeton University Press, 2010). Anne C. Dailey's "Developing Citizens" takes a similar view. For scholarship that incorporates scientific evidence of cognition into legal reform efforts, see Vivian E. Hamilton's "Democratic Inclusion, Cognitive Development, and the Age of Electoral Majority," *Brooklyn Law Review* 77, no. 4 (2012): 1447–1514 and her essay, "Liberty without Capacity: Why States Should Ban Adolescent Driving," *Georgia Law Review* 48, no. 4 (2014): 1019–84. For liberal democratic updates to childhood as a legal category, see Anne C. Dailey and Laura A. Rosenbury, "The New Law of the Child," *Yale Law Journal* 127, no. 6 (2018): 1448–1537 and Clare Huntington and Elizabeth S. Scott, "Conceptualizing Legal Childhood in the Twenty-First Century," *Michigan Law Review* 118, no. 7 (2020): 1371–457.

40. Fábio Perin Shecaira and Noel Struchiner, "Legal Audiences," *Argumentation* 32, no. 2 (2018): 273–91. See also Jane S. Schachter, "*Obergefell*'s Audiences," *Ohio State Law Journal* 77, no. 5 (2014): 1011–38 (reviewing various possible audiences and judicial roles, including the "republican schoolmaster" who educates a nation and serves as a resource that offers frames of argument to social movements for possible future use).

41. Laurence S. Tribe, "America's Constitutional Narrative," *Daedalus* 141, no. 1 (2012): 120. Judicial opinions create and legitimate a narrative about who we are as a people. The "unfolding interpretation and implementation through the crucible of competing stories about constitutional values represent elements of a *practice* essential to the creation and perpetual re-creation of 'We, the People.'" In Tribe, "Constitutional Narrative," 19.

42. Robert A. Ferguson, "The Judicial Opinion as Literary Genre," *Yale Journal of Law and Humanities* 2, no. 1 (1990): 201. James Arnt Aune makes this point about institutionalized judicial review in "Modernity as a Rhetorical Problem: *Phronesis*, Forms, and Forums in *Norms of Rhetorical Culture*," *Philosophy and Rhetoric* 41, no. 4 (2008): 413. As Paul W. Kahn writes, "the courts are always telling us to listen. . . . About a judgment, we are always entitled—and expected—to ask 'why?' The court owes us an explanation." In Kahn, *Making the Case: The Art of the Judicial Opinion* (New Haven: Yale University Press, 2016), 5.

43. It is sometimes said that the law is primarily ideological—merely the expression of the political will of the party who appoints the judges. This idea explains judicial votes, but not opinions. Those texts involve the rhetorical justifications that are part of the development of law. For a deep theoretical look at the ways that law grounds itself as au-

thoritative in the face of social contingency, see Peter Fitzpatrick, *Modernism and the Grounds of Law* (Cambridge: Cambridge University Press, 2001). For criticism of the ways that law claims such authority while legitimizing violence, see Austin Sarat, *When the State Kills: Capital Punishment and the American Condition* (Princeton: Princeton University Press, 2001). Robert Cover highlighted how narrative and myth constitute judicial authority, enabling a "repertoire of moves—a lexicon of normative action—that may be combined into meaningful patterns culled from the meaningful patterns of the past." See Robert M. Cover, "The Supreme Court 1982 Term Foreword: Nomos and Narrative," *Harvard Law Review* 97, no. 4 (1983): 4–68, 9.

44. John Leubsdorf, "The Structure of Judicial Opinions," *Minnesota Law Review* 86, no. 2 (2001): 447.

45. Ferguson, "The Judicial Opinion as Literary Genre."

46. Chaïm Perelman and Lucie Olbrechts-Tyteca, *The New Rhetoric: A Treatise on Argumentation* (South Bend: University of Notre Dame Press, 1973) investigates the role of precedent and analogy in argument, with examples from law. See also Frederick Schauer, "Precedent," *Stanford Law Review* 39, no. 3 (1987): 571–605, and a wide range of scholarship on stare decisis in the legal academy too voluminous to list here.

47. Edward Schiappa, *Defining Reality: Definitions and the Politics of Meaning* (Carbondale: Southern Illinois University Press, 2003) and Douglas Walton and Fabrizio Macagno, "The Importance and Trickiness of Definition Strategies in Legal and Political Argumentation," *Journal of Politics and Law* 8, no. 1 (2015): 137–48.

48. The relationship between character and the rhetorical authority of legal opinions has animated James Boyd White's works such as *When Words Lose Their Meaning: Constitutions and Reconstitutions of Language, Character, and Community* (Chicago: University of Chicago Press, 1984) and *Justice as Translation: An Essay in Cultural and Legal Criticism* (Chicago: University of Chicago Press, 1994). Eugene Garver has assessed the argumentative character of legal opinions in *For the Sake of Argument: Practical Reasoning, Character, and the Ethics of Belief* (Chicago: University of Chicago Press, 2004). Legal scholars exploring this relationship include Jerry Frug, "Argument as Character," *Stanford Law Review* 40, no. 4 (1988): 869–927 and Eileen A. Scallen, "Classical Rhetoric, Practical Reasoning, and the Law of Evidence," *American University Law Review* 44, no. 5 (1995): 1718–1816.

49. Philip Bobbitt, *Constitutional Fate: Theory of the Constitution* (New York: Oxford University Press, 1982) and Jack M. Balkin, "A Night in the Topics: The Reason of Legal Rhetoric and the Rhetoric of Legal Reason," in Peter Brooks and Paul Gewirtz, eds. *Law's Stories: Narrative and Rhetoric in the Law* (New Haven: Yale University Press, 1996), 211–24.

50. Stuart Hampshire, *Justice Is Conflict* (Princeton: Princeton University Press, 2000). Hampshire marks the virtue of fair procedure without specific attention to judicial opinions. At times, the need to appear neutral and objectively fair causes opinions to conceal their rhetorical features due to the uncertain status of rhetorical knowledge. Gerald B. Wetlaufer, "Rhetoric and its Denial in Legal Discourse," *Virginia Law Review* 76, no. 8 (1990): 1545–97.

51. M. M. Bakhtin, "Epic and Novel: Towards a Methodology for the Study of the Novel," in Michael Holquist ed., *The Dialogic Imagination: Four Essays by M. M. Bakhtin,*

trans. by Caryl Emerson and Michael Holquist (Austin: University of Texas Press, 1981), 3–40. Robert Hariman has referenced novelization in "Political Parody and Public Culture," *Quarterly Journal of Speech* 94, no. 3 (2008): 247–72. Hariman credits Ronald W. Greene for the productive possibilities of studying public address as a system. Ronald W. Greene, "Rhetorical Pedagogy as a Postal System: Circulating Subjects through Michael Warner's 'Publics and Counterpublics,'" *Quarterly Journal of Speech* 88, no. 4 (2002): 434–43.

52. Ken Hirschkop, *Mikhail Bakhtin: An Aesthetic for Democracy* (Oxford: Oxford University Press, 1999) (especially pages 225–48). See also Graham Pechey, "On the Borders of Bakhtin: Dialogization, Decolonization," *Oxford Literary Review* 9, no. 1/2 (1987): 59–84. Martha Nussbaum has highlighted the role of the novel in developing key capabilities for democratic citizenship in "Democratic Citizenship and the Narrative Imagination," *Yearbook of the National Society for the Study of Education* 107, no. 1 (2008): 143–57. Nussbaum has applied this argument to the analysis of judicial rhetoric in "Poets as Judges: Judicial Rhetoric and the Literary Imagination," *University of Chicago Law Review* 62, no. 4 (1995): 1477–519. Nussbaum identifies virtues of a "literary judge" who can analyze facts in a manner that sees the totality of relations between people, including the fragile aspects of lives that demonstrate humanity.

53. On the role of dialogue in Bakhtin's thought and its importance for democratic rhetoric, see James P. Zappen, *The Rebirth of Dialogue: Bakhtin, Socrates, and the Rhetorical Tradition* (Albany: SUNY Press, 2004).

54. Readers familiar with this scholarship will no doubt see similarities between this approach and that of scholars in the legal academy whose work relates to the "Law and Literature" movement. In addition to Martha Nussbaum's work "Poets as Judges" (cited previously), Robert Cover made vital contributions in reading judicial opinions and legal rhetoric as narrative. See Robert Cover, "Nomos and Narrative," and "Violence and the Word," *Yale Law Journal* 95, no. 8 (1986): 1601–29. Of course, this work (and the current study) are indebted to Hayden White's approach to narrative. White argued that narrative (and figuration) played a vital role in creating and maintaining social and political order, especially in his collections *The Tropics of Discourse: Essays in Cultural Criticism* (Baltimore: Johns Hopkins Press, 1986), *The Content of the Form: Narrative Discourse and Historical Representation* (Baltimore: Johns Hopkins University Press, 1990), and *Metahistory: The Historical Imagination in Nineteenth Century Europe*, 40th anniversary ed. (Baltimore: Johns Hopkins University Press, 2014).

55. Kenneth Burke refers to this maneuver as casuistic stretching: "introducing new principles while theoretically remaining faithful to old principles." Burke, *Attitudes Toward History* (Berkeley: University of California Press, 1984), 229.

Chapter 1

1. Sanford J. Fox, "Juvenile Justice Reform: An Historical Perspective," *Stanford Law Review* (1970): 1187–89; David M. Schneider, *The History of Public Welfare in New York State 1609–1866*, Chicago: University of Chicago Press 1938), 317; Anthony M. Platt, *The Child Savers: The Invention of Delinquency*, 40th anniversary ed. (New Brunswick, NJ: Rutgers University Press 2009), introduction.

2. Fox, "Juvenile Justice Reform," 1188.

3. "Society for the Prevention of Pauperism in the City of New York, Report on the Subject of Erecting a House of Refuge for Vagrant and Depraved Young People," in Nathaniel Hart, ed., *Society for the Reformation of Juvenile Delinquents, Documents Relative to the House of Refuge* (New York: M. Day), 13.

4. John Adams, "Thoughts on Government," in *The Works of John Adams, Second President of the United States: With a Life of the Author, Notes and Illustrations Thoughts on Government*, vol. 4, edited by Charles Francis Adams (Boston: Little, Brown, 1856), 197.

5. Tyack, "Ways of Seeing"; Tyack and Hansot, "Conflict and Consensus in American Public Education"; Tyack and Hansot; *Managers of Virtue*; and Tyack, *Seeking Common Ground.*

6. As mentioned in the introductory chapter, Archard ("Children, Multiculturalism, and Education") and Callan (*Creating Citizens*) provide a contemporary analysis of this structural issue.

7. Holly Brewer, *By Birth or Consent: Children, Law, and the Anglo-American Revolution in Authority* (Chapel Hill: University of North Carolina Press, 2012), 2.

8. Brewer, *By Birth or Consent*, 4.

9. Brewer, *By Birth or Consent*, 4. Brewer refers to Henry Maine's account of the child's inability to form judgments as important evidence of a shift from (ancient) status relationships to (modern) contract relationships: "The great majority of Jurists are constant to the principle that the [child, orphan, and lunatic] are subject to extrinsic control on the single ground that they do not possess the faculty of forming a judgment." Brewer, 7 (citing Henry Sumner Maine, *Ancient Law: Its Connection with the Early History of Society, and Its Relation to Modern Ideas* [1861; J. Murray: London, 1930], 181.)

10. It was also reflected in their representation in literature and cultural texts of the colonial and early American period. See Courtney Weikle-Mills, *Imaginary Citizens: Child Readers and the Limits of American Independence* (Baltimore: Johns Hopkins University Press, 2013).

11. "This doctrine is meant to apply only to human beings in the maturity of their faculties. We are not speaking of children or of young persons below the age which the law may fix as that of manhood or womanhood." J. S. Mill, "On Liberty," in *On Liberty and Other Writings*, ed. Stefan Collini (Cambridge: Cambridge University Press, 1989), 13.

12. Thomas S. Popkewitz, "Governing the Child and Pedagogicalization of the Parent," in *Governing Children, Families and Education*, eds. Marianne N. Bloch, Kerstin Holmlund, Ingeborg Moqvist, and Thomas S. Popkewitz (New York: Palgrave, 2003), 36; Jay Fliegelman, *Prodigals and Pilgrims: The American Revolution against Patriarchal Authority 1750–1800* (Cambridge: Cambridge University Press, 1982), especially 9–35.

13. Karen Sanchez-Eppler, *Dependent States: The Child's Part in Nineteenth Century American Culture* (Chicago: University of Chicago Press, 2005), 7. See also Weikle-Mills, *Imaginary Citizens.*

14. Holly Brewer, *By Birth or Consent*, especially 1–17.

15. Ex parte Crouse, 4 Whart. 9 (Penn. 1839), 1839 Pa. LEXIS 171. Later references to this case will refer to pagination in the LexisNexis database.

16. *Ex parte Crouse*, 1839 Pa. LEXIS at *2.

17. *Ex parte Crouse*, 1839 Pa. LEXIS at *3.

18. Latin for "by the court," a *per curiam* opinion does not identify an individual author. It reflects a desire for consensus that dates at least back to Chief Justice John Marshall. Laura Krugman Ray, "The History of the *Per Curiam* Opinion: Consensus and Individual Expression on the Supreme Court," *Journal of Supreme Court History* 27, no. 2 (2002): 176–93.

19. This was the first known case to incorporate the parens patriae doctrine into American jurisprudence. See Elizabeth S. Scott, "The Legal Construction of Adolescence," *Hofstra Law Review* 29, no. 2 (2000): 552 (n. 16).

20. T. R. Stevenson, "The Ideal Benefactor and the Father Analogy in Greek and Roman Thought," *Classical Quarterly* 42, no. 2 (1992): 421–36. Closely related to this title was the Roman doctrine of patria potestas, which held that a father possessed his children as chattel. Herbert Felix Jolowicz and Barry Nicholas, *Historical Introduction to the Study of Roman Law* (Cambridge: Cambridge University Press, 1972), 238.

21. The Crown controlled the land of those under its care and took its profit during their lifetimes. Herbert E. Bell, *An Introduction to the History and Records of the Court of Wards and Liveries* (Cambridge: Cambridge University Press, 1953), 128.

22. *Ex parte Crouse*, 1839 Pa. LEXIS at *5.

23. *Ex parte Crouse*, 1839 Pa. LEXIS at *6.

24. *Ex parte Crouse*, 1839 Pa. LEXIS at *6.

25. *Ex parte Crouse*, 1839 Pa. LEXIS at *4.

26. *Ex parte Crouse*, 1839 Pa. LEXIS at *4.

27. *Ex parte Crouse*, 1839 Pa. LEXIS at *5.

28. *Ex parte Crouse*, 1839 Pa. LEXIS at *5.

29. *Ex parte Crouse*, 1839 Pa. LEXIS at *5.

30. *Ex parte Crouse*, 1839 Pa. LEXIS at *5.

31. Platt, *The Child Savers*.

32. *Ex parte Crouse*, 1839 Pa. LEXIS at *5.

33. *Ex parte Crouse*, 1839 Pa. LEXIS at *5.

34. *Ex parte Crouse*, 1839 Pa. LEXIS at *5.

35. Austin Reed's memoir, the earliest known prison memoir written by an African American author, chronicles this abuse, which began when he was committed to the New York House of Refuge. See Austin Reed, *The Life and Adventures of a Haunted Convict* (New Haven: Yale University Press, 2016). Reed's recollection of abuse is corroborated by scholarship concerning the House of Refuge in particular and more broadly the juvenile reformatories throughout the nineteenth century. For a documentation of this abuse, see Alexander W. Pisciotta, "Treatment on Trial: The Rhetoric and Reality of the New York House of Refuge, 1857–1935," *American Journal of Legal History* 29, no. 2 (1985): 151–81. Stern discipline was the norm in the Philadelphia House of Refuge as well. Negley K. Teeters, "The Early Days of the Philadelphia House of Refuge," *Pennsylvania History: A Journal of Mid-Atlantic Studies* 27, no. 2 (1960): 182–84.

36. Arnold Binder and Virginia L. Binder, "The Incarceration of Juveniles, from the Era of *Crouse* to that of Freud and Skinner," *Legal Studies Forum* 18, no. 3 (1994): 352. See also Alexander W. Pisciotta, "Saving the Children: The Promise and Practice of *Parens Patriae*, 1838–98," *Crime and Delinquency* 28, no. 3 (1982): 410–25; and Jean Tre-

panier, "Juvenile Courts after 100 Years: Past and Present Orientations," *European Journal on Criminal Policy and Research* 7, no. 3 (1999): 303–27.

37. *Ex parte Crouse*, 1839 Pa. LEXIS at *1. Lawrence L. Koontz Jr. suggests that Mary Ann was committed for the "crime of being poor." See Lawrence L. Koontz Jr., "Re-assessment Should Not Lead to Wholesale Rejection of the Juvenile Justice System," *University of Richmond Law Review* 31, no. 1 (January 1997): 183. Scholarship in this vein focuses on a critique of juvenile commitments as a way for the state to control poor families. See, for example, Christine Griffin, *Representations of Youth: The Study of Youth and Adolescence in Britain and America* (New York: John Wiley, 2013). The *Ex parte Crouse* opinion itself stated that Mary Ann was committed on a complaint from her mother.

38. Carl F. Kaestle, *Pillars of the Republic: Common Schools and American Society, 1780–1860* (New York: Macmillan 1983); Clarence J. Karier, *The Individual, Society, and Education: A History of American Educational Ideas* (Urbana: University of Illinois Press, 1986); Sherry L. Field, "Citizens for a 'New World Order': A Historical Perspective of Citizenship Education in the United States," in Kerry J. Kennedy ed., *Citizenship Education and the Modern State* (London: Taylor and Francis 1997), 137–47.

39. Carl F. Kaestle, "Social Change, Discipline, and the Common School in Early Nineteenth-Century America," *Journal of Interdisciplinary History* 9, no. 1 (1978): 1–17, 3.

40. Kaestle, "Social Change," 10–11.

41. Kaestle, "Social Change," 11.

42. State v. Pendergrass, 19 N.C. 365, 1837 N.C. LEXIS 42 (North Carolina, 1837); Lander v. Seaver, 32 Vt. 114, 1859 Vt. LEXIS 74 (Vermont, 1859). Later references to these cases will refer to pagination in the LexisNexis database.

43. *Pendergrass*, 1837 N.C. LEXIS at *1.

44. *Pendergrass*, 1837 N.C. LEXIS at *1.

45. *Pendergrass*, 1837 N.C. LEXIS at *1.

46. *Pendergrass*, 1837 N.C. LEXIS at *1.

47. *Pendergrass*, 1837 N.C. LEXIS at *3.

48. *Pendergrass*, 1837 N.C. LEXIS at *4.

49. *Pendergrass*, 1837 N.C. LEXIS at *3.

50. *Pendergrass*, 1837 N.C. LEXIS at *4.

51. *Pendergrass*, 1837 N.C. LEXIS at *4.

52. *Pendergrass*, 1837 N.C. LEXIS at *3.

53. *Pendergrass*, 1837 N.C. LEXIS at *3.

54. *Pendergrass*, 1837 N.C. LEXIS at *4.

55. *Pendergrass*, 1837 N.C. LEXIS at *4.

56. *Pendergrass*, 1837 N.C. LEXIS at *6.

57. *Lander v. Seaver*, 32 Vt. 114, 1859 Vt. LEXIS 74, *1–2.

58. *Lander*, 1859 Vt. LEXIS at *2.

59. *Lander*, 1859 Vt. LEXIS at *2–3.

60. *Lander*, 1859 Vt. LEXIS at *3–4.

61. *Lander*, 1859 Vt. LEXIS at *4.

62. *Lander*, 1859 Vt. LEXIS at *4–5.

63. *Lander*, 1859 Vt. LEXIS at *8.

64. *Lander*, 1859 Vt. LEXIS at *9.

65. *Lander*, 1859 Vt. LEXIS at *9.

66. This tension between elite informal norms—associated with a refined style—and plain-spoken common culture was a recurring tension in nineteenth-century American political life. For a sample of work exploring this dialectic, see Reva B. Siegel, "Why Equal Protection No Longer Protects: The Evolving Forms of Status-Enforcing State Action," *Stanford Law Review* 49, no. 6 (1997): 1111–48 (stratification in racial and gender relationships); and Kenneth Cmiel, *Democratic Eloquence: The Fight over Popular Speech in Nineteenth-Century America* (Berkeley: University of California Press, 1990). For the relationship between status and symbolism, see Joseph R. Gusfield, *Symbolic Crusade: Status Politics and the American Temperance Movement* (Urbana: University of Illinois Press, 1986).

67. The opinion does not explicitly state that reasonableness is a standard for citizen judgment, but it placed reasonableness between the poles of the parent's natural rights and the public official's actions in an official capacity.

68. *Lander*, 1859 Vt. LEXIS at *14.

69. *Lander*, 1859 Vt. LEXIS at *12–13.

70. *Lander*, 1859 Vt. LEXIS at *11.

71. *Lander*, 1859 Vt. LEXIS at *12.

72. *Lander*, 1859 Vt. LEXIS at *18.

73. *Lander*, 1859 Vt. LEXIS at *18.

74. *Lander*, 1859 Vt. LEXIS at *18–19.

75. *Lander*, 1859 Vt. LEXIS at *19.

76. *Lander*, 1859 Vt. LEXIS at *10.

Chapter 2

1. David S. Tanenhaus, "Between Dependency and Liberty: The Conundrum of Children's Rights in the Gilded Age," *Law and History Review* 23, no. 2 (2005): 351–86. Tanenhaus's work comprehensively details the development (and subsequent waning) of a variety of rights claims for children. Exemplary pieces include David S. Tanenhaus, *Juvenile Justice in the Making* (Oxford: Oxford University Press, 2004) and *The Constitutional Rights of Children*: In re Gault *and Juvenile Justice* (Lawrence: University Press of Kansas, 2011).

2. The People v. Turner, 55 Ill. 280 (Illinois 1870); Petition of Ferrier, 103 Ill. 367 (Illinois 1882); County of McLean v. Laura B. Humphreys, 104 Ill. 379 (Illinois 1882). See Tanenhaus, "Between Dependency and Liberty" for this argument, as well as David Tanenhaus, "The Evolution of Juvenile Courts in the Early Twentieth Century: Beyond the Myth of Immaculate Construction," in Margaret K. Rosenheim, Franklin E. Zimring, David S. Tanenhaus, and Bernadine Dohrn, eds., *A Century of Juvenile Justice* (Chicago: University of Chicago Press, 2000), 46.

3. *Turner*, 55 Ill. at 282.

4. For a detailed discussion of the case, see Fox, "Juvenile Justice Reform," especially 1216–19 (see ch. 1, n. 1). "The illogic, confusion, and technical incompetence in failing to deal with relevant cases and doctrine prevented the opinion from having any broader, lasting influence on the course of law." Fox, 1219.

5. *Turner,* 55 Ill. at 283–84.

6. *Turner,* 55 Ill. at 284.

7. *Turner,* 55 Ill. at 284.

8. *Turner,* 55 Ill. at 285.

9. *Turner,* 55 Ill. at 286.

10. *Turner,* 55 Ill. at 286.

11. *Turner,* 55 Ill. at 287.

12. *Turner,* 55 Ill. at 287–88.

13. Tanenhaus, "Evolution of Juvenile Courts," 46.

14. See, for example, Wooster v. Sunderland, et al., 148 P. 959 (Cal. 1915). In *Wooster,* a California appellate court relied on in loco parentis authority in upholding a student's expulsion for criticizing the board of education's management of the school. By this point, there were a host of cases in various state courts to support the court's ruling that the student's conduct was "insubordination to constituted authority, which required correction . . . in order that the discipline of the school might be maintained unimpaired." *Wooster,* 148 P. at 961.

15. Woodhouse, "Who Owns the Child," 1010 (see intro, n. 39).

16. See, for example, Andrew Jay Kleinfeld, "The Balance of Power among Infants, Their Parents, and the State, Part 2," *Family Law Quarterly* 4, no. 4 (1970): 416–19. William G. Ross has argued that *Meyer* and *Pierce* are exemplars of judicial strength to protect minority rights in the face of nativist pressure. See William G. Ross, *Forging New Freedoms: Nativism, Education, and the Constitution, 1917–1927,* Lincoln: University of Nebraska Press, 1994; and William G. Ross, "The Contemporary Significance of *Meyer* and *Pierce* for Parental Rights Issues Involving Education," *Akron Law Review* 34, no. 1 (2000): 177–208. Ross has argued that the cases prioritized economic freedom, while also acknowledging other liberties (to marry and establish a home, for example) whose subsequent legal application has waxed and waned with particular contexts.

17. Laurence Tribe, "*Lawrence* v. *Texas*: The 'Fundamental Right' That Dare Not Speak Its Name," *Harvard Law Review* 117, no. 6 (2004): 1934.

18. Woodhouse, "Who Owns the Child?"1010.

19. Jay S. Bybee, "Substantive Due Process and the Free Exercise of Religion: *Meyer, Pierce,* and the Origins of *Wisconsin v. Yoder,*" *Capital University Law Review* 25, no. 2 (1996): 895, quoting Nebraska District of Evangelical Lutheran Synod v. McKelvie, 175 N.W. 531, 533 (1919).

20. *McKelvie,* 175 N.W. 531, 534.

21. Bybee, "Substantive Due Process," 896.

22. I am indebted to Christopher Capozzola's discussion of *Meyer* in his book *Uncle Sam Wants You: World War I and the Making of the American Citizen* (New York: Oxford University Press, 2008), especially pages 190–98.

23. Meyer v. State, 187 N.W. 100 (1922) at 104 (Letton, J., dissenting) (quoting State v. Ferguson, 144 N.W. 1039, 1043 [1914]).

24. Meyer v. Nebraska, 262 U.S. 390, 400 (1923).

25. *Meyer,* 262 U.S. at 400.

26. *Meyer,* 262 U.S. at 403.

27. Justice Oliver Wendell Holmes dissented (joined by Justice George Sutherland)

in its companion case, Bartels v. Iowa, 262 U.S. 404, 412–13 (1923). Justice Holmes believed that the law was a reasonable restriction on liberty, emphasizing the fact that the statute was limited to youth: "Youth is the time when familiarity with a language is established and if there are sections in a state where a child would hear only [their native language] at home . . . it is [reasonable] to provide that . . . [they] shall hear and speak only English at school." *Bartels*, 262 U.S. at 412.

28. *Meyer*, 262 U.S. at 400.

29. *Meyer*, 262 U.S. at 400.

30. *Meyer*, 262 U.S. at 400.

31. *Meyer*, 262 U.S. at 401. The Nebraska Supreme Court had already interpreted the statute to exempt "'the so-called ancient or dead languages'. . . . Latin, Greek, Hebrew are not proscribed." *Meyer*, at 400 (citing *Nebraska District of Evangelical Lutheran Synod v. McKelvie*, 187 N.W. 927).

32. *Meyer*, 262 U.S. at 401.

33. *Meyer*, 262 U.S. at 401.

34. *Meyer*, 262 U.S. at 401–2.

35. *Meyer*, 262 U.S. at 402.

36. *Meyer*, 262 U.S. at 402.

37. *Meyer*, 262 U.S. at 402.

38. The notion of judgment adducing different perspectives that can improve decision-making has been a persistent focus in rhetorical studies, especially under its virtue analogue, prudence. Significant contributions include James Jasinski, "The Forms and Limits of Prudence in Henry Clay's (1850) Defense of the Compromise Measures," *Quarterly Journal of Speech* 81, no. 4 (1995): 454–78; Beth Innocenti Manolescu, "Style and Spectator Judgment in Fisher Ames's Jay Treaty Speech," *Quarterly Journal of Speech* 84, no. 1 (1998): 62–79; and Michele Kennerly, "Getting Carried Away: How Rhetorical Transport Gets Judgment Going," *Rhetoric Society Quarterly* 40, no. 3 (2010): 269–91.

39. *Meyer*, 262 U.S. at 399.

40. *Meyer*, 262 U.S. at 399.

41. Slaughterhouse Cases. 83 U.S. 36 (1873). These cases limited the Due Process Clause to the few privileges and immunities conferred by federal citizenship, rather than the more expansive privileges and immunities that a particular state may have granted its citizens.

42. Scholarship on this document argues that it stands for a commitment to equality of access to education, and also that it should be considered a "constitutional document" on par with the Federalist Papers as an authoritative source for judicial interpretation. For the former claim, see Harold M. Hyman, *American Singularity: The 1787 Northwest Ordinance, the 1862 Homestead and Morrill Acts, and the 1944 G. I. Bill* (Athens: University of Georgia Press, 2008). For the latter claim, see Denis P. Duffey, "The Northwest Ordinance as a Constitutional Document," *Columbia Law Review* 95 no. 4 (May 1995): 929–68.

43. *Meyer*, 262 U.S. at 400.

44. *Meyer*, 262 U.S. at 400.

45. *Meyer*, 262 U.S. at 402–3.

46. *Meyer*, 262 U.S. at 403.

47. Alexander M. Bickel, *The Least Dangerous Branch*, Indianapolis: Bobbs-Merrill 1962, 71.

48. Anthony T. Kronman, "Alexander Bickel's Philosophy of Prudence," *Yale Law Journal* 94, no. 7 (June 1985): 1587. Kronman highlights a court's ability to not decide a particular controversy, but this passive virtue also applies to the counterfactual strategy deployed in *Meyer*.

49. Pierce v. Society of Sisters, 268 U.S. 510, 530 (1925). Violating the provision was a misdemeanor.

50. The opinion noted the statute's exceptions—for "children who are not normal or who have completed eighth grade, or who reside at considerable distances from any public school, or whose parents or guardians hold special permits from the County Superintendent." *Pierce*, 268 U.S. at 530.

51. See David B. Tyack, "The Perils of Pluralism: The Background of the Pierce Case," *American Historical Review* 74, no. 1 (October 1968): 74–98. Tyack's essay marked the ways that antielitism and working-class anxiety came together with the overt racism of the KKK in the passage of Oregon's law.

52. *Pierce*, 268 U.S. at 531.

53. *Pierce*, 268 U.S. at 531–32.

54. *Pierce*, 268 U.S. at 532.

55. *Pierce*, 268 U.S. at 532.

56. *Pierce*, 268 U.S. at 534–35.

57. *Pierce*, 268 U.S. at 536.

58. *Pierce*, 268 U.S. at 534.

59. *Pierce*, 268 U.S. at 534.

60. *Pierce*, 268 U.S. at 534.

Part II

1. This snippet is taken from a 2007 question and answer session between Professor John Q. Barrett and Gathie Barnett Edmonds in "Recollections of *West Virginia State Board of Education v. Barnette*," *St. John's Law Review* 81, no. 4 (2007): 768–70. Edmonds was one of the named plaintiffs in *Barnette*.

2. For these functions of the judicial opinion, see Patricia M. Wald, "The Rhetoric of Results and the Results of Rhetoric: Judicial Writings," *University of Chicago Law Review* 62, no. 4 (1995): 1371–419.

Chapter 3

1. The court records misspelled the *Minersville* plaintiffs' last name as "Gobitis."

2. Lillian Gobitas, "The Courage to Put God First," *Awake!* July 22, 1993, 13.

3. Noah Feldman, *Scorpions: The Battles and Triumphs of FDR's Great Supreme Court Justices* (New York: Twelve Publishers, 2010), 179–80. Feldman relies on David R. Manwaring's *Render unto Caesar: The Flag Salute Controversy* (Chicago: University of Chicago Press, 1962), 30–31 for Rutherford's speech, and 81–82 for the reaction of the Gobitas children.

4. Feldman, *Scorpions*, 180. Feldman cites Lillian Gobitas, "The Courage to Put God First," 13–14.

5. Feldman, *Scorpions*, 180.

6. Feldman, *Scorpions*, 180.

7. Minersville School Dist. v. Gobitis, 310 U.S. 586, 596 (1940).

8. Lochner v. New York, 198 U.S. 45 (1905).

9. *Lochner*, 198 U.S. at 75 (Holmes, J., dissenting).

10. Jeremy Waldron has estimated that 170 labor statutes were invalidated by *Lochner* era state and federal courts. Jeremy Waldron, "The Core of the Case against Judicial Review," *Yale Law Journal* 115, no. 4 (2006): 1348. Waldron derived his calculations from William E. Forbath's *Law and the Shaping of the American Labor Movement* (Cambridge: Harvard University Press, 1991), appendices A and C, 177–92 and 199–203.

11. For the National Industrial Recovery Act, see Schechter Poultry Corp. v. U.S., 295 U.S. 495 (1935). The court struck down the Agricultural Adjustment Act in United States v. Butler, 297 U.S. 1 (1936), and the Railroad Retirement Act in Railroad Retirement Board v. Alton Railroad Co., 295 U.S. 330 (1935).

12. Morehead v. New York ex rel. Tipaldo, 298 U.S. 587 (1936).

13. These cases include West Coast Hotel v. Parrish, 300 U.S. 379 (1937); NLRB v. Jones & Laughlin Steel Corp., 301 U.S. 1 (1937); Steward Machine Co. v. Davis, 301 U.S. 548 (1937); and Helvering v. Davis, 301 U.S. 619 (1937). *West Coast Hotel* upheld Washington state's minimum wage law, and *Jones & Laughlin Steel* decided that the National Labor Relations Act of 1935 (which set terms under which private companies may deal with labor unions) was constitutional. *Steward Machine* and *Helvering* dealt with unemployment and old-age insurance (respectively) as a part of the Social Security Act.

14. *Gobitis*, 310 U.S. 586, 591 (1940).

15. *Gobitis*, 310 U.S. at 593.

16. *Gobitis*, 310 U.S. at 594.

17. *Gobitis*, 310 U.S. at 594 (citing Hamilton v. Regents of the University of California, 293 U.S. 245 (1934). *Hamilton* upheld compulsory university classes in military training in the face of a conscientious objection by minor members of the Methodist Episcopal Church. Justice Holmes—himself a Civil War veteran—reasoned that the historical source of the right to conscientious objection was statutory, and not a constitutional right. *Hamilton*, 293 U.S. at 264 (citing U.S. v. Macintosh, 283 U.S. 605, 623 [1931]).

18. *Gobitis*, 310 U.S. at 591–92.

19. *Gobitis*, 310 U.S. at 595.

20. *Gobitis*, 310 U.S. at 595.

21. *Gobitis*, 310 U.S. at 595.

22. *Gobitis*, 310 U.S. at 596.

23. *Gobitis*, 310 U.S. at 596.

24. *Gobitis*, 310 U.S. at 596 (quoting Halter v. Nebraska, 205 U.S. 34, 43 (1907)).

25. *Gobitis*, 310 U.S. at 597.

26. *Gobitis*, 310 U.S. at 597–98.

27. *Gobitis*, 310 U.S. at 598.

28. *Gobitis*, 310 U.S. at 598.

29. *Gobitis*, 310 U.S. at 598.

30. *Gobitis*, 310 U.S. at 598.

31. *Gobitis*, 310 U.S. at 599–600.

32. *Gobitis*, 310 U.S. at 600.

33. Justice Harlan Fiske Stone dissented, arguing that the law required the students to violate their personal beliefs. Justice Stone dismissed the importance of national unity, arguing that the Bill of Rights prevented a legislature from deciding that its concerns about civic unity "are more important to the public welfare than the Bill of Rights." *Gobitis*, 310 U.S. at 605 (Stone, J., dissenting).

34. Feldman, *Scorpions*, 185. For a report of the Maine violence, see "Maine Mob Burns Jehovah Sect Home: Action Follows Shooting of Two Kennebunk Men by Group Barricaded in House," *New York Times*, June 10, 1940, 19.

35. West Virginia v. Barnette, 319 U.S. 624, 629 (1943).

36. *Barnette*, 319 U.S. at 630.

37. *Barnette*, 319 U.S. at 635.

38. *Barnette*, 319 U.S. at 638, 641–42.

39. Justices Black and Murphy wrote separate concurrences. Each justice thought that the law's effect on civic unity was minimal.

40. William P. Marshall, "Progressive Constitutionalism, Originalism, and the Significance of Landmark Decisions in Evaluating Constitutional Theory," *Ohio State Law Journal* 72, no. 6 (2011): 1259–60.

41. Kermit L. Hall and John J. Patrick, *The Pursuit of Justice: Supreme Court Decisions That Shaped America* (New York: Oxford University Press, 2006), 101.

42. Barrett, "Recollections," 796. Shawn Francis Peters has argued for the centrality of the Jehovah's Witnesses cases to the Supreme Court's rights revolution in his book *Judging Jehovah's Witnesses: Religious Persecution and the Dawn of the Rights Revolution* (Lawrence: University Press of Kansas, 2000).

43. Nadine Strossen, "The Supreme Court's Role: Guarantor of Individual and Minority Group Rights," *University of Richmond Law Review* 26 (1992): 467.

44. The norm of stare decisis accords value to precedent cases. The norm has spurred a lengthy debate about when the court should overrule past cases, including questions about judicial mistakes and altered cultural circumstances. See for example Henry Paul Monaghan, "*Stare Decisis* and Constitutional Adjudication," *Columbia Law Review* 88, no. 4 (May 1988): 723–73; Jack Knight and Lee Epstein, "The Norm of *Stare Decisis*," *American Journal of Political Science* 40, no. 4 (1996): 1018–35; Richard H. Fallon Jr., "*Stare Decisis* and the Constitution: An Essay on Constitutional Methodology," *NYU Law Review* 76, no. 2 (2001): 570–97; Caleb Nelson, "*Stare Decisis* and Demonstrably Erroneous Precedents," *Virginia Law Review* 87, no. 1 (2001): 1–84; and Frederick Schauer, "*Stare Decisis*—Rhetoric and Reality in the Supreme Court," *Supreme Court Review* 2018 (2018): 121–43.

45. *Barnette*, 319 U.S. at 630.

46. *Barnette*, 319 U.S. at 632.

47. *Barnette*, 319 U.S. at 641.

48. *Barnette*, 319 U.S. at 637.

49. *Barnette*, 319 U.S. at 641.

50. *Barnette*, 319 U.S. at 637–8.

51. *Barnette*, 319 U.S. at 638.

52. *Barnette*, 319 U.S. at 641–42.

53. *Barnette*, 319 U.S. at 646–47.

54. *Barnette*, 319 U.S. at 646–47.

55. *Barnette*, 319 U.S. at 648.

56. *Barnette*, 319 U.S. at 648–49.

57. *Barnette*, 319 U.S. at 651.

58. *Barnette*, 319 U.S. at 651–52.

59. *Barnette*, 319 U.S. at 653.

60. For the ordering function of chiasmus, and its reliance on a "third term," see Robert Hariman, "What Is a Chiasmus? or, Why the Abyss Stares Back," in *Chiasmus and Culture*, eds. Boris Wiseman and Anthony Paul (New York: Berghahn Books, 2014): 45–68.

61. *Barnette*, 319 U.S. at 655.

62. *Barnette*, 319 U.S. at 655.

63. *Barnette*, 319 U.S. at 655.

64. *Barnette*, 319 U.S. at 656.

65. *Barnette*, 319 U.S. at 662.

66. *Barnette*, 319 U.S. at 663–64.

67. *Barnette*, 319 U.S. at 670–71.

Chapter 4

1. Some of these pieces aligned in prior decades. In *Prince v. Massachusetts*, the court upheld a child labor law that restricted the selling of goods and distribution of literature, observing the "general interest in youth's wellbeing, the state, as *parens patriae*, may restrict the parent's control." Prince v. Massachusetts, 312 U.S. 158, 166 (1944). And *Brown v. Board of Education* interpreted the Fourteenth Amendment to end segregation, emphasizing the role of education as "the most important function of state and local government," as well as "the very foundation of good citizenship," and "a principal instrument in awakening the child to cultural values." *Brown v. Board of Ed.*, 347 U.S. 483, 493.

2. Kent v. U.S., 383 U.S. 541, 556 (1966).

3. David S. Tanenhaus, "First Things First: Juvenile Justice Reform in Historical Context." *Texas Tech Law Review* 46 (2013): 284.

4. Tanenhaus, *The Constitutional Rights of Children*, 4 (see ch. 2, n. 1). Tanenhaus provides a thorough history of the case as an expression of legal liberalism.

5. Tanenhaus, "First Things First," 284.

6. In re Gault, 387 U.S. 1, 31–34 (1967).

7. *In re Gault*, 387 U.S. at 34–42.

8. *In re Gault*, 387 U.S. at 44–56 and 57–58.

9. *In re Gault*, 387 U.S. at 79 (Stewart, J., dissenting).

10. *In re Gault*, 387 U.S. at 80. Justices Black and White wrote separate concurring opinions. Justice Harlan concurred in part and dissented in part, objecting to the reach of the court's opinion and desiring more flexibility to give the states the opportunity to evolve a diversity of procedures.

11. Tanenhaus, *Constitutional Rights of Children*, 4. Tanenhaus relied on an internal

memorandum that Warren wrote to Justice Fortas, who wrote the majority opinion in the case.

12. Norman Dorsen and Daniel A. Reznick, "*In re Gault* and the Future of Family Law," *Family Law Quarterly* 1, no. 4 (1967): 28.

13. *In re Gault*, 387 U.S. 1, 14 (1967). The court's emphasis on procedure and the individual deflected attention away from substantive racial inequalities. See Robin Walker Sterling, "Fundamental Unfairness: *In re Gault* and the Road Not Taken," *Maryland Law Review* 72, no. 3 (2013): 607–81.

14. *In re Gault*, 387 U.S. at 15.

15. *In re Gault*, 387 U.S. at 15.

16. *In re Gault*, 387 U.S. at 15.

17. *In re Gault*, 387 U.S. at 16.

18. *In re Gault*, 387 U.S. at 16.

19. *In re Gault*, 387 U.S. at 16.

20. *In re Gault*, 387 U.S. at 16.

21. *In re Gault*, 387 U.S. at 16–17.

22. *In re Gault*, 387 U.S. at 17.

23. *In re Gault*, 387 U.S. at 17–18.

24. The references in the opinion to peculiarity and benevolent motivations raise the implicit comparison to slavery. Eric Foner has argued that slavery was typically equated with arbitrary rule in common political discourse. A Southern slaveholder reconciled that unjust practice with liberty in part because slaves were not entitled to freedom, and slave ownership enabled freedom. The Northerners saw equal capabilities as a crucial warrant for categorical equality, consonant with a freedom to work. See, for example, *Free Labor, Free Soil, Free Men* (Oxford: Oxford University Press, 1995) and *The Story of American Freedom* (New York: Norton, 1999), especially chapter 2. In the same way, the child was categorically equal and was therefore entitled to the same treatment in terms of criminal procedure.

25. *In re Gault*, 387 U.S. at 20.

26. *In re Gault*, 387 U.S. at 21.

27. *In re Gault*, 387 U.S. at 21–22.

28. *In re Gault*, 387 U.S. at 25–26.

29. *In re Gault*, 387 U.S. at 27.

30. *In re Gault*, 387 U.S. at 28.

31. *In re Gault*, 387 U.S. at 28.

32. *In re Gault*, 387 U.S. at 28–29.

33. *In re Gault*, 387 U.S. at 29.

34. *In re Gault*, 387 U.S. at 34.

35. *In re Gault*, 387 U.S. at 36. Quoting Powell v. Alabama, 287 U.S. 45, 61 (1932).

36. *In re Gault*, 109 387 U.S. at 46–47.

37. *In re Gault*, 387 U.S. at 58.

38. *In re Gault*, 387 U.S. at 78–79.

39. *In re Gault*, 387 U.S. at 79.

40. *In re Gault*, 387 U.S. at 79.

41. *In re Gault*, 387 U.S. at 79–80.

Chapter 5

1. Tinker v. Des Moines Independent Community School District (no. 21), 393 U.S. 503 (1969). All of the facts are taken from the majority opinion.

2. The children filed the claim under 42 U.S.C. Section 1983, which allows plaintiffs to file civil lawsuits against state actors for civil rights violations.

3. At the time, the Fifth Circuit Court of Appeals had already considered a similar protest (Burnside v. Byars, 363 F.2d 744 (5th Cir. 1966)) and had decided that schools could not prohibit the action of wearing armbands unless it "materially and substantially interfere[d] with the requirements of appropriate discipline in the operation of the school." (*Burnside*, 363 F.2d at 749). The Eighth Circuit was not bound by this decision.

4. This means that every member of the appellate court was on the panel. Normally, an appeal would consist of a three-judge panel.

5. Six justices joined his opinion.

6. *Tinker*, 393 U.S. at 506.

7. *Tinker*, 393 U.S at 515. Justice Harlan also dissented, advocating for a rule placing the burden of proof on the students to demonstrate that the rule was motivated by something other than school concerns. *Tinker*, 393 U.S. at 526.

8. *Tinker*, 393 U.S. at 507.

9. *Tinker*, 393 U.S. at 504.

10. *Tinker*, 393 U.S. at 504.

11. *Tinker*, 393 U.S. at 504.

12. *Tinker*, 393 U.S. at 505–6.

13. *Tinker*, 393 U.S. at 505–6.

14. *Tinker*, 393 U.S. at 508.

15. *Tinker*, 393 U.S. at 508.

16. *Tinker*, 393 U.S. at 507–8.

17. *Tinker*, 393 U.S. at 508.

18. *Tinker*, 393 U.S. at 507–8.

19. *Tinker*, 393 U.S. at 507–8.

20. *Tinker*, 393 U.S. at 510.

21. *Tinker*, 393 U.S. 503 at 515.

22. Robert Asen's work in rhetorical studies has drawn attention to the democratic practice of school board meetings, and it has also noted barriers to policy implementation and the persistence of value conflicts in such meetings. See, for example, Robert Asen et al., "Research Evidence and School Board Deliberations Lessons from Three Wisconsin School Districts," *Educational Policy* 27, no. 1 (2013): 33–63.

23. *Tinker*, 393 U.S. at 516.

24. *Tinker*, 393 U.S. at 516.

25. *Tinker*, 393 U.S. at 517.

26. This is the argument of the Federalist Papers, typified by Madison's argument for representative democracy to restrain the passions of the people in Fed. 57 and Fed. 63.

27. *Tinker*, 393 U.S. at 518.

28. *Tinker*, 393 U.S. at 522.

29. *Tinker*, 393 U.S. at 524.

30. *Tinker*, 393 U.S. at 518.

31. Black referred to *Lochner*, *Meyer*, and *Pierce*. He argued that the *Tinker* majority substituted its own views of what was reasonable for those of the (democratically elected) legislatures: "This test . . . brought on President Franklin Roosevelt's well known Court fight. His proposed legislation did not pass, but the fight left the 'reasonableness' constitutional test dead on the battlefield." *Tinker*, 393 U.S. at 519 (Black, J. dissenting).

32. Justice Black cited Ferguson v. Skrupa, 372 U.S. 726 (1963). *Tinker*, 393 U.S. at 519–20.

33. *Tinker*, 393 U.S. at 524.

34. *Tinker*, 393 U.S. at 524.

35. *Tinker*, 393 U.S. at 524.

36. *Tinker*, 393 U.S. at 525.

37. *Tinker*, 393 U.S. at 525.

Part III Introduction

1. The most prominent recent appraisal of the Burger Court's legacy is that it did indeed begin a long conservative movement in constitutional decision-making. See Michael J. Graetz and Linda Greenhouse, *The Burger Court and the Rise of the Judicial Right* (New York: Simon and Schuster, 2016).

2. Other notable decisions included Wisconsin v. Yoder, 406 U.S. 205 (1972); Goss v. Lopez, 419 U.S. 565 (1975); Planned Parenthood v. Danforth, 428 U.S. 52 (1976); and FCC v. Pacifica, 438 U.S. 726 (1978). The cases I have selected demonstrate the direct efforts of the Burger Court to obtain a majority in the area of limited due process and free speech rights.

Chapter 6

1. Ingraham v. Wright, 430 U.S. 651, 655 (1977) (citing Fla. Stat. Ann. section 232.27 [1961]).

2. *Ingraham*, 430 U.S. at 657.

3. *Ingraham*, 430 U.S. at 657.

4. *Ingraham*, 430 U.S. at 657.

5. *Ingraham*, 430 U.S. at 657.

6. Ingraham v. Wright, 525 F.2d 909 (5th Cir. 1976).

7. *Ingraham*, 430 U.S. 651, 700–702. Stevens, J., dissenting.

8. *Ingraham*, 430 U.S. at 653.

9. I am not arguing that the cases in this chapter were the only places where the Burger Court limited individual rights. I am arguing that these cases provided an opportunity to use a counterdiscourse of "tradition" (among other maneuvers) strategically to reconfigure a constitutional narrative about the relationship between the citizen and the state.

10. *Ingraham*, 430 U.S. at 659–60.

11. *Ingraham*, 430 U.S. at 660.

12. *Ingraham*, 430 U.S. at 660.

13. *Ingraham*, 430 U.S. at 660–61.

14. *Ingraham*, 430 U.S. at 661.

15. *Ingraham*, 430 U.S. at 662.

16. *Tinker v. Des Moines*, 393 U.S. 503, 512.

17. For an argument that marked the various flawed psychological assumptions in the court's decision, as well as some of the practical barriers in the briefing process that prevented social scientific evidence of corporal punishment's prevalence and effects, see Irwin A. Hyman, "A Social Science Review of Evidence Cited in Litigation on Corporal Punishment in the Schools," *Journal of Clinical Child & Adolescent Psychology* 7, no. 3 (1978): 195–99.

18. *Ingraham*, 430 U.S. at 669.

19. *Ingraham*, 430 U.S. at 670.

20. *Ingraham*, 430 U.S. at 664–70. For an argument that the court (mis)represented the state of precedent, see Irene Merker Rosenberg, "Ingraham v. Wright: The Court's Whipping Boy," *Columbia Law Review* 78, no. 1 (1978): 83–85.

21. *Ingraham*, 430 U.S. at 675.

22. *Ingraham*, 430 U.S. at 677.

23. *Ingraham*, 430 U.S. at 677–78.

24. *Ingraham*, 430 U.S. at 680.

25. *Ingraham*, 430 U.S. at 684 (White, J., dissenting).

26. *Ingraham*, 430 U.S. at 685.

27. *Ingraham*, 430 U.S. at 685–86.

28. *Ingraham*, 430 U.S. at 690.

29. *Ingraham*, 430 U.S. at 692.

30. *Ingraham*, 430 U.S. at 693, citing *Goss v. Lopez*, 419 U.S. at 565, 580–84. *Goss* reversed a student's suspension for property damage because the student was denied a hearing. Justice Powell dissented on grounds that hearing requirements in schools would overwhelm local school governance: "In many of these situations . . . the pupil can advance the same types of speculative and subjective injury" in a variety of analogous cases. *Goss*, 419 U.S. at 597–99. *Ingraham* and *Goss* are difficult to reconcile. Justice Potter Stewart—the justice who famously wrote "I know it when I see it" when articulating standards for obscenity—was in the *Goss* majority, but also the *Ingraham* majority.

31. *Ingraham*, 430 U.S. at 700 (quoting *Goss v. Lopez*, 419 U.S. at 581).

32. After *Ingraham*, many states acted to regulate corporal punishment. However, the practice persists. Even three decades later, over two hundred thousand children were punished in this way in a given school year, sending between ten to twenty thousand to seek medical attention for their injuries. Lewis M. Wasserman, "Corporal Punishment in K-12 Public School Settings: Reconsideration of its Constitutional Dimensions Thirty Years after *Ingraham v. Wright*," *Touro Law Review* 26, no. 5 (2011): 1029.

Chapter 7

1. Parham v. J. R., 442 U.S. 584, 590 (1979).

2. *Parham*, 442 U.S. at 590.

3. *Parham*, 442 U.S. at 590.

4. *Parham*, 442 U.S. at 590.

5. *Parham*, 442 U.S. at 590.

6. *Parham*, 442 U.S. at 592.

7. J. R. was a ward of the state. There was no parental right at issue.

8. *Parham*, 442 U.S. at 590–91.

9. *Parham*, 442 U.S. at 592–95.

10. *Parham*, 442 U.S. at 597. See J. L. v. Parham, 412 F. Supp. 112, 137–38 (M.D. Ga. 1976).

11. *J. L. v. Parham*, 412 F. Supp. 112.

12. *Parham*, 442 U.S. 584, 625–26 (Brennan, J., dissenting). Justice Brennan also argued that preconfinement hearings should have been required for wards of the state.

13. For an argument interpreting *Parham* as a case about the child's diminished decision-making capacity, see Lois A. Weithorn, "A Constitutional Jurisprudence of Children's Vulnerability," *Hastings Law Journal* 69, no. 1 (2017): 209.

14. *Parham*, 442 U.S. at 587.

15. *Parham*, 442 U.S. at 589.

16. *Parham*, 442 U.S. at 598.

17. Amartya Sen, "Description as Choice," *Oxford Economic Papers* 32, no. 3 (1980): 353–69. Sen argues that good descriptions contain an element of value related to a purpose.

18. For an argument that criticized the opinion's factual assumptions, see Gail S. Perry and Gary B. Melton, "Precedential Value of Judicial Notice of Social Facts: *Parham* as an Example," *Journal of Family Law* 22, no. 4 (1983): 633–76 and Winsor C. Schmidt Jr., "Considerations of Social Science in a Reconsideration of *Parham v. J. R.* and the Commitment of Children to Mental Institutions," *Journal of Psychiatry & Law* 13, no. 3 (1985): 339–59.

19. *Parham*, 442 U.S. at 589–90.

20. *Parham*, 442 U.S. at 590.

21. *Parham*, 442 U.S. at 596.

22. *Parham*, 442 U.S. 584, 596.

23. *Parham*, 442 U.S. at 596.

24. *Parham*, 442 U.S. at 597–98.

25. This is known as the tu quoque fallacy, an attack on the person engaging in conduct of which the person complains. For its structure and use in argument, see Douglas N. Walton, "The *Ad Hominem* Argument as an Informal Fallacy," *Argumentation* 1, no. 3 (1987): 317–31, particularly pages 312–25. For its use in legal argumentation, see Kevin W. Saunders, "Informal Fallacies in Legal Argumentation," *South Carolina Law Review*, 44 (1992): 343, 373–74.

26. *Parham*, 442 U.S. 584, 598.

27. *Parham*, 442 U.S. at 599.

28. *Parham*, 442 U.S. at 598.

29. Abram Chayes, "The Role of the Judge in Public Law Litigation," *Harvard Law Review* 89, no. 7 (1976): 1281–318. Chayes argued that the use of litigation to accomplish public regulatory aims created a regime of on-going judicial involvement extending beyond the litigants, in contrast to the traditional judicial function of doing justice to a dispute between two private parties. Chayes believed this new role to be a necessary means for judicial practice to come to terms with the modern regulatory state.

30. *Parham*, 442 U.S. 584, 600.

31. *Parham*, 442 U.S. at 602.

32. *Parham*, 442 U.S. at 602–3.
33. *Parham*, 442 U.S. at 603–4.
34. *Parham*, 442 U.S. at 625–26 (Brennan, J. dissenting).
35. *Parham*, 442 U.S. at 627.
36. *Parham*, 442 U.S. at 628.
37. *Parham*, 442 U.S. at 629.
38. *Parham*, 442 U.S. at 629.
39. *Parham*, 442 U.S. at 629.
40. *Parham*, 442 U.S. at 630.
41. *Parham*, 442 U.S. at 630.
42. *Parham*, 442 U.S. at 631.
43. *Parham*, 442 U.S. at 631.
44. *Parham*, 442 U.S. at 632.
45. *Parham*, 442 U.S. at 632.
46. *Parham*, 442 U.S. at 633.

Chapter 8

1. The Burger Court followed this approach in its decisions approving of parental consent laws for obtaining an abortion, including Bellotti v. Baird, 443 U.S. 622 (1979) and Planned Parenthood v. Ashcroft, 462 U.S. 476 (1983). These cases permitted laws requiring parental consent before a minor could obtain an abortion so long as there was a "judicial bypass" procedure whereby a judge could grant permission in cases where parental consent was not possible. This legal procedure requires youth to "perform their maturity." Amsden, "Performing Maturity" (see intro, n. 19).
2. FCC v. Pacifica, 438 U.S. 726 (1978).
3. *Pacifica*, 438 U.S. at 749.
4. Bethel School District no. 403 et al. v. Fraser, 478 U.S. 675, 678 (1986).
5. *Fraser*, 478 U.S. at 678.
6. *Fraser*, 478 U.S. at 678–79.
7. Justices O'Connor, Powell, Rehnquist, and White joined Burger's opinion.
8. *Fraser*, 478 U.S. at 683–85.
9. *Fraser*, 478 U.S. at 686.
10. *Fraser*, 478 U.S. at 680.
11. *Fraser*, 478 U.S. at 677.
12. *Fraser*, 478 U.S. at 678.
13. *Fraser*, 478 U.S. at 680.
14. *Fraser*, 478 U.S. at 681 (citing Charles A. Beard and Mary R. Beard, *New Basic History of the United States* [New York: Doubleday, 1968], 268).
15. *Fraser*, 478 U.S. at 681.
16. *Fraser*, 478 U.S. at 683.
17. *Fraser*, 478 U.S. at 683–84.
18. *Fraser*, 478 U.S. at 684.
19. *Fraser*, 478 U.S. at 681.
20. *Fraser*, 478 U.S. at 681–82.
21. *Fraser*, 478 U.S. at 682.

22. John Rawls's *A Theory of Justice* (Cambridge: Belknap Press of Harvard University Press, 1999), rev. ed., argued that the pursuit of justice should focus on proper procedures for determining fair and equitable distributions of goods.

23. *Fraser*, 478 U.S. at 683.

24. *Fraser*, 478 U.S. at 682.

25. Erwin Chemerinsky, "Students Do Leave Their First Amendment Rights at the Schoolhouse Gates: What's Left of *Tinker*?" *Drake Law Review* 48, no. 3 (2000): 537.

26. *Fraser*, 478 U.S. at 686 (quoting New Jersey v. T.L.O., 469 U.S. 325 at 340 [1985] and Arnett v. Kennedy, 416 U.S. 134, 161 [1974] ([Rehnquist, J., concurring]).

27. *Fraser*, 478 U.S. at 686.

28. *Fraser*, 478 U.S. at 686.

29. Justice Brennan concurred with the result. He argued that the school officials had the authority to suppress the speech because it wanted the "assembly to proceed in an orderly manner." *Fraser*, 478 U.S. at 689. Justice Marshall dissented, observing briefly that the school simply hadn't demonstrated that the remarks were disruptive. *Fraser*, 478 U.S. at 690.

30. *Fraser*, 478 U.S. at 692.

31. *Fraser*, 478 U.S. at 692.

32. *Fraser*, 478 U.S. at 693.

33. The reference raises the problem of the speaking child as a problem of parrhesia. Michel Foucault's description of speaking truth to power indexed "courage in the face of danger." Michel Foucault, *Fearless Speech*, ed. Joseph Pearson (Cambridge: MIT Press, 2001), 16. Of course, "use of *parrhesia* requires that the *parrhesiastes* know his own genealogy, his own status; i.e. usually one must first be a male citizen to speak the truth." Foucault, 16. The place of the child indexes just this dilemma—on the one hand, the child is an individual citizen, but on the other hand, courts require the child to earn that status through a performance of risk assessment.

34. *Fraser*, 478 U.S. at 695.

35. Elizabeth Markovits investigates this effect in *The Politics of Sincerity: Plato, Frank Speech, and Democratic Judgment* (University Park: Pennsylvania State University Press, 2008), 25–36.

Chapter 9

1. The court noted that this prepublication review process—which courts typically treat as a disfavored prior restraint of speech—appeared to be routine.

2. Hazelwood v. Kuhlmeier, 484 U.S. 260 263 (1988).

3. *Hazelwood*, 484 U.S. at 263.

4. *Hazelwood*, 484 U.S. at 265 (citing the lower appellate court's decision, Kuhlmeier v. Hazelwood School Dist., 795 F.2d 1368, 1372–73 [8th Cir.]).

5. *Hazelwood*, 484 U.S. at 265 (citing 795 F.2d 1368, 1375).

6. Chief Justice Rehnquist, Justice Stevens, Justice O'Connor, and Justice Scalia joined the opinion.

7. *Hazelwood*, 484 U.S. at 272.

8. Brian Amsden focused on the tension between speech and action in these cases. Amsden wants to advocate for youth because their "identity places them often on the

outside of the boundaries of the law." "Student Advocacy and the Limits of (Action-) Free Speech: Figurations of Materiality in *Tinker, Bethel,* and *Hazelwood,*" *Communication and Critical/Cultural Studies* 8, no. 4 (2011): 354. My focus on judicial performances tracks the shifting nature of citizenship. The child is but one example about how marginal figures are used as the other of citizenship. Because they also are paradoxically citizens themselves, the child is both inside and outside the boundaries of the law at the same time.

9. An example of work that emphasized the decision's support for the role of institutions to nurture First Amendment rights is Bruce C. Hafen's "*Hazelwood School District* and the Role of First Amendment Institutions," *Duke Law Journal* 37, no 4. (1988): 685–705. Hafen stated the child's speaking right as "the right to develop their own educated capacity for self-expression." This idea covered tradition: the "sources of social and political continuity for society." Hafen, "*Hazelwood,*" 704.

10. *Hazelwood,* 484 U.S. at 266.

11. *Hazelwood,* 484 U.S. at 267.

12. Hague v. CIO, 307 U.S. 496, 515 (1939).

13. *Hazelwood,* 484 U.S. at 267 (citing Perry Education Assn. v. Perry Local Educators' Assn., 460 U.S. 37, 47 [1983], and *Perry* at 46, n. 7).

14. *Hazelwood,* 484 U.S. at 268.

15. *Hazelwood,* 484 U.S. at 268–69.

16. *Hazelwood,* 484 U.S. at 269.

17. *Hazelwood,* 484 U.S. at 269.

18. *Hazelwood,* 484 U.S. at 269.

19. *Hazelwood,* 484 U.S. at 273.

20. *Hazelwood,* 484 U.S. at 274–75.

21. *Hazelwood,* 484 U.S. at 275.

22. While an analysis of cases applying *Hazelwood* found that the decision had a substantial effect on "strengthen[ing] the authority of public schools," it also concluded that this authority was important as a way to "facilitate development of [students'] long-term actual autonomy." Bruce C. Hafen and Jonathan O. Hafen, "The *Hazelwood* Progeny: Autonomy and Student Expression in the 1990s," *St. John's Law Review* 69, nos. 3–4 (1995): 379. The censorship trend in schools appears to be continuing. See Catherine J. Ross, *Lessons in Censorship: How Schools and Courts Subvert Students' First Amendment Rights* (Cambridge: Harvard University Press, 2015). It is also apparently broadening to college campuses. David L. Hudson Jr., "Thirty Years of *Hazelwood* and Its Spread to Colleges and University Campuses," *Howard Law Journal* 61, no. 3 (2018): 491–522.

23. *Hazelwood,* 484 U.S. at 277 (Brennan, J., dissenting).

24. *Hazelwood,* 484 U.S. at 282 and 290 (Brennan J., dissenting).

25. *Hazelwood,* 484 U.S. at 277.

26. *Hazelwood,* 484 U.S. at 278.

27. *Hazelwood,* 484 U.S. at 278.

28. Justice Brennan relied on *Brown*'s recognition that public education prepares students for "the duties of citizenship in our democratic republic." *Hazelwood,* 484 U.S. at 278, citing *Brown v. Board of Ed.,* 347 U.S. 483, 493. At the same time, *Ambach* reminded the court that public schools inculcate "in tomorrow's leaders the 'fundamental values

necessary to the maintenance of a democratic political system." *Hazelwood,* 484 U.S. at 278, citing Ambach v. Norwick, 441 U.S. 68, 77 (1979). *Board of Ed. v. Pico* (which considered the authority of school boards to remove books from junior high and high school libraries) noted the role of "the public educator [in] nurtur[ing] students' social and moral development by transmitting to them an official dogma of 'community values.'" *Hazelwood,* 484 U.S. at 278, citing Board of Education v. Pico, 457 U.S. 853, 864 (1982).

29. *Hazelwood,* 484 U.S. at 278.

30. *Hazelwood,* 484 U.S. at 280.

31. *Hazelwood,* 484 U.S. at 281–82.

32. *Hazelwood,* 484 U.S. at 279–80.

33. *Hazelwood,* 484 U.S. at 285.

34. *Hazelwood,* 484 U.S. at 285.

35. *Hazelwood,* 484 U.S. at 289.

36. In fact, *Hazelwood* shifted away from a value of viewpoint diversity and toward a hegemonic conception of community values. See, for example, the impact analysis of the decision in Rosemary C. Salomone, "Free Speech and School Governance in the Wake of *Hazelwood,*" *Georgia Law Review* 26, no. 2 (1992): 253–322.

Chapter 10

1. DeShaney v. Winnebago County, 489 U.S., 189, 194 (1989).

2. Justices White, Stevens, O'Connor, Scalia, and Kennedy joined this opinion.

3. *DeShaney,* 418 U.S. 189, 211 (Brennan, J., dissenting). Justices Marshall and Blackmun joined Justice Brennan's opinion.

4. *DeShaney,* 418 U.S. 189, 212 (Blackmun, J., dissenting).

5. *DeShaney,* 418 U.S. 189, 213 (Blackmun, J., dissenting).

6. Aviam Soifer argued that the opinion used abstraction and formal categories to misrepresent the historical significance of the Fourteenth Amendment. "Moral Ambition, Formalism, and the Free World of *DeShaney,*" *George Washington Law Review* 57, no. 6 (1989): 1513–32.

7. For a detailed analysis of the arguments, stories, and personalities of the case, see Lynne Curry, *The* DeShaney *Case: Child Abuse, Family Rights, and the Dilemma of State Intervention* (Lawrence: University Press of Kansas, 2007).

8. *DeShaney,* 489 U.S. at 192.

9. *DeShaney,* 489 U.S. at 192.

10. *DeShaney,* 489 U.S. at 192.

11. *DeShaney,* 489 U.S. at 194.

12. *DeShaney,* 489 U.S. at 195.

13. I have written about the features of Justice Rehnquist's interpretive style. See Timothy Barouch, "The Judicial Character of Late Liberal Prudence: *Paul v. Davis,*" *Rhetoric and Public Affairs* 21, no. 3 (2018): 417–46.

14. This parsimonious style is consonant with certain canons of statutory construction, such as *Expressio Unius Est Exclusio Alterius.* That principle stands for the interpretive practice of excluding certain members of a class where a statute doesn't mention them (but does mention other members of the class).

15. *DeShaney,* 489 U.S. at 196. Rehnquist wrote two of the majority opinions for the

cases he cited, and each one limited of the state's liability for injuries suffered by prison inmates. See Davidson v. Cannon, 474 U.S. 344 (1986) (a prison guard ignoring an inmate's note saying that he was in danger; the guard's mere negligence wasn't covered by the Due Process Clause). Daniels v. Williams, 474 U.S. 331 (1986) addressed a suit from a prisoner who had slipped on a pillow that a deputy had left on a staircase.

16. *DeShaney*, 489 U.S. at 197.

17. *DeShaney*, 489 U.S. at 198, citing Estelle v. Gamble, 429 U.S. 97, 103–4 (1976).

18. *DeShaney*, 489 U.S. at 199, citing Youngberg v. Romeo, 457 U.S. 307, 315–16 (1982).

19. *DeShaney*, 489 U.S. at 199–200.

20. *DeShaney*, 489 U.S. at 200.

21. For an argument that criticized the decision's neglect of democratic norms, see Jack M. Beerman, "Administrative Failure and Local Democracy: The Politics of *DeShaney*," *Duke Law Journal* 39, no. 5 (1990): 1078–112.

22. *DeShaney*, 489 U.S. at 201.

23. Judith Shklar, "The Liberalism of Fear," in *Liberalism and the Moral Life*, ed. Nancy L. Rosenblum (Cambridge: Harvard University Press, 1991), 21–37, 23.

24. *DeShaney*, 489 U.S. at 203.

25. It also used emotion as a persuasive appeal. For an excellent analysis of this type of claim, see Jamal Greene, "Pathetic Argument in Constitutional Law," *Columbia Law Review* 113, no. 6 (2013): 1389–481. Justice Brennan also dissented. He argued that a trier of fact should at least hear the claim. *DeShaney*, 489 U.S. at 203–12 (Brennan, J. dissenting).

26. *DeShaney*, 489 U.S. at 212.

27. Scholarship on the proper role of emotion in judgment includes Richard A. Posner's *How Judges Think* (Cambridge: Harvard University Press, 2010) and Martha C. Nussbaum's *Upheavals of Thought: The Intelligence of Emotions* (Cambridge: Cambridge University Press, 2003).

28. *DeShaney*, 489 U.S. at 212. Blackmun cited Robert Cover's *Justice Accused* here, again activating the extended comparison between childhood and slavery.

29. *DeShaney*, 489 U.S. at 213. Benjamin Zipursky argued that compassion should have influenced interpretation in *DeShaney* in "*DeShaney* and the Jurisprudence of Compassion," *New York University Law Review* 65, no. 4 (1990): 1101–47.

30. Laura Krugman Ray has termed this "situational emotionalism," based on the emotional reaction to a litigant's plight. Ray criticized this approach for its lack of analytical rigor. Laura Krugman Ray, "Judicial Personality: Rhetoric and Emotion in Supreme Court Opinions," *Washington and Lee Law Review* 59, no. 1 (2002): 230.

31. Alan A. Stone, *Law, Psychiatry, and Morality: Essays and Analysis* (Washington, DC: American Psychiatric Press, 1984).

32. *DeShaney*, 489 U.S. at 213.

33. *DeShaney*, 489 U.S. at 213.

34. *DeShaney*, 489 U.S. at 213.

35. It also implicated the debate about negative and positive liberties. For an argument that *Obergefell v. Hodges* (576 U.S. 644 [2015]), which held that the Fourteenth

Amendment required states to perform and recognize same sex marriages, opened the door to reevaluate this distinction (and the *DeShaney* result), see Kenji Yoshino, "A New Birth of Freedom? *Obergefell v. Hodges*," *Harvard Law Review* 129, no. 1 (2015): 168.

36. Whether institutions have obligations to address bad luck has been a recurring topic in political and legal philosophy. See, for example, Bernard Arthur Owen Williams and Thomas Nagel, "Moral Luck," *Proceedings of the Aristotelian Society, Supplementary Volumes* 50 (1976): 115–51. More recent interventions include Kok-Chor Tan, *Justice, Institutions, and Luck: The Site, Ground, and Scope of Equality* (Oxford: Oxford University Press, 2012) and Shlomi Segall, *Equality and Opportunity* (Oxford: Oxford University Press, 2013).

37. *DeShaney*, 489 U.S. at 213.

38. Akhil Reed Amar and Daniel Widawsky, "Child Abuse as Slavery: A Thirteenth Amendment Response to *DeShaney*," *Harvard Law Review* 105, no. 6 (1992): 1359–85. See also Jane Kim, "Taking Rape Seriously: Rape as Slavery," *Harvard Journal of Law and Gender* 35, no. 1 (2012): 263–310 and Susan H. Bitensky, "Analytical Ode to Personhood: The Unconstitutionality of Corporal Punishment of Children Under the Thirteenth Amendment," *Santa Clara Law Review* 53, no. 1 (2013): 1–71. For an argument that the prevalent understanding of slavery at the time of the founding was domination and subordination, see Jack M. Balkin and Sanford Levinson, "The Dangerous Thirteenth Amendment," *Columbia Law Review* 112, no. 7 (2012): 1459–99. For examples of political projects grounded in alternate interpretations of the Thirteenth Amendment, see Maria Linda Ontiveros, "A Strategic Plan for Using the Thirteenth Amendment to Protect Immigrant Workers," *Wisconsin Journal of Law, Gender and Society* 27, no. 2 (2012): 134–61 and D. S. Sidhu, "The Unconstitutionality of Urban Poverty," *DePaul Law Review* 62, no. 1 (2012): 1–63.

Chapter 11

1. Morse v. Frederick, 551 U.S. 393, 398 (2007).

2. *Morse*, 551 U.S. at 398.

3. *Morse*, 551 U.S. at 398–99.

4. When someone sues a government official for violating their constitutional rights, the official can argue for immunity on the grounds that the right was not "clearly established" when the official acted.

5. *Morse*, 551 U.S. at 43 (Stevens, J., dissenting).

6. *Morse*, 551 U.S. at 397.

7. *Morse*, 551 U.S. at 398.

8. *Morse*, 551 U.S. at 397.

9. *Morse*, 551 U.S. at 401.

10. *Morse*, 551 U.S. at 401.

11. *Morse*, 551 U.S. at 402.

12. *Morse*, 551 U.S. at 402.

13. *Morse*, 551 U.S. at 403.

14. *Morse*, 551 U.S. at 403.

15. *Morse*, 551 U.S. at 403–4.

16. This approach also arguably abandoned any role for the court to guide lower courts in applying the new principles. See Frederick Schauer, "Abandoning the Guidance Function: *Morse v. Frederick*," *Supreme Court Review* 2007, no. 1 (2007): 205–35.

17. *Morse*, 551 U.S. at 404 (quoting *Fraser*, 478 U.S. at 683).

18. *Morse*, 551 U.S. at 404–5.

19. *Fraser* relied on *Tinker*. Chief Justice Burger never explicitly repudiated *Tinker* and Justice Brennan wrote separately to emphasize *Tinker*'s viability. *Fraser*, 478 U.S. at 688 (quoting *Tinker*).

20. Wetlaufer, "Rhetoric and Its Denial in Legal Discourse" (see intro, n. 49).

21. *Morse*, 551 U.S. at 405.

22. In a 2006 address at Georgetown University, Chief Justice Roberts stated, "If it's not necessary to decide more to dispose of a case, in my view, it is necessary not to decide more." See Associated Press, "Chief Justice Says His Goal Is More Consensus on the Court," *New York Times*, May 22, 2006, http://www.nytimes.com/2006/05/22/washington/22justice.html?_r=0.

23. *Morse*, 551 U.S. at 406 (citing New Jersey v. T. L. O., 469 U.S. 325, 340 [1985]) and at 406 (citing Board of Ed. v. Earls, 536 U.S. 822, 829–30 (2002)).

24. *Morse*, 551 U.S. at 407.

25. *Morse*, 551 U.S. at 407.

26. *Morse*, 551 U.S. at 408.

27. The ruling also implicated student speech on the internet. See, for example, Brannon P. Denning and Molly C. Taylor, "*Morse v. Frederick* and the Regulation of Student Cyberspeech," *Hastings Constitutional Law Quarterly* 35, no. 4 (2008): 835–96.

28. *Morse*, 551 U.S. at 402–3.

29. Justice Thomas concurred on grounds that *Tinker* should be overruled because the child has no right to free speech. For him, *Tinker* undid a long tradition of cases that granted schools in loco parentis authority: "In the earliest public schools, teachers taught, and students listened. Teachers commanded, and students obeyed. Teachers did not rely solely on the power of ideas to persuade; they relied on discipline to maintain order." *Morse*, 551 U.S. at 412. Justice Alito also wrote a concurring opinion emphasizing the continuing importance of political and social commentary. Justice Breyer wrote a partial dissent, partial concurrence: he agreed that Morse should win the case based on her qualified immunity defense and disagreed with the court's potentially broad speech prohibitions.

30. *Morse*, 551 U.S. at 435.

31. *Morse*, 551 U.S. at 435.

32. *Morse*, 551 U.S. at 436.

33. *Morse*, 551 U.S. at 437.

34. *Morse*, 551 U.S. at 438 (citing Justice Brandeis's concurrence in Whitney v. California, 274 U.S. 357, 376 (1927)).

35. *Morse*, 551 U.S. at 440.

36. *Morse*, 551 U.S. at 441–42.

37. *Morse*, 551 U.S. at 448.

38. *Morse*, 551 U.S. at 448.

Conclusion

1. Jeremy Raff, "'The Separation Was So Long.'" *Atlantic*, September 7, 2018, https://www.theatlantic.com/politics/archive/2018/09/trump-family-separation-children-border/569584/.

2. Donald J. Trump (@realDonaldTrump), "Democrats are the problem. They don't care about crime and want illegal immigrants, no matter how bad they may be, to pour into and infest our Country, like MS-13. They can't win on their terrible policies, so they view them as potential voters!" Twitter, June 19, 2018, 9:52 a.m., https://twitter.com/realdonaldtrump/status/1009071403918864385?lang=en. Like all of Donald Trump's tweets, this one is no longer viewable on Twitter since the company permanently banned him from their platform in the aftermath of the January 2021 insurrection at the US Capitol: Twitter Inc., "Permanent suspension of @realDonaldTrump," Twitter.com, January 8, 2021, https://blog.twitter.com/en_us/topics/company/2020/suspension.html. Timothy Snyder has drawn parallels between the rise of the Nazi regime and the current American president's governing tactics. See Timothy Snyder, *The Road to Unfreedom: Russia, Europe, America* (New York: Tim Duggan Books, 2018).

3. Mallory Shelbourne, "'Fox & Friends' Host: Many Migrant Children 'Turn into MS-13,'" *Hill*, June 19, 2018, https://thehill.com/homenews/media/392968-fox-friends-host-many-migrant-children-turn-into-ms-13.

4. PBS NewsHour, "WATCH: Sessions Cites Bible to Defend Separating Immigrant Families," June 14, 2018, https://www.pbs.org/newshour/politics/watch-live-attorney-general-jeff-sessions-talks-about-immigration.

5. Sarah Huckabee Sanders, press briefing, June 14, 2018. https://www.whitehouse.gov/briefings-statements/press-briefing-press-secretary-sarah-sanders-061418/. For opposition to the Trump administration's policy, see David Bier, "Defenses of Separating Children from Parents—And Why They're Wrong," Cato Institute, June 20, 2018, https://www.cato.org/blog/defenses-separating-children-parents-why-theyre-wrong.

6. Daniel Arken and Ben Popkin, "How the Internet's Conspiracy Theorists Turned Parkland Students into 'Crisis Actors,'" NBC, February 21, 2018, https://www.nbcnews.com/news/us-news/how-internet-s-conspiracy-theorists-turned-parkland-students-crisis-actors-n849921?icid=related. This tactic rose to prominence after the Sandy Hook killings in 2012 and was also used in the child separation controversy. See Tom Porter, "Ann Coulter Claims Crying Immigrant Children Are 'Crisis Actors,' but Author She Cited Slams Her as Illiterate," *Newsweek*, June 19, 2018, https://www.newsweek.com/ann-coulter-claims-crying-children-crisis-actors-author-she-slams-her-983497. Coulter, a prominent conservative pundit, said, "these child actors weeping and crying on all the other networks 24/7 right now—do not fall for it, Mr. President."

7. Courtney Kirchoff, "Parkland Survivor Admits to Bullying the Shooter. And She's Not Sorry," *Louder with the Crowder*, March 27, 2018, https://www.louderwithcrowder.com/parkland-survivor-admits-to-bullying-the-shooter-and-shes-not-sorry/.

8. *PBS News*, "Fabricated Photo Shows Parkland Shooting Survivor Emma Gonzalez Destroying Constitution," March 26, 2018, https://www.pbs.org/newshour/politics/fabricated-photo-shows-parkland-shooting-survivor-emma-gonzalez-destroying-constitution.

9. Donald J. Trump (@realDonaldTrump), "So ridiculous. Greta must work on her Anger Management problem, then go to a good old fashioned movie with a friend! Chill Greta, Chill!" Twitter, December 12, 2019, 7:22 a.m., https://twitter.com/realDonaldTrump/status/1205100602025545730.

10. Miranda Devine, "Irresponsible Adults Have Caused the Climate Fear Plaguing Greta Thunberg," *New York Post*, September 25, 2019, https://nypost.com/2019/09/25/devine-irresponsible-adults-have-caused-the-climate-fear-plaguing-greta-thunberg/.

11. Robby Soave, "Here's What's Wrong with *Time* Declaring Greta Thunberg Person of the Year," *Reason*, December 11, 2019, https://reason.com/2019/12/11/greta-thunberg-time-person-of-the-year/.

12. Yascha Mounk, *The People vs. Democracy: Why Our Freedom Is in Danger and How to Save It* (Cambridge: Harvard University Press, 2018).

13. See, for example, Martha C. Nussbaum, *Frontiers of Justice: Disability, Nationality, Species Membership* (Cambridge: Belknap Press, 2007); Amartya K. Sen and Geoffrey Hawthorn, eds., *The Standard of Living* (Cambridge: Cambridge University Press, 1988); Amartya K. Sen, *Inequality Reexamined* (Oxford: Clarendon, 1992); Amartya K. Sen, *Commodities and Capabilities* (New York: Oxford University Press, 1999); and Amartya K. Sen, "Capabilities, Lists, and Public Reason: Continuing the Conversation," *Feminist Economics* 10, no. 3 (2004): 77–80.

14. Amartya K. Sen, "Human Rights and Capabilities," *Journal of Human Development* 6, no. 2 (2005): 151–66, 153.

15. Rosalind Dixon and Martha C. Nussbaum, "Children's Rights and a Capabilities Approach: The Question of Special Priority," *Cornell Law Review* 97, no. 3 (2012): 593. Dixon and Nussbaum argue that the social contract's focus on naturally free and equal people ignores the realities of status markers of wealth, birth, and physical ability.

16. Nussbaum, *Frontiers of Justice*, 77.

WORKS CITED

Adams, John. "Thoughts on Government." In *The Works of John Adams, Second President of the United States: With a Life of the Author, Notes and Illustrations Thoughts on Government*, vol. 4, edited by Charles Francis Adams. Boston: Little, Brown, 1856.

Amar, Akhil Reed, and Daniel Widawsky. "Child Abuse as Slavery: A Thirteenth Amendment Response to *DeShaney*." *Harvard Law Review* 105, no. 6 (1992): 1359–85.

Ambach v. Norwick. 441 U.S. 68 (1979).

Amsden, Brian S. "Democratic Prudence and the Youth Suffrage Debate." *Argumentation and Advocacy* 48, no. 1 (2011): 22–38.

———. "Negotiating Liberalism and Bio-Politics: Stylizing Power in Defense of the Mall Curfew." *Quarterly Journal of Speech* 94, no. 4 (2008): 407–29.

———. "Performing Maturity in the Parental Consent and Notification Judicial Bypass Procedure." *Communication and Critical/Cultural Studies* 12, no. 1 (2015): 1–18.

———. "Student Advocacy and the Limits of (Action-) Free Speech: Figurations of Materiality in *Tinker*, *Bethel*, and *Hazelwood*." *Communication and Critical/Cultural Studies* 8, no. 4 (2011): 353–75.

Archard, David. "Children, Multiculturalism, and Education." In *The Moral and Political Status of Children*, edited by David Archard and Colin M. Mcleod, 142–59. New York: Oxford University Press, 2002.

Aries, Philippe. *Centuries of Childhood: A Social History of Family Life*. New York: Vintage, 1965.

Arken, Daniel, and Ben Popkin. "How the Internet's Conspiracy Theorists Turned Parkland Students into 'Crisis Actors.'" *NBC News*, February 21, 2018. https://www.nbcnews.com/news/us-news/how-internet-s-conspiracy-theorists-turned-parkland-students-crisis-actors-n849921?icid=related.

Arnett v. Kennedy. 416 U.S. 134 (1974).

Asen, Robert. "A Discourse Theory of Citizenship." *Quarterly Journal of Speech* 90, no. 2 (2004): 189–211.

Asen, Robert, Deb Gurke, Pamela Conners, Ryan Solomon, and Elsa Gumm. "Research Evidence and School Board Deliberations: Lessons from Three Wisconsin School Districts." *Educational Policy* 27, no. 1 (2013): 33–63.

Associated Press. "Chief Justice Says His Goal Is More Consensus on the Court." *New*

York Times, May 22, 2006. http://www.nytimes.com/2006/05/22/washington/22justice.html?_r=0.

Aune, James Arnt. "Modernity as a Rhetorical Problem: *Phronesis*, Forms, and Forums in *Norms of Rhetorical Culture*." *Philosophy and Rhetoric* 41, no. 4 (2008): 402–20.

Bakhtin, M. M. "Epic and Novel: Towards a Methodology for the Study of the Novel." In *The Dialogic Imagination: Four Essays by M. M. Bakhtin*, edited by Michael Holquist, 3–40. Translated by Caryl Emerson and Michael Holquist. Austin: University of Texas Press, 1981.

Balkin, Jack M. "A Night in the Topics: The Reason of Legal Rhetoric and the Rhetoric of Legal Reason." In *Law's Stories: Narrative and Rhetoric in the Law*, edited by Peter Brooks and Paul Gewirtz, 211–24. New Haven: Yale University Press, 1996.

Balkin, Jack M., and Sanford Levinson. "The Dangerous Thirteenth Amendment." *Columbia Law Review* 112, no. 7 (2012): 1459–99.

Barouch, Timothy. "The Judicial Character of Late Liberal Prudence: *Paul v. Davis*." *Rhetoric & Public Affairs* 21, no. 3 (2018): 417–46.

Barrett, John Q., and Gathie Barnett Edmonds. "Recollections of *West Virginia State Board of Education v. Barnette*." *St. John's Law Review* 81, no. 4 (2007): 755–96.

Bartels v. Iowa. 262 U.S. 404 (1923).

Beard, Charles A., and Mary R. Beard. *New Basic History of the United States*. New York: Doubleday, 1968.

Beerman, Jack M. "Administrative Failure and Local Democracy: The Politics of *DeShaney*." *Duke Law Journal* 39, no. 5 (1990): 1078–112.

Bell, Herbert E. *An Introduction to the History and Records of the Court of Wards and Liveries*. Cambridge: Cambridge University Press, 1953.

Bellotti v. Baird. 443 U.S. 622 (1979).

Berlant, Lauren. "The Theory of Infantile Citizenship." *Public Culture* 5, no. 3 (1993): 395–410.

Bernstein, Robin. *Racial Innocence: Performing American Childhood from Slavery to Civil Rights*. New York: NYU Press, 2011.

Bethel School District no. 403 et al. v. Fraser. 478 U.S. 675 (1986).

Bickel, Alexander M. *The Least Dangerous Branch*. Indianapolis: Bobbs-Merrill, 1962.

Bier, David. "Defenses of Separating Children from Parents—And Why They're Wrong." Cato Institute, June 20, 2018. https://www.cato.org/blog/defenses-separating-children-parents-why-theyre-wrong.

Binder, Arnold, and Virginia L. Binder. "The Incarceration of Juveniles, from the Era of *Crouse* to that of Freud and Skinner." *Legal Studies Forum* 18, no. 3 (1994): 349–68.

Bitensky, Susan H. "Analytical Ode to Personhood: The Unconstitutionality of Corporal Punishment of Children Under the Thirteenth Amendment." *Santa Clara Law Review* 53, no. 1 (2013): 1–71.

Board of Education v. Earls. 536 U.S. 822 (2002).

Board of Education v. Pico. 457 U.S. 853 (1982).

Bobbitt, Philip. *Constitutional Fate: Theory of the Constitution*. New York: Oxford University Press, 1982.

Borter, Gabriella. "Parkland Massacre Survivors Post Sweeping U.S. Gun-Control Plan ahead of 2020 Election." Reuters, August 21, 2019. https://www.reuters.com

/article/us-usa-guns/parkland-massacre-survivors-post-sweeping-u-s-gun-control-plan-ahead-of-2020-election-idUSKCN1VB1KE.

Brewer, Holly. *By Birth or Consent: Children, Law, and the Anglo-American Revolution in Authority*. Chapel Hill: University of North Carolina Press, 2012.

Brown v. Board of Education. 347 U.S. 483, 493 (1954).

Brown, Gillian. *The Consent of the Governed: The Lockean Legacy in Early American Culture*. Cambridge: Harvard University Press, 2001.

Brummett, Barry. "Burke's Representative Anecdote as a Method in Media Criticism." *Critical Studies in Mass Communication* 1, no. 2 (1984): 161–76.

Burke, Kenneth. *Attitudes toward History*. Berkeley: University of California Press, 1984.

———. *A Grammar of Motives*. Berkeley: University of California Press, 1962.

———. *Language as Symbolic Action*. Berkeley: University of California Press, 1966.

———. *Permanence and Change*. Berkeley: University of California Press, 1965.

———. *Philosophy of Literary Form*. Berkeley: University of California Press, 1967.

Burnside v. Byars. 363 F.2d 744 (5th Cir. 1966).

Bybee, Jay S. "Substantive Due Process and the Free Exercise of Religion: *Meyer, Pierce*, and the Origins of *Wisconsin v. Yoder*." *Capital University Law Review* 25, no. 2 (1996): 887–932.

Callan, Eamonn. *Creating Citizens: Political Education and Liberal Democracy*. Oxford: Clarendon, 1997.

Capozzola, Christopher. *Uncle Sam Wants You: World War I and the Making of the American Citizen*. New York: Oxford University Press, 2008.

Chayes, Abram. "The Role of the Judge in Public Law Litigation." *Harvard Law Review* 89, no. 7 (1976): 1281–318.

Chemerinsky, Erwin. "Students Do Leave Their First Amendment Rights at the Schoolhouse Gates: What's Left of *Tinker*?" *Drake Law Review* 48 (1999): 527–46.

Cheng, Martha S., and Julian C. Chambliss. "The 1909 *Plan of Chicago* as Representative Anecdote: Constituting New Citizens for the Commercial American City." *Rhetoric Review* 35, no. 2 (2016): 91–107.

Child's World America. n.d. "Petition from Mental Health Professionals: Stop Border Separation of Children from Parents!" https://childsworldamerica.org/stop-border-separation/stop-border-separation-text-preview/. Accessed November 4, 2020.

Chuck, Elizabeth, Alex Johnson, and Corky Siemaszko. "17 Killed in Mass Shooting in High School." *NBC News*, February 15, 2018. https://www.nbcnews.com/news/us-news/police-respond-shooting-parkland-florida-high-school-n848101.

Cmiel, Kenneth. *Democratic Eloquence: The Fight over Popular Speech in Nineteenth-Century America*. Berkeley: University of California Press, 1990.

CNN News. "Transcript: Stoneman Students' Questions to Lawmakers and the NRA at the CNN Town Hall." CNN, February 22, 2018. https://www.cnn.com/2018/02/22/politics/cnn-town-hall-full-video-transcript/index.html.

Cohen, Elizabeth F. "Neither Seen Nor Heard: Children's Citizenship in Contemporary Democracies." *Citizenship Studies* 9, no. 2 (2005): 221–40.

———. *Semi-Citizenship in Democratic Politics*. Cambridge: Cambridge University Press, 2009.

Coker, Calvin. "Romney, Obama, and the 47%: Gaffes and Representative Anecdotes in the 2012 Presidential Campaign." *Argumentation and Advocacy* 53, no. 4 (2017): 327–43.

County of McLean v. Laura B. Humphreys. 104 Ill. 379 (Illinois 1882).

Cover, Robert M. "The Supreme Court 1982 Term Foreword: Nomos and Narrative." *Harvard Law Review* 97, no. 4 (1983): 4–68.

———. "Violence and the Word." *Yale Law Journal* 95, no. 8 (1986): 1601–29.

Crable, Bryan Crable. "Burke's Perspective on Perspectives: Grounding Dramatism in the Representative Anecdote." *Quarterly Journal of Speech* 86, no. 3 (2000): 318–33.

Curry, Lynne. *The* DeShaney *Case: Child Abuse, Family Rights, and the Dilemma of State Intervention*. Lawrence: University Press of Kansas, 2007.

Dailey, Anne C. "Developing Citizens." *Iowa Law Review* 91, no. 2 (2006): 431–504.

Dailey, Anne C., and Laura A. Rosenbury. "The New Law of the Child." *Yale Law Journal* 127, no. 6 (2018): 1448–537.

Daniels v. Williams. 474 U.S. 331 (1986).

Davidson v. Cannon. 474 U.S. 344 (1986).

Denning, Brannon P., and Molly C. Taylor. "*Morse v. Frederick* and the Regulation of Student Cyberspeech." *Hastings Constitutional Law Quarterly* 35, no. 4 (2008): 835–96.

DeShaney v. Winnebago County. 489 U.S. 189 (1989).

Devine, Miranda. "Irresponsible Adults Have Caused the Climate Fear Plaguing Greta Thunberg." *New York Post*, September 25, 2019. https://nypost.com/2019/09/25/devine-irresponsible-adults-have-caused-the-climate-fear-plaguing-greta-thunberg/.

Dixon, Rosalind, and Martha C. Nussbaum. "Children's Rights and a Capabilities Approach: the Question of Special Priority." *Cornell Law Review* 97, no. 3 (March 2012): 549–94.

Dorsen, Norman, and Daniel A. Reznick. "*In re Gault* and the Future of Family Law." *Family Law Quarterly* 1, no. 4 (1967): 1–46.

Duffey, Denis P. "The Northwest Ordinance as a Constitutional Document." *Columbia Law Review* 95, no. 4 (May 1995): 929–68.

Estelle v. Gamble. 429 U.S. 97 (1976).

Ex parte Crouse. 4 Whart. 9 (Pa. 1839).

Fallon Richard H., Jr. "*Stare Decisis* and the Constitution: An Essay on Constitutional Methodology." *NYU Law Review* 76, no. 2 (2001): 570–97.

FCC v. Pacifica. 438 U.S. 726 (1978).

Feldman, Noah. *Scorpions: The Battles and Triumphs of FDR's Great Supreme Court Justices*. New York: Twelve Publishers, 2010.

Ferguson, Robert A. "The Judicial Opinion as Literary Genre." *Yale Journal of Law and Humanities* 2, no. 1 (1990): 201–20.

Ferguson v. Skrupa. 372 U.S. 726 (1963).

Field, Sherry L. "Citizens for a 'New World Order': A Historical Perspective of Citizenship Education in the United States." In *Citizenship Education and the Modern State*, edited by Kerry J. Kennedy, 137–47. London: Taylor and Francis 1997.

Fitzpatrick, Peter. *Modernism and the Grounds of Law*. Cambridge: Cambridge University Press, 2001.

Fliegelman, Jay. *Prodigals and Pilgrims: The American Revolution against Patriarchal Authority 1750–1800*. Cambridge: Cambridge University Press, 1982.

Foner, Eric. *Free Labor, Free Soil, Free Men: The Ideology of the Republican Party before the Civil War*. Oxford: Oxford University Press, 1995.

———. *The Story of American Freedom*. New York: Norton, 1999.

Forbath, William E. *Law and the Shaping of the American Labor Movement*. Cambridge: Harvard University Press, 1991.

Foucault, Michel. *Fearless Speech*. Edited by Joseph Pearson. Cambridge: MIT Press, 2001.

Fox, Sanford J. "Juvenile Justice Reform: An Historical Perspective." *Stanford Law Review* 22, no. 4 (1970): 1187–239.

Frug, Jerry. "Argument as Character." *Stanford Law Review* 40, no. 4 (1988): 869–927.

Garver, Eugene. *For the Sake of Argument: Practical Reasoning, Character, and the Ethics of Belief*. Chicago: University of Chicago Press, 2004.

Gobitis, Lillian. "The Courage to Put God First." *Awake!* July 22, 1993, 13.

Goss v. Lopez. 419 U.S. 565 (1975).

Graetz, Michael J., and Linda Greenhouse. *The Burger Court and the Rise of the Judicial Right*. New York: Simon and Schuster, 2016.

Graham, David A. "Are Children Being Kept in 'Cages' at the Border?" *Atlantic*, June 18, 2018. https://www.theatlantic.com/politics/archive/2018/06/ceci-nest-pas-une-cage/563072/.

Greene, Jamal. "Pathetic Argument in Constitutional Law." *Columbia Law Review* 113, no. 6 (2013): 1389–481.

Greene, Ronald W. "Rhetorical Pedagogy as a Postal System: Circulating Subjects through Michael Warner's 'Publics and Counterpublics.'" *Quarterly Journal of Speech* 88, no. 4 (2002): 434–43.

Griffin, Christine Griffin. *Representations of Youth: The Study of Youth and Adolescence in Britain and America*. New York: John Wiley, 2013.

Gusfield, Joseph R. *Symbolic Crusade: Status Politics and the American Temperance Movement*. Urbana: University of Illinois Press, 1986.

Hafen, Bruce C. "*Hazelwood School District* and the Role of First Amendment Institutions." *Duke Law Journal* 37, no 4. (1988): 685–705.

Hafen, Bruce C., and Jonathan O. Hafen. "The *Hazelwood* Progeny: Autonomy and Student Expression in the 1990s." *St. John's Law Review* 69, no. 3–4 (1995): 379–420.

Hague v. CIO. 307 U.S. 496 (1939).

Hall, Kermit L., and John J. Patrick. *The Pursuit of Justice: Supreme Court Decisions That Shaped America*. New York: Oxford University Press, 2006.

Halter v. Nebraska. 205 U.S. 34 (1907).

Hamilton v. Regents of the University of California. 293 U.S. 245 (1934).

Hamilton, Vivian E. "Democratic Inclusion, Cognitive Development, and the Age of Electoral Majority." *Brooklyn Law Review* 77, no. 4 (2012): 1447–514.

———. "Liberty without Capacity: Why States Should Ban Adolescent Driving." *Georgia Law Review* 48, no. 4 (2014): 1019–84.

Hampshire, Stuart. *Justice Is Conflict*. Princeton: Princeton University Press, 2000.

Hariman, Robert. "Political Parody and Public Culture." *Quarterly Journal of Speech* 94, no. 3 (2008): 247–72.

———. "What Is a Chiasmus? or, Why the Abyss Stares Back." In *Chiasmus and Culture*, edited by Boris Wiseman and Anthony Paul, 45–68. New York: Berghahn, 2014.

Hariman, Robert and John Louis Lucaites. *No Caption Needed: Iconic Photographs, Public Culture, and Liberal Democracy*. Chicago: University of Chicago Press, 2007.
Hazelwood v. Kuhlmeier. 484 U.S. 260 (1988).
Helvering v. Davis. 301 U.S. 619 (1937).
Hirschkop, Ken. *Mikhail Bakhtin: An Aesthetic for Democracy*. Oxford: Oxford University Press, 1999.
Hudson, David L., Jr. "Thirty Years of *Hazelwood* and Its Spread to Colleges and University Campuses." *Howard Law Journal* 61, no. 3 (2018): 491–522.
Huntington, Clare, and Elizabeth S. Scott. "Conceptualizing Legal Childhood in the Twenty-First Century." *Michigan Law Review* 118, no. 7 (2020): 1371–457.
Hyman, Harold M. *American Singularity: The 1787 Northwest Ordinance, the 1862 Homestead and Morrill Acts, and the 1944 G. I. Bill*. Athens: University of Georgia Press, 2008.
Hyman, Irwin A. "A Social Science Review of Evidence Cited in Litigation on Corporal Punishment in the Schools." *Journal of Clinical Child & Adolescent Psychology* 7, no. 3 (1978): 195–99.
In re Cassandra C. 112 A.3d 158 (Conn. 2015).
In re Gault. 387 U.S. 1 (1967).
Ingraham v. Wright. 430 U.S. 651, 655 (1977).
Isin, Engin F., and Greg M. Nielsen, eds. *Acts of Citizenship*. Chicago: Zed Books, 2008.
J. L. v. Parham. 412 F. Supp. 112 (M.D. Ga. 1976).
James, Allison. "To Be (Come) or Not to Be (Come): Understanding Children's Citizenship." *ANNALS of the American Academy of Political and Social Science* 633, no. 1 (2010): 167–79.
Jasinski, James. "The Forms and Limits of Prudence in Henry Clay's (1850) Defense of the Compromise Measures." *Quarterly Journal of Speech* 81, no. 4 (1995): 454–78.
Jolowicz, Herbert Felix, and Barry Nicholas. *Historical Introduction to the Study of Roman Law*. Cambridge: Cambridge University Press, 1972.
Jones, Van. "'This Week' Transcript." *ABC News*, March 4, 2018. https://abcnews.go.com/Politics/week-transcript-11-18-white-house-chief-staff/story?id=53487441.
Kaestle, Carl F. Kaestle. *Pillars of the Republic: Common Schools and American Society, 1780–1860*. New York: Macmillan 1983.
———. "Social Change, Discipline, and the Common School in Early Nineteenth-Century America." *Journal of Interdisciplinary History* 9, no. 1 (1978): 1–17.
Kahn, Paul W. *Making the Case: The Art of the Judicial Opinion*. New Haven: Yale University Press, 2016.
Kanno-Youngs, Zolan. "Poor Conditions Persist for Migrant Children Detained at the Border, Democrats Say." *New York Times*, August 29, 2019. https://www.nytimes.com/2019/08/29/us/politics/homeland-security-migrant-children.html.
Karier, Clarence J. *The Individual, Society, and Education: A History of American Educational Ideas*. Urbana: University of Illinois Press, 1986.
Kennerly, Michele. "Getting Carried Away: How Rhetorical Transport Gets Judgment Going." *Rhetoric Society Quarterly* 40, no. 3 (2010): 269–91.
Kent v. U.S. 383 U.S. 541 (1966).

Kerber, Linda K. "The Republican Mother: Women and the Enlightenment–An American Perspective." *American Quarterly* 28, no. 2 (1976): 187–205.

———. *Women of the Republic: Intellect and Ideology in Revolutionary America*. Chapel Hill: University of North Carolina Press, 2000.

Kim, Jane. "Taking Rape Seriously: Rape as Slavery." *Harvard Journal of Law and Gender* 35, no. 1 (2012): 263–310.

Kirchoff, Courtney. "Parkland Survivor Admits to Bullying the Shooter. And She's Not Sorry." *Lowder with Crowder*, March 27, 2018. https://www.louderwithcrowder.com/parkland-survivor-admits-to-bullying-the-shooter-and-shes-not-sorry/.

Kleinfeld, Andrew Jay. "The Balance of Power among Infants, Their Parents, and the State, Part 2." *Family Law Quarterly* 4, no. 4 (1970): 409–43.

Knight, Jack, and Lee Epstein. "The Norm of *Stare Decisis*." *American Journal of Political Science* 40, no. 4 (1996): 1018–35.

Kock, Christian, and Lisa S. Villadsen. "Rhetorical Citizenship: Studying the Discursive Crafting and Enactment of Citizenship." *Citizenship Studies* 21, no. 5 (2017): 570–86.

Koontz, Lawrence L., Jr. "Reassessment Should Not Lead to Wholesale Rejection of the Juvenile Justice System." *University of Richmond Law Review* 31, no. 1 (January 1997): 179–90.

Kronman, Anthony T. "Alexander Bickel's Philosophy of Prudence." *Yale Law Journal* 94, no. 7 (1985): 1567–616.

Kulynych, Jessica. "No Playing in the Public Sphere: Democratic Theory and the Exclusion of Children." *Social Theory and Practice* 27, no. 2 (2001): 231–64.

Lander v. Seaver. 32 Vt. 114, 1859 Vt. LEXIS 74 (1859).

Leubsdorf, John. "The Structure of Judicial Opinions." *Minnesota Law Review* 86, no. 2 (2001): 447–88.

Lister, Ruth. "Why Citizenship: Where, When, and How Children?" *Theoretical Inquiries in Law* 8, no. 2 (2007): 693–718.

Lochner v. New York. 198 U.S. 45 (1905).

"Maine Mob Burns Jehovah Sect Home: Action Follows Shooting of Two Kennebunk Men by Group Barricaded in House." *New York Times*, June 10, 1940.

Maine, Henry Sumner. *Ancient Law: Its Connection with the Early History of Society, and Its Relation to Modern Ideas*. 1861. J. Murray: London, 1930.

Manolescu, Beth Innocenti. "Style and Spectator Judgment in Fisher Ames's Jay Treaty Speech." *Quarterly Journal of Speech* 84, no. 1 (1998): 62–79.

Manwaring, David R. *Render unto Caesar: The Flag Salute Controversy*. Chicago: University of Chicago Press, 1962.

Markovits, Elizabeth. *The Politics of Sincerity: Plato, Frank Speech, and Democratic Judgment*. University Park: Pennsylvania State University Press, 2008.

Marshall, William P. "Progressive Constitutionalism, Originalism, and the Significance of Landmark Decisions in Evaluating Constitutional Theory." *Ohio State Law Journal* 72, no. 6 (2011): 1251–77.

McFarland, Susan. "Fla. Governor Signs School Security, Gun Control Bill; NRA Sues to Challenge." *United Press International*, March 9, 2018. https://www.upi.com/Top

_News/US/2018/03/09/Fla-governor-signs-school-security-gun-control-bill-NRA-sues-to-challenge/5961520617500/.
Meiners, Erica R. *For the Children? Protecting Innocence in the Carceral State.* Minneapolis: University of Minnesota Press, 2016.
Mengistu, Amdé. "This Teenager Made History and Pissed Off Racists Everywhere." *Vice,* February 27, 2018. https://www.vice.com/en_us/article/8xdkj5/this-teenager-made-history-and-pissed-off-racists-everywhere.
Meyer, Robinson. "Why Greta Makes Adults Uncomfortable." *Atlantic,* September 23, 2019. https://www.theatlantic.com/science/archive/2019/09/why-greta-wins/598612/.
Meyer v. Nebraska. 262 U.S. 390 (1923).
Meyer v. State. 187 N.W. 100 (1922).
Mill, J. S. "On Liberty." In *On Liberty and Other Writings,* edited by Stefan Collini, 1–116. 1859. Cambridge: Cambridge University Press, 1989.
Minersville School Dist. v. Gobitis. 310 U.S. 586 (1940).
Monaghan, Henry Paul. "*Stare Decisis* and Constitutional Adjudication." *Columbia Law Review* 88, no. 4 (May 1988): 723–73.
Moosa-Mitha, Mehmoona. "A Difference Centered Alternative to Theorization of Children's Citizenship Rights." *Citizenship Studies* 9, no. 4 (2005): 369–88.
Morehead v. New York ex rel. Tipaldo. 298 U.S. 587 (1936).
Morse v. Frederick. 551 U.S. 393 (2007).
Mounk, Yascha. *The People vs. Democracy: Why Our Freedom Is in Danger and How to Save It.* Cambridge: Harvard University Press, 2018.
Neale, Bren. "Dialogue with Children: Children, Divorce, and Citizenship." *Childhood* 9, no. 4 (2002): 455–75.
Nebraska District of Evangelical Lutheran Synod v. McKelvie. 175 N.W. 531 (1919).
Nelson, Caleb. "*Stare Decisis* and Demonstrably Erroneous Precedents." *Virginia Law Review* 87, no. 1 (2001): 1–84.
New Jersey v. T. L. O. 469 U.S. 325 (1985).
Newcomb, Alyssa. "How Parkland's Social Media-Savvy Teens Took Back the Internet—and the Gun Control Debate." *NBC News,* February 22, 2018, https://www.nbcnews.com/tech/tech-news/how-parkland-students-are-using-social-media-keep-gun-control-n850251.
NLRB v. Jones & Laughlin Steel Corp. 301 U.S. 1 (1937).
Nussbaum, Martha C. "Democratic Citizenship and the Narrative Imagination." *Yearbook of the National Society for the Study of Education* 107, no. 1 (2008): 143–57.
———. *Frontiers of Justice: Disability, Nationality, Species Membership.* Cambridge: Belknap, 2007.
———. "Poets as Judges: Judicial Rhetoric and the Literary Imagination." *University of Chicago Law Review* 62, no. 4 (1995): 1477–519.
———. *Upheavals of Thought: The Intelligence of Emotions.* Cambridge: Cambridge University Press, 2003.
Obergefell v. Hodges. 576 U.S. 644 (135 S. Ct. 2071) (2015).
Ontiveros, Maria Linda. "A Strategic Plan for Using the Thirteenth Amendment to Pro-

tect Immigrant Workers." *Wisconsin Journal of Law, Gender and Society* 27, no. 2 (2012): 134–61.

Parham v. J. R. 442 U.S. 584 (1979).

PBS News. "Fabricated Photo Shows Parkland Shooting Survivor Emma Gonzalez Destroying Constitution." PBS, March 26, 2018. https://www.pbs.org/newshour/politics/fabricated-photo-shows-parkland-shooting-survivor-emma-gonzalez-destroying-constitution.

PBS NewsHour. "WATCH: Sessions Cites Bible to Defend Separating Immigrant Families." PBS, June 14, 2018. https://www.pbs.org/newshour/politics/watch-live-attorney-general-jeff-sessions-talks-about-immigration.

Pechey, Graham. "On the Borders of Bakhtin: Dialogization, Decolonization." *Oxford Literary Review* 9, no. 1/2 (1987): 59–84.

People v. Turner. 55 Ill. 280 (Illinois 1870).

Perelman, Chaïm, and Lucie Olbrechts-Tyteca. *The New Rhetoric: A Treatise on Argumentation*. South Bend: University of Notre Dame Press, 1973.

Perry Education Assn. v. Perry Local Educators' Assn. 460 U.S. 37 (1983).

Perry, Gail S., and Gary B. Melton. "Precedential Value of Judicial Notice of Social Facts: *Parham* as an Example." *Journal of Family Law* 22, no. 4 (1983): 633–76.

Peters, Shawn Francis. *Judging Jehovah's Witnesses: Religious Persecution and the Dawn of the Rights Revolution*. Lawrence: University Press of Kansas, 2000.

Petition of Ferrier. 103 Ill. 367 (Illinois 1882).

Pierce v. Society of Sisters. 268 U.S. 510 (1925).

Pisciotta, Alexander W. "Saving the Children: The Promise and Practice of *Parens Patriae*, 1838–98." *Crime and Delinquency* 28, no. 3 (1982): 410–25.

———. "Treatment on Trial: The Rhetoric and Reality of the New York House of Refuge, 1857–1935." *American Journal of Legal History* 29, no. 2 (1985): 151–81.

Planned Parenthood v. Ashcroft. 462 U.S. 476 (1983).

Planned Parenthood v. Danforth. 428 U.S. 52 (1976).

Platt, Anthony M. *The Child Savers: The Invention of Delinquency*. 40th anniversary edition. New Brunswick, NJ: Rutgers University Press, 2009.

Popkewitz, Thomas S. "Governing the Child and Pedagogicalization of the Parent." In *Governing Children, Families and Education*, edited by Marianne N. Bloch, Kerstin Holmlund, Ingeborg Moqvist, and Thomas S. Popkewitz, 35–61. New York: Palgrave, 2003.

Porter, Tom. "Ann Coulter Claims Crying Immigrant Children Are 'Crisis Actors,' but Author She Cited Slams Her as Illiterate." *Newsweek*, June 19, 2018. https://www.newsweek.com/ann-coulter-claims-crying-children-crisis-actors-author-she-slams-her-983497.

Posner, Richard A. *How Judges Think*. Cambridge: Harvard University Press, 2010.

Postman, Neil. *The Disappearance of Childhood*. New York: Vintage, 1994.

Powell v. Alabama. 287 U.S. 45 (1932).

Prince v. Massachusetts. 312 U.S. 158 (1944).

Raff, Jeremy. "'The Separation Was So Long. My Son Has Changed So Much.'" *Atlantic*, September 7, 2018. https://www.theatlantic.com/politics/archive/2018/09/trump-family-separation-children-border/569584/.

Railroad Retirement Board v. Alton Railroad Co. 295 U.S. 330 (1935).

Rawls, John. *A Theory of Justice*. Rev. ed. Cambridge: Belknap Press of Harvard University Press, 1999.

Ray, Laura Krugman. "The History of the *Per Curiam* Opinion: Consensus and Individual Expression on the Supreme Court." *Journal of Supreme Court History* 27, no. 2 (2002): 176–93.

———. "Judicial Personality: Rhetoric and Emotion in Supreme Court Opinions." *Washington and Lee Law Review* 59, no. 1 (2002): 193–234.

Reed, Austin. *The Life and Adventures of a Haunted Convict*. New Haven: Yale University Press, 2016.

Roche, Jeremy. "Children: Rights, Participation, and Citizenship." *Childhood* 6, no. 4 (1999): 475–93.

Rosenberg, Irene Merker. "Ingraham v. Wright: The Court's Whipping Boy." *Columbia Law Review* 78, no. 1 (1978): 75–110.

Ross, Catherine J. *Lessons in Censorship: How Schools and Courts Subvert Students' First Amendment Rights*. Cambridge: Harvard University Press, 2015.

Ross, William G. "The Contemporary Significance of *Meyer* and *Pierce* for Parental Rights Issues Involving Education." *Akron Law Review* 34, no. 1 (2000): 177–208.

———. *Forging New Freedoms: Nativism, Education, and the Constitution, 1917–1927*. Lincoln: University of Nebraska Press, 1994.

Sacchetti, Maria. "'Kids in Cages': House Hearing Examines Immigration Detention as Democrats Push for More Information." *Washington Post*, July 10, 2019. https://www.washingtonpost.com/immigration/kids-in-cages-house-hearing-to-examine-immigration-detention-as-democrats-push-for-more-information/2019/07/10/3cc53006-a28f-11e9-b732-41a79c2551bf_story.html.

Salomone, Rosemary C. "Free Speech and School Governance in the Wake of *Hazewlood*." *Georgia Law Review* 26, no. 2 (1992): 253–322.

Sanchez-Eppler, Karen. *Dependent States: The Child's Part in Nineteenth Century American Culture*. Chicago: University of Chicago Press, 2005.

Sanders, Sarah Huckabee. White House Press Briefing. June 14, 2018. https://www.whitehouse.gov/briefings-statements/press-briefing-press-secretary-sarah-sanders-061418/.

Sarat, Austin. *When the State Kills: Capital Punishment and the American Condition*. Princeton: Princeton University Press, 2001.

Saunders, Kevin W. "Informal Fallacies in Legal Argumentation." *South Carolina Law Review* 44 (1992): 343–82.

Scallen, Eileen A. "Classical Rhetoric, Practical Reasoning, and the Law of Evidence." *American University Law Review* 44, no. 5 (1995): 1718–816.

Scanlan, Quinn. "Florida Teen Shooting Survivors Announce 'March for Our Lives' Demonstration in Washington." *ABC News*, February 18, 2018. https://abcnews.go.com/Politics/florida-teen-shooting-survivors-announce-march-washington-demand/story?id=53178265.

Schachter, Jane S. "*Obergefell*'s Audiences." *Ohio State Law Journal* 77, no. 5 (2014): 1011–38.

Schauer, Frederick. "Abandoning the Guidance Function: *Morse v. Frederick*." *Supreme Court Review* 2007, no. 1 (2007): 205–35.
———. "Precedent." *Stanford Law Review* 39, no. 3 (1987): 571–605.
———. "*Stare Decisis*—Rhetoric and Reality in the Supreme Court." *Supreme Court Review* 2018 (2018): 121–43.
Schechter Poultry Corp. v. U.S. 295 U.S. 495 (1935).
Schiappa, Edward. *Defining Reality: Definitions and the Politics of Meaning*. Carbondale: Southern Illinois University Press, 2003.
Schmidt, Winsor C., Jr. "Considerations of Social Science in a Reconsideration of *Parham v. J. R.* and the Commitment of Children to Mental Institutions." *Journal of Psychiatry and Law* 13, no. 3 (1985): 339–59.
Schneider, David M. *The History of Public Welfare in New York State 1609–1866*. Chicago: University of Chicago Press, 1938.
Scott, Elizabeth S. "The Legal Construction of Adolescence." *Hofstra Law Review* 29, no. 2 (2000): 547–98.
Segall, Shlomi. *Equality and Opportunity*. Oxford: Oxford University Press, 2013.
Sen, Amartya K. "Capabilities, Lists, and Public Reason: Continuing the Conversation." *Feminist Economics* 10, no. 3 (2004): 77–80.
———. *Commodities and Capabilities*. New York: Oxford University Press, 1999.
———. "Description as Choice." *Oxford Economic Papers* 32, no. 3 (1980): 353–69.
———. "Human Rights and Capabilities." *Journal of Human Development* 6, no. 2 (2005): 151–66.
———. *Inequality Reexamined*. Oxford: Clarendon, 1992.
Sen, Amartya K., and Geoffrey Hawthorn, eds. *The Standard of Living*. Cambridge, UK: Cambridge University Press, 1988.
Shecaira, Fábio Perin, and Noel Struchiner. "Legal Audiences." *Argumentation* 32, no. 2 (2018): 273–91.
Shelbourne, Mallory. "'Fox & Friends' Host: Many Migrant Children 'Turn into MS-13.'" *Hill*, June 19, 2018. https://thehill.com/homenews/media/392968-fox-friends-host-many-migrant-children-turn-into-ms-13.
Sherman, Christopher, Martha Mendoza, and Garance Burke. "U.S. Held a Record Number of Migrant Kids in Custody This Year." *Frontline* and the Associated Press, November 12, 2019. https://www.pbs.org/wgbh/frontline/article/u-s-held-record-69-thousand-migrant-children-in-custody-in-2019/.
Shklar, Judith. "The Liberalism of Fear." In *Liberalism and the Moral Life*, edited by Nancy L. Rosenblum, 21–37. Cambridge: Harvard University Press, 1991.
Sidhu, D. S. "The Unconstitutionality of Urban Poverty." *DePaul Law Review* 62, no. 1 (2012): 1–63.
Siegel, Reva B. "Why Equal Protection No Longer Protects: The Evolving Forms of Status-Enforcing State Action." *Stanford Law Review* 49, no. 6 (1997): 1111–48.
Slaughterhouse Cases. 83 U.S. 36 (1873).
Snyder, Timothy. *The Road to Unfreedom: Russia, Europe, America*. New York: Tim Duggan Books, 2018.
Soave, Robby. "Here's What's Wrong With *Time* Declaring Greta Thunberg Person of

the Year." *Reason*, December 11, 2019. https://reason.com/2019/12/11/greta-thunberg-time-person-of-the-year/.

"Society for the Prevention of Pauperism in the City of New York, Report on the Subject of Erecting a House of Refuge for Vagrant and Depraved Young People." In *Society for the Reformation of Juvenile Delinquents, Documents Relative to the House of Refuge*, edited by Nathaniel Hart, 11–36. New York: M. Day, 1832.

Soifer, Aviam. "Moral Ambition, Formalism, and the Free World of *DeShaney*." *George Washington Law Review* 57, no. 6 (1989): 1513–32.

State v. Pendergrass. 19 N.C. 365 (1837).

Sterling, Robin Walker. "Fundamental Unfairness: *In re Gault* and the Road Not Taken." *Maryland Law Review* 72, no. 3 (2013): 607–81.

Stevenson, T. R. "The Ideal Benefactor and the Father Analogy in Greek and Roman Thought." *Classical Quarterly* 42 (1992): 421–36.

Steward Machine Co. v. Davis. 301 U.S. 548 (1937).

Stone, Alan A. *Law, Psychiatry, and Morality: Essays and Analysis*. Washington, DC: American Psychiatric Press, 1984.

Strossen, Nadine. "The Supreme Court's Role: Guarantor of Individual and Minority Group Rights." *University of Richmond Law Review* 26, no. 3 (1992): 467–70.

Tan, Kok-Chor. *Justice, Institutions, and Luck: The Site, Ground, and Scope of Equality*. Oxford: Oxford University Press, 2012.

Tanenhaus, David S. "Between Dependence and Liberty: The Conundrum of Children's Rights in the Gilded Age." *Law and History Review* 23, no. 2 (2005): 351–85.

———. *The Constitutional Rights of Children*: In re Gault *and Juvenile Justice*. Lawrence: University Press of Kansas, 2011.

———. "The Evolution of Juvenile Courts in the Early Twentieth Century: Beyond the Myth of Immaculate Construction." In *A Century of Juvenile Justice*, edited by Margaret K. Rosenheim, Franklin E. Zimring, David S. Tanenhaus, and Bernadine Dohrn, 42–73. Chicago: University of Chicago Press, 2000.

———. "First Things First: Juvenile Justice Reform in Historical Context." *Texas Tech Law Review* 46, no. 1 (2013): 281–90.

———. *Juvenile Justice in the Making*. Oxford: Oxford University Press, 2004.

Taylor, Charles. *Modern Social Imaginaries*. Durham: Duke University Press, 2004.

Teeters, Negley K. "The Early Days of the Philadelphia House of Refuge." *Pennsylvania History: A Journal of Mid-Atlantic Studies* 27, no. 2 (April 1960): 165–87.

Thompson, Ginger. "A Border Patrol Agent Reveals What It's Really Like to Guard Migrant Children." ProPublica, July 16, 2019, https://www.propublica.org/article/a-border-patrol-agent-reveals-what-its-really-like-to-guard-migrant-children.

———. "Listen to Children Who've Just Been Separated from Their Parents at the Border." ProPublica, June 18, 2018. https://www.propublica.org/article/children-separated-from-parents-border-patrol-cbp-trump-immigration-policy.

Thunberg, Greta. "Transcript: Speech at the U.N. Climate Action Summit." *NPR*, September 23, 2019. https://www.npr.org/2019/09/23/763452863/transcript-greta-thunbergs-speech-at-the-u-n-climate-action-summit.

Tinker v. Des Moines Independent Community School District. 393 U.S. 503 (1969).

Trepanier, Jean. "Juvenile Courts after 100 Years: Past and Present Orientations." *European Journal on Criminal Policy and Research* 7, no. 3 (1999): 303–27.

Tribe, Laurence S. "America's Constitutional Narrative." *Daedalus* 141, no. 1 (2012): 18–42.

———. "*Lawrence v. Texas*: The 'Fundamental Right' That Dare Not Speak Its Name." *Harvard Law Review* 117, no. 6 (2004): 1894–955.

Trump, Donald J. @realDonaldTrump. "Democrats are the problem. They don't care about crime and want illegal immigrants, no matter how bad they may be, to pour into and infest our Country, like MS-13. They can't win on their terrible policies, so they view them as potential voters!" Twitter. June 19, 2018, 9:52 a.m. https://twitter.com/realdonaldtrump/status/1009071403918864385?lang=en.

———. "So ridiculous. Greta must work on her Anger Management problem, then go to a good old fashioned movie with a friend! Chill Greta, Chill!" Twitter. December 12, 2019, 7:22 a.m. https://twitter.com/realDonaldTrump/status/1205100602025545730. Note: Donald Trump's tweets are no longer viewable on Twitter since the company permanently banned him from their platform in the aftermath of the January 2021 insurrection at the US Capitol: Twitter Inc., "Permanent suspension of @realDonaldTrump," Twitter.com, January 8, 2021, https://blog.twitter.com/en_us/topics/company/2020/suspension.html. Timothy

Tyack, David. "The Perils of Pluralism: The Background of the Pierce Case." *American Historical Review* 74, no. 1 (October 1968): 74–98.

———. *Seeking Common Ground: Public Schools in a Diverse Society*. Cambridge: Harvard University Press, 2003.

———. "Ways of Seeing: An Essay on the History of Compulsory Schooling." *Harvard Educational Review* 46, no. 3 (1976): 355–89.

Tyack, David B., and Elisabeth Hansot. "Conflict and Consensus in American Public Education." *Daedalus* 110, no. 3 (1981): 1–25.

———. *Managers of Virtue: Public School Leadership in America, 1820–1980*. New York: Basic Books, 1982.

United States v. Butler. 297 U.S. 1 (1936).

United States. v. Macintosh. 283 U.S. 605 (1931).

Wald, Patricia M. "The Rhetoric of Results and the Results of Rhetoric: Judicial Writings." *University of Chicago Law Review* 62, no. 4 (1995): 1371–419.

Waldron, Jeremy. "The Core of the Case against Judicial Review." *Yale Law Journal* 115, no. 4 (2006): 1347–406.

Wall, John. "Can Democracy Represent Children? Towards a Politics of Difference." *Childhood* 19, no. 1 (2011): 86–100.

Walton, Douglas N. "The *Ad Hominem* Argument as an Informal Fallacy." *Argumentation* 1, no. 3 (1987): 317–31.

Walton, Douglas, and Fabrizio Macagno. "The Importance and Trickiness of Definition Strategies in Legal and Political Argumentation." *Journal of Politics and Law* 8, no. 1 (2015): 137–48.

Wasserman, Lewis M. "Corporal Punishment in K-12 Public School Settings: Reconsideration of its Constitutional Dimensions Thirty Years after *Ingraham v. Wright*." *Touro Law Review* 26, no. 5 (2011): 1029–101.

Weikle-Mills, Courtney. *Imaginary Citizens: Child Readers and the Limits of American Independence*. Baltimore: Johns Hopkins University Press, 2013.

Weir, Bill. "Greta Thunberg: The Teenage Old Soul of the Climate Crisis." CNN, September 20, 2019. https://www.cnn.com/2019/09/20/us/greta-thunberg-profile-weir/index.html.

Weithorn, Lois A. "A Constitutional Jurisprudence of Children's Vulnerability." *Hastings Law Journal* 69, no. 1 (2017): 179–274.

West Coast Hotel v. Parrish. 300 U.S. 379 (1937).

West Virginia v. Barnette. 319 U.S. 624 (1943).

Wetlaufer, Gerald B. "Rhetoric and Its Denial in Legal Discourse." *Virginia Law Review* 76, no. 8 (1990): 1545–97.

White, Hayden. *The Content of the Form: Narrative Discourse and Historical Representation*. Baltimore: Johns Hopkins University Press, 1990.

———. *Metahistory: The Historical Imagination in Nineteenth Century Europe*. 40th anniversary edition. Baltimore: Johns Hopkins University Press, 2014.

———. *The Tropics of Discourse: Essays in Cultural Criticism*. Baltimore: Johns Hopkins University Press, 1986.

White, James Boyd. *Justice as Translation: An Essay in Cultural and Legal Criticism*. Chicago: University of Chicago Press, 1994.

———. *When Words Lose Their Meaning: Constitutions and Reconstitutions of Language, Character, and Community*. Chicago: University of Chicago Press, 1984.

Whitney v. California. 274 U.S. 357 (1927).

Williams, Bernard Arthur Owen, and Thomas Nagel. "Moral Luck." *Proceedings of the Aristotelian Society, Supplementary Volumes* 50 (1976): 115–51.

Wisconsin v. Yoder. 406 U.S. 205 (1972).

Woodhouse, Barbara Bennett. *Hidden in Plain Sight: The Tragedy of Children's Rights from Ben Franklin to Lionel Tate*. Princeton: Princeton University Press, 2010.

———. "Who Owns the Child? *Meyer* and *Pierce* and the Child as Property." *William and Mary Law Review* 33, no. 4 (1992): 995–1122.

Wooster v. Sunderland, et al. 148 P. 959 (Cal. 1915).

Yoshino, Kenji. "A New Birth of Freedom? *Obergefell v. Hodges*." *Harvard Law Review* 129, no. 1 (2015): 147–79.

Youngberg v. Romeo. 457 U.S. 307 (1982).

Zappen, James P. *The Rebirth of Dialogue: Bakhtin, Socrates, and the Rhetorical Tradition*. Albany: SUNY Press, 2004.

Zelizer, Viviana. *Pricing the Priceless Child: The Changing Social Value of Children*. Princeton: Princeton University Press, 1994.

Zipursky, Benjamin. "*DeShaney* and the Jurisprudence of Compassion." *New York University Law Review* 65, no. 4 (1990): 1101–47.

INDEX